I0796840

DEATH IN A SHALLOW POND

Death in a Shallow Pond

A PHILOSOPHER, A DROWNING CHILD, AND STRANGERS IN NEED

DAVID EDMONDS

PRINCETON UNIVERSITY PRESS
PRINCETON & OXFORD

Published by Princeton University Press

41 William Street, Princeton, New Jersey 08540
99 Banbury Road, Oxford OX2 6JX

press.princeton.edu

GPSR Authorized Representative: Easy Access System Europe - Mustamäe tee 50, 10621 Tallinn, Estonia, gpsr.requests@easproject.com

ISBN 9780691254029
ISBN (e-book) 9780691254043

Library of Congress Control Number: 2025931197

British Library Cataloging-in-Publication Data is available

Editorial: Rob Tempio and Chloe Coy
Production Editorial: Theresa Liu
Jacket/Cover Design: Karl Spurzem
Production: Erin Suydam
Publicity: Maria Whelan and Carmen Jimenez
Copyeditor: Francis Eaves

This book has been composed in Arno

Printed in the United States of America

10 9 8 7 6 5 4 3 2 1

CONTENTS

PREFACE AND ACKNOWLEDGMENTS

AS I WAS writing this book, dreadful events were unfolding in Israel and Palestine. The brutal massacre of Israeli civilians on October 7, 2023 was followed by a devastating Israeli air and land attack. The situation was fraught in many ways, politically, militarily, ethically.

Philosophers, like everyone else, had opinions. Some of them felt that their opinions were of special weight on account of their philosophical expertise, yet they offered no distinctive insights—moral or otherwise—into this historically and politically layered conflict. Nor, let's be honest, did the influential actors in the conflict pay the slightest attention to their views.

The news from far away was profoundly depressing. A trifling matter in the grand scheme of things; but I also found the philosophical impotence disheartening. After tearing myself away from the media, however, and returning to this book, there was some solace. For the Shallow Pond is an example of a very specific philosophical contribution, that has had an enormous if contested impact. It has persuaded many people to give away a lot of money to help faraway strangers.

Today's philosophers don't tend to be public figures, at least in the Anglo-American world. Nor do they tend to be activists. Yet, agree or disagree with them, Peter Singer, and the founders of the effective altruism movement he inspired, Toby Ord and Will MacAskill, are all activists. They each want to make an impact beyond academia. As a testament to their public significance, each has been given the much coveted profile treatment in the *New Yorker*.

Although *Death in a Shallow Pond* is a short book, the list of those to whom it is indebted is long. I must start my acknowledgments with Peter Singer. Singer is a kind of anti–Bernard-Henri Lévy, referring to the French philosopher who flamboyantly bestrides the globe with his flowing locks and his open-to-the navel tailored shirt (once earning him the memorable description "a clothes rack in search of a war zone").[1] There is nothing flamboyant about Singer (and he has no locks to flow). He looks and sounds like the sort of provincial accountant one can rely upon for sound advice on what expenses to claim on the annual tax return. Patient and down-to-earth, he has been generous with his time, happily answering all my questions, never dodging, or dissembling.

Both Will MacAskill and Toby Ord also took chunks out of busy schedules to talk to me several times. Angus Deaton, the Nobel Prize-winning economist, has been ridiculously kind to me, generous with both his time and attention. We met in person in Princeton, had several meetings online, and he carefully annotated an early version of this manuscript.

Angus was important in particular for chapter 17, on the "effectiveness critique" of effective altruism. Putting philosophy to one side, the question "Does effective altruism work?" is rather fundamental! You might think that there would be by now a settled answer to this question; but you would be wrong. And several economists and political scientists spoke to me about this, including Tim Besley, Stefan Dercon, Alex de Waal, and Ravi Kanbur.

Several other people read the manuscript in part or whole, and made many useful suggestions. These readers were Lucius

Caviola, Elie Hassenfeld, Theron Pummer, Neville Shack, Stefan Schubert, and Maurice Walsh.

Princeton University Press approached two referees to assess the book. Referee 1 responded quickly, but Referee 2 was tardier. While awaiting the judgment of Ref. 2, I wrote to Richard Chappell (an excellent philosopher who's written about effective altruism), to ask if he would be interested in reading the manuscript. "I'm Referee 2," he responded. Thank you to Ref. 2 for some very useful feedback, and thanks also to Brad Hooker, who revealed himself to be Ref. 1.

The following people each helped me in one way or another. My thanks go to Grace Adams, Richard Armitage, Edmond Awad, Nicola Banks, Owen Bennett Jones, Alexander Berger, Lewis Bollard, Nigel Bowles, Clare Chambers, Robin Darwall-Smith, Hannah Edmonds, Gareth Evans, Alan Fenwick, Luke Freeman, Aaron Gertler, Jonathan Glover, Megan Goodwin, Wendy Harrison , Shakeel Hashim, Jonathan Haskel, Elie Hassenfeld, Jenny Hodgson, Tom Hurka, Michelle Hutchinson, Guy Kahane, Richard Keshen, Jessica La Mesa, Matthew Lindauer, Jenny Linford, Francesca Minerva, Michalis Moatsos, Hannah Newman, Kate Newman, Alex Oliver, James Pliskin, Jonathan Rée, Emma Richter, James Robinson, Jonathan Salter, Philip Schofield, Stefan Schubert, Kieran Setiya, Pablo Stafforini, Larry Temkin, Ben Todd, Cari Tuna, Peter Unger, Leif Wenar, and Richard Zeckhauser. I'm sure I've forgotten others, to whom I apologize.

As always, I'd like to thank my agent Veronique Baxter and my excellent Princeton University Press team, Chloe Coy, Francis Eaves, Lachlan Brooks, Theresa Liu, David Luljak, Carmen Jimenez, Maria Whelan, and most especially the ever cheery Rob Tempio, who was supportive whenever I had the feeling that in the Shallow Pond I was way out of my depth.

DEATH IN A SHALLOW POND

INTRODUCTION

Death and the Shallow Pond

> More than half the people of the world are living in conditions approaching misery. . . . For the first time in history, humanity possesses the knowledge and skill to relieve the suffering of these people.
>
> —HARRY TRUMAN, INAUGURAL ADDRESS, JANUARY 20, 1949

ON YOUR WAY TO WORK, you pass a small pond. On hot days, children sometimes play in the pond, which is only about knee-deep. The weather's cool today, though, and the hour is early, so you are surprised to see a child splashing around in it. As you get closer, you see that she is a very young child, a toddler, and that she is flailing about, unable to stay upright or walk out of the pond. You look for the parents or babysitter, but there is no one in the vicinity. The child is unable to keep her head above the water for more than a few seconds at a time. If you don't wade in and pull her out, she seems likely to drown. Wading in is easy and safe, but you will ruin the new shoes you bought only a few days ago and get your suit wet and muddy. By the time you hand over the child to someone responsible for her, and change your clothes, you'll be late for work. What should you do?[1]

Philosophers sometimes posit scenarios, or "thought experiments," in which it's not clear how you should act. This is not one of those cases. It is not offered as a genuine dilemma. You are not supposed to scratch your chin and seriously weigh up the options. "What should you do?" here is a purely rhetorical question. Indeed, when I present the imaginary situation to my (nonphilosopher) friends, as I have done numerous times, a typical reaction is awkward laughter. The idea that a person could be concerned about being late for an appointment or about getting their garments muddy when a child's life is at stake is obviously preposterous. We'd regard anybody who worried about their clothes in such a situation as morally warped, and quite possibly dangerous.

So if the answer to the thought experiment is not in doubt, what is its point? Well, one philosopher, Peter Singer, uses it as evidence for a radical claim. Over the years, the exact wording of this claim has evolved a little, but the original version went like this. "If it is in our power to prevent something bad from happening, without thereby sacrificing anything of comparable moral importance, we ought, morally, to do it."[2]

Why is this so radical? Because, according to Singer, most of us in the affluent world metaphorically walk past such a shallow pond every day of our lives. You, reader, are probably one of those to whom Singer's argument is addressed. There are people dying of poverty and disease every day. Obviously, that is an extremely regrettable state of affairs. What's more, Singer thinks, these people can easily be helped. There are multiple charities that operate in the developing world with a mission to help those most in need. Many of us are sufficiently well-off to donate to these charities with money that we would otherwise spend on relatively trivial things. We could donate enough to save a life (or indeed lives). That is what we are morally required to do. If we know we can save a life, and fail to do so, we're no better than the person who ignores the toddler's cries, choosing instead to keep their clothes clean.

It's been described as "the most famous argument in modern philosophy."[3] And it is unlikely that any article has been assigned so frequently on university ethics courses as "Famine, Affluence, and Morality," in which the Shallow Pond makes its first appearance. Nor—at least in the Anglo-American world—is there any philosopher better known outside philosophy than its author, Peter Singer, who is, according to taste, admired or despised.

The Shallow Pond has spawned an enormous literature. My aim in this book is to explain its peculiar philosophical power and appeal, as well as the trenchant philosophical criticism to which it has been subjected. But there are more dimensions to the Shallow Pond than just the philosophical. There are riveting psychological, economic, and sociological angles, all of which I explore. Nor is the Shallow Pond of mere academic interest. I will tell the story of how the thought experiment came about and how it has had a huge real-world effect—for the better, it seems to me, though much for the worse according to some detractors.

Its success has derived principally from a movement known as "effective altruism," which began in Oxford more than three decades after the original publication of Singer's article. The founders were two young Oxford-based philosophers, Toby Ord and Will MacAskill. Effective altruism encourages the relatively well-off to give more, but also directs donations toward particular "effective" causes. We might wonder, for example, whether to give money to a college scholarship fund for poor kids, an art museum, a charity to fund lifeboats, a charity supporting military veterans or one supporting sick animals, a cancer research institute, or a charity providing emergency support for victims of natural disasters. Effective altruists say they can help here. They've been successful in persuading many people—including some mega-rich people—to join their moral crusade. This in turn, they say, has transformed (for the better) the lives of those at the receiving end of these funds. Others deride the benefits of aid as illusionary.

Is the argument from the Shallow Pond watertight? Does this pond provide a compelling analogy with the real world? Should we all be effective altruists? Opponents scattergun those who take seriously the supposed implications of the thought experiment with a range of objections. I will endeavor to impose some order on these misgivings, though the criticisms overlap. One feature they share is that they are expressed in surprisingly trenchant, often *ad hominem* ways. Effective altruists are bad philosophers, and their philosophy is "repugnant."[4] Repugnant! It has always been fascinating to me that individuals dedicated to giving away a not-insubstantial percentage of their income have attracted so much abuse and opprobrium.

While the first half of this book tells the story of how the Shallow Pond thought experiment arose, and its impact, the second half is mainly focused on objections to it. *Death in a Shallow Pond* is not a polemic. It presents and attempts to grapple with the arguments. I hope it is evenhanded in its assessment.

If, by the end, you are unpersuaded by the analogy, you will feel justified in carrying on as normal. If, on the other hand, you find it compelling, you may feel duty bound to rethink how you live your life.

PART 1

The Giving Philosophy

1

Vienna, Melbourne

> Philosophers have so far *interpreted* the world. The point, however, is to *change* it.
>
> —KARL MARX

THERE HAS BEEN NO MORE passionate champion of Karl Marx's message than Peter Singer. Marx and Singer have in common their philosophical activism. Marx sought to change the world and, for good or ill (overwhelmingly ill), change it he eventually did—though not in his lifetime. He died in 1883 and it would be another thirty-four years before his followers seized power in Russia. Other communist governments followed, in Europe, Africa, Asia, and the Americas. Singer wrote a short book on Marx, critiquing him for maintaining that human nature is more elastic than it actually is—a great deal of what drives us is innate and not, as Marx would have it, a by-product of economic and social relationships. But, as Singer pointed out in his preface, "For much of the second half of the twentieth century, nearly four of every ten people on earth lived under governments that considered themselves Marxist. . . . In these countries Marx was a kind of secular Jesus; his writings were the ultimate source of truth and authority; his image was everywhere reverently displayed."[1]

There is no such idolatry of Singer. But he has had one up on Marx. He has lived to witness the impact of his ideas.

The world's most influential moral philosopher, as he is frequently tagged, was born in Australia on July 6, 1946, and grew up in Melbourne in a middle-class secular Jewish family. Singer's mother was a doctor with a particular interest in psychology; his father ran a coffee-importing business. Both his parents had been born and raised in Vienna, managing to flee Austria four months after the 1938 Anschluss with Germany, the catalyst for a frenzied eruption of anti-Semitism.

His grandparents were less fortunate. They included Singer's maternal grandfather, David Oppenheim, a teacher of Greek and Latin who had coauthored a paper with Sigmund Freud, and the main protagonist in a book Singer wrote about his family.[2] Having fought for the Austro-Hungarians during World War I, and been decorated for his bravery, Oppenheim was slow to see that in post-Anschluss Austria assimilation and professional status were no protection: "I have risked my life for this country. . . . They can't do anything to me."[3] Dithering cost vital time. He perished in Theresienstadt concentration camp, in what is now the Czech Republic. As it happens, a direct ancestor, another David Oppenheim, had been Prague's chief rabbi.

The Australian government was largely indifferent to the plight of European Jewry. At a notorious international conference in Evian, northern France, in July 1938, to discuss the refugee crisis, the Australian delegate articulated the official mindset: "It will no doubt be appreciated that as we have no racial problem, we are not desirous of importing one."[4] A cap on refugees meant that in the prewar period after Hitler's seizure of power, the Singers were among only 8,200 Jews allowed in.[5]

Singer's family settled in Hawthorn, about four miles east of Melbourne city center, a tree-lined neighborhood with some splendid period homes (not that the family could afford to live in one of them). There were few other émigrés around. Peter was offered the chance of having a bar mitzvah, but there was no parental pressure, and he declined. There was little Jewish ritual. The family had meals with both milk and meat, ate bacon, and continued to eat bread at Passover. Singer's parents spoke German to each other and English to Peter and his elder sister. It would require the psychological skills of David Oppenheim's erstwhile coauthor to trace the exact connections between this refugee background and Singer's values—but it seems implausible that he was not affected by it. Singer himself points to his lifelong abhorrence of racism and fascism, and posits a link with his empathy for nonhuman animals, quoting a character in a novel from the Nobel prizewinner Isaac Bashevis Singer (no relation): "For the animals, every day is Treblinka."[6]

It was in other ways a fairly typical Australian upbringing and Singer engaged in typical childhood activities; he dreamt of becoming a train driver or pilot, made model aircraft, collected stamps, joined the boy scouts, played tennis, and developed an enduring passion for the local Australian rules football club, the Hawthorn Hawks. During holidays, there was winter skiing, and summer outings to the beach, where Singer snorkeled. He read a lot, including Bertrand Russell's *History of Western Philosophy*—a book that doesn't even name-check one of Singer's subsequent intellectual heroes, the nineteenth-century British moral philosopher Henry Sidgwick.

He was sent to a nearby Presbyterian school (Scotch College). Although not off-the-scale brilliant, he was one of the top academic performers with a reputation for enjoying an argument. The legal profession was an obvious destination for a young man who relished debate, but hedging his bets, Singer applied for and was accepted to study a combined law and arts degree at the University of Melbourne, beginning in 1964.

It was here that he first became fascinated by philosophy and, in 1967, having completed his BA, he embarked on a philosophy MA course, which he completed in eighteen months, writing a dissertation on whether and why one should be moral. That morality should be lived, as well as studied, became a life-defining principle. His main philosophy teacher at university was H. J. McCloskey, a decent but pedantic, old-fashioned man, who always wore a suit. Singer took McCloskey's ethics course in 1965. McCloskey was an intuitionist, maintaining that ethics is not governed by a single moral principle; there are many duties and obligations, and the answer to how one should act in a particular case is available through intuition, and not by formula.

Singer was heavily influenced by McCloskey, but unimpressed by his intuitionism. McCloskey contrasted intuitionism with utilitarianism, which offers a simple method (in theory at least) for determining how to act. According to the utilitarian, we should act so as to produce the most happiness or least suffering. But to every criticism McCloskey leveled against utilitarianism, Singer thought there was a satisfactory response.

Take this hypothetical example of McCloskey's that would have felt uncomfortably topical in the 1960s. Suppose you are the sheriff in a small town in the American South. A White woman reports that she has been raped by a Black man, and in vengeful fury a White mob round up six random Black men, place nooses over their heads and is about to hang them from a nearby tree. As sheriff, you can't stop them entirely. You can, however, lie, and claim to have evidence that identifies one of the six as guilty—thus saving the other five. Nobody will ever discover your lie. Nonetheless, to McCloskey it was obvious that this would be wrong. To Singer it was equally obvious that it would be right; after all, if you fail to lie, the person you falsely accuse will die anyway.[7]

Ordinarily, thought Singer, we should abide by rules such as "Tell the truth," "Don't frame an innocent person," "Stick to the norms and accepted procedures of your chosen job or profession." Such commonsense rules are helpful because they engender trust and stability. They are justifiable in utilitarian terms. They make our lives easier. The discovery that a police officer or judge had framed an innocent person would undermine the whole system of justice. But McCloskey's case—in which by hypothesis the stitch-up remains secret and there are no bad consequences—is an exception, when the normal rules should be overridden.

Utilitarianism is a calculating approach to ethics—possible actions should be judged by adding up the good they would produce and subtracting the bad. In the psychological literature a distinction is drawn between two rough systems of thinking—fast and slow,[8] also characterized as the difference between instinct and emotion on the one hand, and reason and calculation on the other. Sometimes these systems complement each other; at other times they conflict.

The most distinctive aspect of Singer's personality was the dominance of slow over fast; of calculation over emotion. He was rarely angry about intellectual or personal matters, and possessed a remarkably attenuated sense of repugnance—practices that might immediately disgust others were instead subjected to dispassionate analysis. Perhaps it is relevant—Singer believes it might be—that he grew up in an unusually broadminded family, with progressive attitudes to sex and few hang-ups about the body and bodily functions. "Boys might say at school, 'Have you seen a naked woman?', and I'd say, 'Of course': my mother or my sister coming out of the shower."[9]

During his Melbourne studies, Singer became a committed utilitarian—following in the tradition of Jeremy Bentham (1748–1832), John Stuart Mill (1806–1873) and the aforementioned Sidgwick (1838–1900). Then, as now, it was a controversial outlook. In the late eighteenth century Bentham had proposed such preposterous ideas as equal rights for women, the legalization of homosexuality, and the abolition of slavery and capital punishment. On Friday evenings in mid-twentieth-century Melbourne, the new recruit to utilitarianism, along with a smattering of fellow students and lecturers, would migrate to the down-at-heel Naughton's Pub, close to the university, where philosophical debate would continue.

Outside his studies, Singer was revealing activist instincts, involving himself in various progressive causes. One was opposition to the war in Vietnam, and particularly conscription; a 1964 law required all twenty-year-old Australians to register and potentially serve abroad if, through a lottery system, they were called up. Keen to cement its strategic relationship with the United States, Australia had committed units of its regular army to serve in Vietnam. Singer was president of Melbourne University Campaign Against Conscription. When US president Lyndon B. Johnson paid a visit to Melbourne in October 1966, Singer was among the crowd who turned up to protest, enthusiastically joining in with the chant, "Hey, Hey, LBJ, how many kids did you kill today?" (The notoriously thin-skinned LBJ believed opponents of the war were communist sympathizers, whom he began to see "under every bed and behind every tree.")[10]

A second cause was adopted after Singer had written a harrowing story for the student newspaper, about women unable to access abortion services. Abortion was illegal, but clinics in which doctors were willing to carry out abortions were tolerated—that is, until the arrival of the new head of the homicide squad, Frank Holland, a "rock-ribbed" Roman Catholic.[11] Singer joined the legalization campaign and then became a committee member of the statewide Abortion Law Reform Association. In April 1968, he and the future Australian foreign minister Gareth Evans participated on the same side in a debate at Melbourne University supporting the motion that "this house would legalize abortion." They won. Evans recalls that even then Singer would state his opinions in an unemotional but nonetheless "follow-the-argument-where-it goes/take-no-prisoners" way.[12] This approach to philosophical argument would blossom (or harden) over the next few years in England.

2

Oxford

PHILOSOPHY AWAKES

OXFORD WAS THE UNIVERSITY to which the brightest Australian would-be philosophers were encouraged to apply. After completing his MA, the twenty-three-year-old Singer was awarded an Arthur Sims scholarship—named after a cricketer, industrialist, and philanthropist—and moved to University College, Oxford in 1969. He was accompanied by his wife Renata (née Diamond), who was born in Poland, the daughter of Jewish Holocaust survivors, and who grew up in a Polish- and Yiddish-speaking family. They'd met in history class, and married in December 1968. As the college had no graduate lodgings, they had to seek private accommodation, finding a cheap house in Cumnor Hill, a twenty-minute cycle ride away. It had a large, unkempt garden, part of which the Singers cleared to grow vegetables. The house itself was damp, and in the evening the only warmth was provided by a small electric radiator. The makeshift plastic sheets they hung on the windows to shut out the draft billowed inward whenever the wind blew.

Nevertheless, "it was a thrilling time to be in Oxford,"[1] says Singer. Unquestionably the heart of the Anglo-American philosophical world, the City of Dreaming Spires was home to many of the philosophers whose books and papers Singer had devoured in Australia—such as R. M. Hare, Peter Strawson, John Mackie (a fellow Australian), and the eminent legal scholar H.L.A. Hart.

When the Singers arrived, moral philosophy was in the midst of a snail's-pace revolution (the maximum speed permitted for an Oxford revolution). The influence of two philosophical titans was very much on the wane. The first, A. J. Ayer, a gregarious, mildly autistic, half-Jewish, old-Etonian football fanatic, womanizer, and provocative and much-in-demand public intellectual, had imported the ideas of the Vienna Circle into the Anglo-American world with the publication of his book *Language, Truth and Logic* (1936). The Vienna Circle had been active in the Austrian capital for a decade in the 1920s and early 1930s, and Ayer had spent several months in its ambit as a young graduate. The members of the Circle were proponents of logical positivism: "logical" in holding that techniques of modern logic were required to build a new philosophy, and "positivist" because they believed positive knowledge could only be derived from the natural world. Famously, they proposed a Verification Principle, which maintained that propositions that were not true by definition ("A triangle has three sides"), or that were not testable ("It is raining outside"), were meaningless. Such propositions included moral statements such as "Abortion is wrong," or "One should never frame an innocent person," or "The rich should give away money to the poor": all of these failed to meet either criterion.

For a period, logical positivism was in vogue. The edifice, however, was supported by some central pillars that wobbled and crumbled under scrutiny. The Verification Principle, for example, while easy to state, was hard to pin down. What counts as verification? Does verification require direct observation (in which case, what of scientific theories about entities that can't be directly observed, such as quarks)? Is it enough that a proposition can be verifiable in theory, or must it be verifiable in practice? And doesn't the Verification Principle fail its own test? It is, after all, neither true by definition, nor testable.

Ayer had a long-running rivalry with a second Oxford titan, J. L. Austin. Austin had made a heartening and surprising discovery: that philosophical ability was transferable to other domains. His exceptional analytic skills were pivotal—and this is no hyperbole—to Allied success in World War II. In particular, he helped pinpoint the most favorable locations (specific beaches in Normandy) for troops to launch the D-Day counteroffensive.[2] In doing so, he saved thousands of lives; the citation for his subsequent OBE declared that his war effort had "without any doubt, been one of the greatest contributions intelligence has made in this campaign towards the defeat of the enemy."[3]

Austin is far less renowned for his war-winning exploits, however, than as the leading exponent of "ordinary language philosophy." This was a movement influenced by the later philosophy of the Austrian-born genius Ludwig Wittgenstein (1889–1951). It held that we should attend to how language is typically used: using ordinary language to address philosophical problems was akin to taking language on holiday (to use a Wittgensteinian expression), and what was needed was to bring it back home. What can we *really* know? Well, don't drag the concept of knowledge away on a philosophical excursion—instead, look at how we typically assign ascriptions of knowledge. As Austin put it, "words are our tools, and at a minimum we should use clean tools: we should know what we mean and what we do not, and we must forearm ourselves against the traps that language sets us."[4]

Was achieving conceptual clarity, in Austin's view, the end point for philosophers, or merely a vital way station, before they could address deeper, more substantial problems? That was never entirely clear. At one point he wrote that "ordinary language is *not* the last word. . . . Only remember, it is the *first* word."[5] He believed that some problems disappeared once we realized how language had befuddled us. But he implied that for other problems, linguistic analysis was merely a necessary preliminary stage in the philosophical process.

In any case, it was not a stage he himself was inclined to move beyond. Why would he? Linguistic inquiry was hard but, by golly, as someone from Austin's background might say, it was fun. Nobody could compete with Austin in identifying the nuances and complexity of language: he reveled in its intricacy. He loved words. He read dictionaries for pleasure. He was a virtuoso lexicographer.

A characteristic modus operandi was to contrast two or more apparently similar words or phrases. What was the difference between acting on purpose, and acting deliberately? Or between doing something with care, and doing it with attention? In one famous essay, "A Plea for Excuses," Austin sought to draw a distinction between an unfortunate outcome brought about "by mistake," and one brought about "by accident," burying this example in a footnote:

> You have a donkey, so have I, and they graze in the same field. The day comes when I conceive a dislike for mine. I go to shoot it, draw a bead on it, fire: the brute falls in its tracks. I inspect the victim, and find to my horror that it is your donkey. I appear on your doorstep with the remains and say—what? "I say, old sport, I'm awfully sorry, etc., I've shot your donkey *by accident*"? Or "*by mistake*"? Then again, I go to shoot my donkey as

> before, draw a bead on it, fire—but as I do so, the beasts move, and to my horror yours falls. Again the scene on the doorstep—what do I say? "By mistake"? Or "by accident"?[6]

One fascinating dimension to language is how we are perfectly competent to follow rules that we can't instantly explain. It is only by attending to the subtle uses to which words are put that we can articulate the rules that they follow. Delicate distinctions might have important real-life implications. Excuses are connected to responsibility. Think of an elderly person driving with great concentration down the middle of the road—driving, that is, with attention, but hardly with care.[7] Following an accident, a court might determine that lack of care and lack of attention do not merit the same sanction.

No territory is more fertile for feuds than academia, and Austin and Ayer bickered for years. Austin believed that some of Ayer's central positions were the product of linguistic confusion—including Ayer's claim that when we perceive an ordinary object, say a cucumber, we only have access to sense-data (how it appears to us: tubelike shape, green colour, texture, etc.) rather than direct access to the object itself. The concept of "sense data," beloved of philosophers, served only to confuse them—or so Austin thought.

Ayer applied for his Oxford job in part to combat Austin's influence. He regarded Austin as pedantic and dull; Austin thought Ayer glib and superficial. Austin was formal and (despite the levity of some of his prose) austere; Ayer was flamboyant and garrulous. J. L. Austin was to be called "Austin," A. J. Ayer was "Freddie." Austin ran an invitation-only philosophical discussion group that met on a Saturday; it included many younger members and was sometimes referred to as "the Kindergarten."[8] Ayer set up his Tuesday Group, also invitation-only, motivated in large measure by the desire to exclude Austin. Austin's gathering was in the morning, and teetotal; Ayer's was late afternoon and proceedings were halted midway to allow for the serving of a stiff drink.

Austin died of lung cancer in 1960, aged just forty-eight. When Singer arrived in Oxford, however, Ayer was still the Wykeham Professor of Logic, though close to retirement. Both logical positivism and ordinary language philosophy were now passé. The *Encyclopaedia of Philosophy* in 1967 declared logical positivism to be as "dead, or as dead as a philosophical movement ever becomes."[9] There were still moral philosophers who felt that their role was to analyze the terms of ethical discourse—concepts such as "good," "wrong," "duty"—but the preoccupation with language had subsided.[10] And there was a fresh and exciting development. A group of ethicists had emerged who were interested less in ethical terms, or the status of ethical statements (whether they are objective, say, or merely expressions of emotions), and more in the practical application of ethics.

Oxford philosophers had never entirely shunned real-life issues, of course. In 1956, for example, Elizabeth Anscombe (an authority on, and former student of, Wittgenstein), almost alone among Oxford academics, objected to the conferring of an honorary degree on the former US president Harry Truman. A politician who had intentionally killed tens of thousands of innocents by ordering atomic bombs to be dropped on Hiroshima and Nagasaki in 1945, was, to be blunt, a mass murderer, and totally unworthy of such an accolade. Although heavily defeated in the university vote, she later published a pamphlet, *Mr Truman's Degree*, that spelled out her objections more fully.

So there were occasions when philosophers weighed in on contemporary controversies, and they were obviously not prevented from doing so. But engagement with the outside world was sporadic and ad hoc. "Applied ethics" was not an official subcategory within moral philosophy. Philosophers opting to engage in debates about matters of general interest risked exposing themselves to sneering condescension from colleagues—applied ethics was not "real" or "serious" philosophy. This attitude began to soften at a time that roughly coincided with Singer's graduate studies.[11] So what brought about this new disciplinary tolerance? Why did it happen at this particular moment?

World War II had roused some moral philosophers from their metaethical slumbers. For them, the emaciated bodies in the concentration camps and a logical positivist conception of ethics could not be reconciled. To condemn the Nazis was not to indulge in meaningless verbiage, nor was it to be interpreted as a mere expression of emotion—"Nazis boo!"—as Ayer maintained.

But while the camps prompted revulsion and a revisiting of the status of moral claims, argument remained stuck at the theoretical level. The war forced some philosophers to challenge the idea that morality was subjective; few took the next step: to ask, "So what's to be done; how should we evaluate and respond to contemporary debates?" That move required the sweeping upheavals that were to come in the 1960s.

Applying Ethics

When the Singers moved to Oxford at the tail-end of the 1960s, miniskirts for women and garish shirts for men were still à la mode. The Beatles' album *Abbey Road* topped the charts, though the band, soon to break up, barely bothered to promote it. The grim X-rated film *Midnight Cowboy* was showing in the cinema. Cannabis had become the student drug of choice.

Britain in 1969 was a wealthy country; there had been sustained growth in earnings for well over a decade, accompanied by a consumer boom. More than two-thirds of households now owned a fridge, and 90 percent had acquired a TV—regular color broadcasts began in November, shortly after the Singers' arrival. Package holidays to sunshine destinations were taking off.

There were unmistakable signs, however, that economic woes lay around the corner. The pound sterling had been devalued in 1967. Strikes were on the increase and the national economy, though still expanding, was in relative decline. In the previous two decades, Britain's share of global manufacturing exports had plummeted from one quarter to 10 percent.

Northern Ireland's so-called Troubles (they would last three decades) escalated just as the Singers were preparing to leave Australia. There had already been big civil rights marches a year earlier when, in August 1969, three days of rioting followed a provocative Protestant ("loyalist") march through a Catholic area of Londonderry. On the recommendation of his home secretary, the Labour prime minister (and former Oxford don) Harold Wilson ordered the deployment of British troops to restore order.

Abroad, the British Empire had been unraveling. In parts of the world the process had been peaceful; in others it had followed, or was accompanied by, bloody conflict. The United Kingdom was having to acclimatize psychologically to a shrunken role as a medium-sized European power. This inevitably led to introspection about nationalism and the relationship between individuals and the state.

The dominant foreign issue was the Vietnam War. Opposition to what was perceived as the unjust, and ultimately futile,

US military campaign in Southeast Asia was the last major cause of the grand old man of British philosophy, Bertrand Russell. Russell provocatively compared America's campaign in Vietnam with Hitler's in eastern Europe.[12] On December 1, 1967, an unofficial international war crimes tribunal established by the ninety-five-year-old Russell—and including Ayer and the French existentialists Jean-Paul Sartre and Simone de Beauvoir—found the United States, to no one's surprise, guilty of genocide.

An important turning point in the conflict was the Tet Offensive (so-called because the day the operation began in January 1968 was the Tet holiday, celebrating the lunar new year). Forces from the North Vietnamese army and Viet Cong launched a surprise attack on American and South Vietnamese troops. They were soon repelled, but the fighting was savage, casualties mounted, and public sentiment in the West turned decisively and stridently anti-war. Student unrest in the UK escalated: Vietnam and the lack of democracy in the universities were the principal grievances.

The demonstrators had an unlikely philosopher poster boy. Few had read his convoluted prose, but his forthright denunciations of the Vietnam conflict made the neo-Marxist German émigré Herbert Marcuse, now based in California, an academic superstar. It helped that he fitted the caricature image of the intellectual: he was a "white-maned, craggy-faced, cigar-puffing septuagenarian,"[13] with a strong Mitteleuropean accent. Various death threats addressed to this "very dirty Communist dog" forced him into temporary hiding in late summer 1968.[14] A secret intelligence report, commissioned by the UK government, warned of a student "explosion" fired by a nihilistic Marcusian worldview.[15] The mandarins were not alone in predicting revolt. "The revolution's here," went the lyrics of a song by the band Thunderclap Newman that climbed to number one in the charts in the summer of 1969.[16]

Vietnam was not a subject toward which philosophers could retain an attitude of parochial and lofty disregard. But there was just as much moral turbulence domestically, following years of agitation. The 1967 Abortion Act in Britain granted women the right to abortion on several grounds. Homosexuality was legalized the same year. Capital punishment was abolished in 1969.

In 1967, philosopher Philippa Foot published an article on abortion in the *Oxford Review*, which included a now famous (or notorious) thought experiment. The brakes have failed on a train that is hurtling down a track on which, unfortunately, five people are tied. You can save their lives by redirecting the train down a side track, where, again regrettably, one person is tied. What should you do? Most people believe you should turn the train, thus saving five lives at the cost of one.

This imaginary case launched an entire subgenre of moral philosophy, so-called "trolleyology," featuring multiple and often surreal dilemmas with out-of-control trains (or trolleys) and individuals who may or may not be killed by them, depending on what choices you make.[17] Foot's article was entitled *The Problem of Abortion and the Doctrine of the Double Effect*, and it interrogated various moral distinctions deployed by protagonists on either side of the abortion debate—the distinction, for example, between "doing" and "allowing," "intending," and merely "foreseeing."

This, then, was the philosophical background to Singer's arrival in Oxford. But perhaps the most notable evidence of a shift toward practical ethics was a new seminar series set up by three young Oxford philosophers, Jonathan Glover, James Griffin, and Derek Parfit, who would each go on to achieve considerable eminence in their own right. The series had the catchy title "Death, Misery, and Morality," and made its first appearance in 1970, proving an instant student hit.

Singer was particularly impressed by Parfit. Much later he would write, "Of all the philosophers I have known since I began to study the subject more than fifty years ago, Parfit was the closest to a genius. Getting into a philosophical argument with him was like playing chess with a grandmaster: he had already thought of every response I could make to his arguments, considered several possible replies, and knew the objections to each reply as well as the best counters to those objections."[18]

It was in the Death, Misery, and Morality seminar that Parfit first introduced some of his famous conundrums about how we should think about possible future people—people who will exist but are not yet born. "Population ethics," like trolleyology, has since become a subgenre within moral philosophy. Singer attended these seminars and recalls other subjects that came up. Glover gave a talk on whether acts with negligible effects can still be bad. To use a contemporary example, if I use more electricity than I need, have I done anything wrong? After all, the effect on global warming will be so minuscule as to be unmeasurable.

Glover contended that such acts, however tiny their impact, were still wrong—as he showed with a thought experiment of his own: the baked-bean bandits. Imagine a village with one hundred inhabitants living in one hundred homes, each of whom has a hundred baked beans they are about to consume for lunch. Just then, a hundred bandits ride into the village, and each bandit goes to one dwelling and robs one villager, seizing their entire baked-bean meal. Each bandit has clearly wronged an individual villager. But suppose the now full-bellied bandits feel a twinge of guilt about their behavior. They decide to adjust their methods. The following week they raid the village again, but this time each of the hundred bandits pilfers a negligible quantity—one baked bean—from each of the hundred villagers. The bandits then ride off into the sunset, convinced that this time they have done no real harm—though no villager is left with so much as a bean. Clearly, thought Glover, the second raid is no improvement on the first.[19]

Singer was captivated: for him, there was no class more stimulating.

Old hierarchies were crashing down, not just in the UK but throughout much of the developed world.[20] There were calls for racial and sex equality, demands for liberalization and more personal freedoms, and a notable erosion of deference toward those in power. In the United States, the Civil Rights Act of 1964 and the Voting Rights Act of 1965 were landmark legal moves designed to tackle entrenched discrimination against African Americans. Jack Baker and Michael McConnell made the news in 1970 as the first gay couple to apply for a marriage license—which they were denied. The right to an abortion was guaranteed under the US Constitution by the *Roe v. Wade* ruling in 1973.

In the United States, just as in Oxford, the philosophical community began to engage more with the outside world. In 1969, the American Philosophical Association formed a division devoted to public affairs and the Society for Ethical and

Legal Philosophy (SELF) was created in part to respond to the moral and legal exigencies of the Vietnam War. SELF met in New York and Cambridge, Massachusetts, and was attended by Harvard's most renowned political theorist.

At the time, John Rawls was working on his magnum opus, *A Theory of Justice*, which would pump oxygen into the semi-comatose discipline of political theory. Although it did not deal head-on with contentious dilemmas of the day, its arguments had practical implications. It offered a framework for how we should—according to Rawls—balance equality and liberty. Its most radical conclusion was that inequality could only be justified if it was to the benefit of the least well-off. That would almost certainly require a major rethink of taxation and wealth distribution.

A Theory of Justice appeared in 1971. But for our story, the most significant development of that year was the establishment of a new quarterly journal, *Philosophy & Public Affairs* (*PPA*). This was supported by Princeton University Press and backed by some of the brightest philosophical luminaries. It declared that its purpose was to use philosophy to help clarify and resolve issues of public concern. The founding editor was Marshall Cohen, Rawls was one of the two advisory editors, and the associate editors were Tom Nagel and Tim Scanlon.

Looking back, it's remarkable how many seminal articles first appeared in the pages of *PPA*. In Volume 1, Issue 1, Judith Jarvis Thomson published what became a much cited paper, "A Defense of Abortion." Many people who oppose abortion do so on the grounds that the fetus is a human being from the moment of conception. Thomson did not believe a fetus had the same moral status as a fully developed human, but insisted that even if we granted that premise, even if there was no difference between the moral status of a fetus and, say, that of the woman who was carrying it, abortion would still sometimes be permissible. She asks us to picture an unusual morning in which you wake up

> and find yourself back-to-back in bed with an unconscious violinist. A famous unconscious violinist. He has been found to have a fatal kidney ailment, and the Society of Music Lovers has canvassed all the available medical records and found that you alone have the right blood type to help. They have therefore kidnapped you, and last night the violinist's circulatory system was plugged into yours, so that your kidneys can be used to extract poisons from his blood as well as your own. The director of the hospital now tells you, "Look, we're sorry the Society of Music Lovers did this to you—we would never have permitted it if we had known. But still, they did it, and the violinist now is plugged into you. To unplug you would be to kill him. But never mind, it's only for nine months. By then he will have recovered from his ailment, and can safely be unplugged from you."[21]

Is it morally incumbent on you to comply with this strange situation? Thomson thought not. It would no doubt be kind of you to let the violinist remain attached to your body, but you were not under an obligation to do so. The analogy with some pregnancies (for example, those resulting from rape) is obvious.

The most philosophically durable article from Issue 2 of *PPA* was Tom Nagel's "War and Massacre," in which Nagel took aim at public apathy in response to news of atrocities in Vietnam and argued that there was a powerful moral basis for the restriction of certain military activities during war. He concluded, however, that moral dilemmas are inevitable, that there can be instances where every course of action is wrong, and that there is not necessarily a solution to every problem. The article closes with two gloomy lines: “We have always known that the world is a bad place. It appears that it may be an evil place as well.”[22]

As for Volume 1, Issue 3—well, without that, this book would never have been written.

3

Vietnam, East Pakistan

IN JANUARY 1970, in protest at the Vietnam conflict, the Danish artist Bjørn Nørgaard publicly slaughtered an old and exhausted workhorse in a field, stuffing pieces of it into dozens of glass jam jars which he then displayed on a set of shelves. *The Horse Sacrifice*, as the artist entitled his stunt, succeeded in its aim of attracting attention—most of it in the form of outrage.

Civil disobedience in protest against the war in Vietnam took many forms, including draft resisters publicly setting fire to their draft cards, and army deserters being smuggled across the US border to safety in Canada. Peter Singer was interested in the legitimacy, or otherwise, of the myriad forms of civil disobedience, and later that year he chose the issue as the topic for his BPhil dissertation.

Advising on his thirty-thousand-word dissertation was the White's Chair of Moral Philosophy, R. M. Hare. Soon after arriving in Oxford, Singer had tentatively dropped an essay he'd written, with a covering note, into Hare's pigeonhole in Corpus Christi College, critiquing some aspect of Hare's writings on the language of morality—tentatively because Hare had a fierce reputation for responding badly to negative comments. In fact, the professor got in contact, explaining patiently why Singer was entirely mistaken, but then offered to supervise the young Australian.

The crux of Singer's dissertation conclusion was this: in an ideal democracy, we have compelling reasons to obey laws. However, in our flawed Western democracies, in which the rich have more power than the poor, and some voting systems disadvantage minority groups, civil disobedience is more easily justified, especially when the aim is to prevent wrongdoing. It was an extended piece of writing that exemplified what were to become Singer's trademark intellectual virtues: logic and clarity. He expressed ideas in simple, jargon-free, unpretentious sentences, and he followed arguments to their conclusion, even when the conclusion seemed antithetical to common sense. One of the BPhil examiners, the eminent legal scholar Herbert Hart, was sufficiently impressed to encourage Singer to publish the eventual *Democracy and Disobedience*[1]—Singer's first book.

As well as a dissertation, BPhil students wrote essays and studied for three exams, one of which had to be on an "authority." Singer opted for the moral philosophy and political philosophy papers, and for his chosen authority proposed that he study Karl Marx. "Not a real philosopher," was the sniffy rejoinder from the faculty, but as a compromise they agreed that he could take a joint paper on Marx and the philosopher to whom Marx was most intellectually indebted, Georg Wilhelm Friedrich Hegel. Singer would later publish introductory guides to both German thinkers.[2]

By this stage he had become involved with a group of disgruntled postgraduates. Although the Death, Misery, and Morality seminars on ethics constituted a stretching of Oxford's philosophical horizons, some students remained frustrated by the aloofness and dryness of mainstream Oxford philosophy. In response, and along with a few graduates and young lecturers from philosophy departments elsewhere in the UK, they founded the journal *Radical Philosophy*. One of the early editors was a gifted writer, Jonathan Rée, a BPhil student in Singer's year. Rée was "appalled by the conservatism and complacency" of Oxford and had a low opinion of his fellow students, most of whom "seemed to think they were the cleverest people in the greatest department at the world's top university, and their only aim in life was to suck up to the dons, emulate their tics, mannerisms and put-downs, and follow them into gilded academic careers."[3]

For £1 (discounted to 60p for students), subscribers to *Radical Philosophy* would receive three editions per year. There would be speaking events too: the Oxford branch would be "the only University philosophy society that invites speakers from outside Oxford; and I think we will have achieved something if we get Oxford philosophers to realise that Oxford isn't the centre of the philosophical world."[4]

Radical Philosophy wanted the study of philosophy to be less ahistorical, less fixated on conceptual analysis, and more open to ideas from other disciplines. The movement had a strong strain of Marxism, but the journal also introduced thinkers snubbed by Oxford—such as the impenetrable German Martin Heidegger and the more accessible Frenchman Michel Foucault. The aim was to combat what the radicals regarded as a pernicious isolationism from the tumultuous national and international events in the outside world. Looking back at this period, Rée explained that he and his peers had sought to "liberate ourselves from our brainwashing and . . . to 'raise consciousness' about the arrogance, aggression and narrow-mindedness" of the intellectual culture that had shaped them.[5]

It's the inevitable fate of the progressive to be eventually outflanked, to be seen, in time, as tame, even reactionary. What was radical in 1971 appears far less so today. It is notable that in the early days the movement was almost entirely male, and that male pronouns were used unreflectingly in sentences where the gender was arbitrary. Philosophers, fulminated the first issue, are a "self-perpetuating clique, like freemasons" forcing "eager young flatterers" to undertake ordeals, such as degrees, and "if the candidate survives these he wins a 'license to practise his trade and mystery.'"[6]

Singer initially embraced the *Radical Philosophy* program, and dutifully went along to meetings. But he quickly became disillusioned. One of the putative aims of the movement was to include writings relevant to people's lives, but Singer came to believe that the radicals had exchanged one brand of smug complacency for another. They may have self-identified as radical, but sitting around smoking cigarettes while discussing Louis Althusser and the overthrow of capitalism involved much talk, rather less action.

Singer, by contrast, was increasingly engaged by the two practical issues that would come to dominate the rest of his life.

Rust-Colored Sauce

As well as giving his joint seminars with Derek Parfit and James Griffin, Jonathan Glover delivered a series of lectures in Michaelmas Term 1970 at New College, where he was a fellow. In effect, these recycled material from a book he'd just completed, with the same name as the lecture series: *Responsibility*. The book, and the lectures, suggested that determinism—the view that all our actions and beliefs are determined by preexisting causes—might be valid, but we could still hold people responsible for their actions: I might be responsible—and therefore blameworthy—for shoplifting a lettuce or a packet of spaghetti, even if the conditions and circumstances that brought me to that point determined that I chose to pilfer the food.

The Wednesday lectures took place at midday—and at the end of one of them (exactly which one, nobody can recall), Singer drew the attention of the audience by challenging Glover from the floor. Afterward, a fellow student approached him. Singer had never spoken to him before, but the young man wanted to know what Singer thought of Glover's response to his question. He had a Canadian accent; in general Singer found it easier to get along with his "fellow colonials" than with the more reserved English.[7] In any case, the two of them began to chat, and the Canadian, Richard Keshen, proposed that they walk for five minutes down Broad Street, back to his college, Balliol, for lunch, in order to continue the discussion. Singer agreed.

It was wise to approach college meals with low culinary expectations. This was the era of prawn cocktails, vegetables boiled to within seconds of their disintegration, and peach melba. Courgettes and aubergines occasionally popped up on the plate but were considered exotic. So was pasta. Only thirteen years earlier, the BBC had run a spoof documentary on April Fool's Day, in which a family was shown harvesting spaghetti from a spaghetti tree; many viewers had rung in to ask for information about how they too could grow spaghetti.

Spaghetti was one option for lunch that day. The other was salad. This apparently innocuous choice would prove hugely consequential. The pasta came with an unappetizing rust-colored sauce—it was probably so-called spaghetti bolognaise (popularly truncated as "spag bol"), and Keshen inquired of the college server whether it contained meat. Told it did, he opted for the salad. Singer had the spaghetti. As they sat eating in the imposing Balliol dining hall, with its vaulted ceiling, long benches, stained-glass windows, and walls adorned with portraits of Balliol grandees, Singer asked why Keshen had wanted to know about the sauce and Keshen, a vegetarian, explained that he felt that it was unjustifiable for animals to be treated the way that they were in the food production process.

It had never occurred to Singer to become vegetarian. He enjoyed meat, though in England he'd noted it was not as tasty as, and far more expensive than, back home. He was also no animal lover: for a few years growing up, the Singers had had a pet cat called Buddy, but Buddy mysteriously disappeared when Peter was six, and after that there was just a succession of boring goldfish. Singer was generally unmoved by cute dogs, rabbits, or guinea pigs. However, after his lunch with Keshen he discussed the moral objections to meat eating with Renata, and they became vegetarian a few weeks later, at the beginning of 1971. They also became part of a close-knit group who'd committed to vegetarianism and who later named themselves the Oxford Group.

Vegetarians at the time were a tiny fringe in White British society. Vegans were rarer still, regarded as fruitcakes and nutjobs. (The best-known vegetarian restaurant was called Cranks.) Animal welfare was barely a consideration. University labs experimented with almost no oversight on a variety of animals, from mice to cats and monkeys. Indeed, a leading member of the Oxford Group, a psychologist called Richard Ryder, was himself a reformed animal experimenter. (Unlike Singer, he had grown up surrounded by pets, as a child even sharing a bedroom for a few months with a monkey.) The Oxford Group organized a few feebly attended demonstrations and in Cornmarket, the city's busiest shopping street, they tried a more imaginative tactic, exhibiting a replica veal calf in the narrow stalls in which such calves were then confined, and battery hens in the small wire cages in which they lived. The hen was constructed from papier-mâché, and realistic enough for one lady to berate Singer for confining the animal in such cruel conditions.

Then, in 1971, a few members of the Oxford Group published a book of essays, *Animals, Men and Morals*—already in press before Singer joined the group, so he was not a contributor.[8] It sank like a meatball in minestrone. Singer was a regular reader of the *New York Review of Books*, however, and—to jump ahead of our story—it was the book's lack of impact that would prompt him to write to Robert Silvers, legendary editor of the *NYRB*, offering to review the soon-to-be-published American edition. It is unlikely that any other editor of a major publication would have considered giving much space to this unpromising subject but, without committing himself, the open-minded, ever curious, philosophically inclined Silvers agreed to read whatever Singer came up with. It may have helped that Singer, having been awarded a distinction in his BPhil degree, had been appointed for two years as a Radcliffe lecturer at University College, and so could legitimately use college stationery and an Oxford academic's byline.

Bob Silvers's office was referred to as a "black hole," because submissions could enter and then disappear for months. But so persuaded was Silvers by Singer's draft that he responded quickly and enthusiastically—and then himself gave up eating meat. The article was published in April 1973, and later expanded into a book: *Animal Liberation* (1975). Now often referred to as the bible of the animal rights movement, it had an arresting preface:

> This book is about the tyranny of human over nonhuman animals. This tyranny has caused and today is still causing an

> amount of pain and suffering that can only be compared with that which resulted from the centuries of tyranny by white humans over black humans.[9]

The book detailed the cruel and inhumane (perhaps a misnomer as it was all too human) treatment of animals in food production and scientific research. The brutal production of broiler chickens, for example, who were kept in windowless sheds from birth, with every aspect of their environment controlled to maximize size, was described as follows:

> Toward the end of the eight- or nine-week life of the chicken, there may be as little as half of a square foot of space per chicken—or less than the area of a sheet of quarto paper for a three-and-one-half-pound bird. Under these conditions with normal lighting the stress of crowding and the absence of natural outlets for the birds' energies lead to outbreaks of fighting, with birds pecking at each other's feathers and sometimes killing and eating one another. Very dim lighting has been found to reduce this and so the birds are likely to live out their last weeks in near-darkness.[10]

Pre-Singer, there had already existed an animal welfare movement—a movement of people who believed that we should treat some nonhuman animals better. Indeed, as well as its National Society for the Prevention of Cruelty to Children, Britain had then, and still has, a Royal Society for the Prevention of Cruelty to Animals. The animal welfare movement tended to focus on those animals that humans love most, however: dogs, cats, horses. Almost no attention was paid to factory farming. Singer's move was to generalize the narrow disquiet about some animal suffering to all animals. We should improve the lives not just of pets, or of those animals we find cute, but of all sentient creatures. Animals, cute or not, have interests and moral claims upon us.

The ugly term "speciesism" had already been coined by Richard Ryder. He had sought an "ism" to shock people and make the parallels with other "isms" explicit, but Singer gave it philosophical heft. Of course, there are relevant moral differences between most humans and most nonhuman animals. Humans have complex and sometimes detailed future projects, for example (e.g., at the time of writing, I want to finish this book). The fact that humans and nonhuman animals vary in certain capacities can justify differential treatment. Killing a chicken can't thwart its philosophy-book-writing plans. That animals don't have sophisticated projects is one reason why killing a nonhuman animal is, according to Singer, less bad than killing a human. But chickens, just like humans, can feel pain, and the mere fact that humans and nonhuman animals belong to a different species is not in itself a reason to discount this pain. Believing "species" is morally relevant per se is speciesist, akin to believing that "race" or "skin color" is morally relevant per se. When it comes to pain, Singer concurred with the English utilitarian Jeremy Bentham, who held that the important question about animals "is not, Can they reason?, nor Can they talk? but, Can they suffer?"[11]

Bentham was one of very few philosophers who had seriously addressed the ethics of animal welfare. It was precisely because it had been relatively overlooked as a topic that Singer thought it worthwhile to devote effort to thinking and writing about it—for the more neglected a topic, the easier it is to make a distinctive contribution.

Besides animals, there was a second cause—charity. As with his work on animals, Singer's philosophy of charity was bound to be of widespread interest. After all, the philosophy of animals concerned what we eat, whereas the philosophy of charity concerned what we do with our money—and we all eat and spend.

Singer Song of Sixpence

At around the time that they became vegetarian, and as part of a conscious decision to live a more ethical life, Renata and Peter had begun to donate around 10 percent of their income to worthy causes. Renata had forced the issue: "How can you make the case that people should act morally, and then not do so yourself?" she asked. That sentiment is expressed in the article that gives rise to this book: "What is the point of relating philosophy to public (and personal) affairs if we do not take our conclusions seriously?"[12] Oxfam, with its headquarters in Oxford, was an obvious choice of charity and, as it happened, Philippa Foot, of trolleyology fame, was one of its early supporters.

Oxfam was active in the late 1960s in the Biafran crisis in Nigeria. But there was another ongoing international crisis that was on Singer's mind when he was approached by a charismatic, garrulous American legal scholar. Ronald Dworkin had recently been appointed chair of jurisprudence at Oxford and, like Singer, was now based at University College. He was on the board of the new journal *Philosophy & Public Affairs*. Might Singer be interested in writing an article for them? "So that's what got me thinking."[13] And when he did, his thoughts turned to South Asia.

East Pakistan

When Britain withdrew from India in 1947, the two majority-Muslim regions, in the northwest and northeast of the country, were artificially amalgamated in order to create a single, separate

Muslim nation, Pakistan. Not only did West and East Pakistan have no common border, but they were miles distant from each other: about 1,250 miles, in fact.

The double-headed entity was always going to struggle to survive. From the start, West Pakistan established itself as the dominant military, economic, political, and cultural partner, the source of bubbling tension between west and east. The British colonialists may have been ejected, but to many Bengalis it seemed as if the West Pakistanis had taken their place. One specific complaint was that the Bengali language was not recognized as a national language. Nationalist sentiment in East Pakistan grew, reinforced in November 1970 by a hopelessly inadequate response from the government to a devastating cyclone (winds of 115 mph) and tidal waves that rolled through densely populated coastal areas. Half a million people lost their lives.

It therefore came as no surprise when, the following month, Bengali nationalists triumphed at the polls. Several months of futile negotiations with West Pakistan ensued and the opening of the National Assembly was postponed. A new opening date was set: March 25, 1971. That night, after it had become clear that constitutional talks designed to hold Pakistan together had collapsed, the president of the country, General Yahya Khan, flew back from East to West Pakistan. As he drank scotch and soda on the plane, the fate of Bangladesh was sealed: but the planned operation would only be activated after confirmation of Khan's safe arrival home.

Almost as soon as Khan touched down, "the genocide began."[14] The West Pakistani troops were in vengeful mood: they'd been trapped for several week in their barracks, for fear of being attacked by Bengali activists. A subsequent commission of inquiry into the events of 1971 reported that it was "as if a ferocious animal having been kept chained and starved was suddenly let loose."[15]

The crackdown (known as Operation Searchlight) targeted nationalists in particular. There was rampant extrajudicial killing. Over ten thousand civilians were massacred within the first three days, some shot, some burned, others bombed. Intellectuals, politicians, students: all were victims; Hindus were marked out, too.

A Bengali soldier (and future president of Bangladesh), Major Zia ur Rehman, refused to be complicit. He ordered the arrest of his commanding officer and then addressed his fellow soldiers. "We have mutinied. From this moment on we are in independent Bangladesh. Pakistan is no more."[16]

The Bangladesh Liberation War had begun.

Bangladesh was forged from conflict. The total number of lives lost in the war remains disputed. Millions of desperate refugees poured across the border into India, the majority taking shelter in West Bengal.

The UN refugee body, the UNHRC, swung into action, trying to coordinate international support. But the rich developed world seemed largely indifferent, and the United States, which regarded Pakistan as a vital anti-communist ally, did nothing to impede hostilities: the Pakistan army fought with US-manufactured arms.

There were dissenting US voices. Archer Blood, the solid, straight-talking American consul-general in Dhaka, put his name to a telegram sent to the US Department of State on April 6, signed also by twenty other members of the US diplomatic staff. The signatories warned that there was a danger of genocide and charged the US government with being guilty of "moral bankruptcy" for failing to denounce the atrocities. The Blood Telegram, as it became known, "was probably the most blistering denunciation of U.S. foreign policy ever sent by its own diplomats."[17] Blood's reward was to be recalled to Washington, DC. His card was marked, and his career never fully recovered.

The Pakistan government did its best to block news of what was happening from reaching the wider world. The censorship forced Anthony Mascarenhas, a middle-aged Pakistani journalist of Christian Goan descent, to approach the British press. On June 13, with Mascarenhas and his family now safely out of Pakistan, the *Sunday Times*—a paper Singer read—splashed with a lengthy feature. The article contained graphic details of what Mascarenhas had eye-witnessed, including near the civic administrative headquarters, Circuit House, in the southeastern city of Comilla. The episode is also described in a book he wrote that same year. "Just before the curfew was sounded at 6 o'clock," he saw four companions,

> all tied loosely by a single rope, march down the street and into the compound of the Circuit House. Minutes later I heard screams and the madding sound of clubs beating on flesh and bone. Then the screaming stopped, as though turned off with a switch. The silence, to my anguished ears, suddenly became the loudest sound in all the world.[18]

India was unable to cope with the tide of gaunt bodies streaming across its border. Hundreds of makeshift camps were set up, lacking basic sanitation and access to clean water. Disease and diarrhea were rife; many of the youngest children died of malnourishment. The camps echoed with cries of the bereaved and the half-crazy.

On August 1, four months after the conflict had begun, Beatle George Harrison and his friend the Bengali sitarist Ravi Shankar organized a concert for Bangladesh at Madison Square Gardens in New York, to raise funds for the United Nations relief effort—actually two concerts on the same day, both sold out. Harrison convinced some famous friends to join in, including Ringo Starr and Eric Clapton. There was a surprise appearance from Bob Dylan.

Not used to being the front man, Harrison seemed nervous. But the concert and the subsequent release of a charity song raised millions of dollars as well as international awareness of the unfolding South Asian disaster. The concert itself received a positive press, though there were one or two discordant voices. "How glorious," *The Village Voice* sniffed, "to be able to launder one's conscience by laying out a few tax-deductible dollars to hear the biggies."[19]

Events in East Pakistan raised a simple question. Were we morally obliged to come to the aid of strangers if we could?

Singer had a simple answer. We were. The Indian government needed—according to the World Bank—£300 million to keep the refugees alive. At the time Singer wrote his article, Britain had given just shy of £15 million, and Singer compared this to the whopping £275 million the government had already spent on the Anglo-French Concorde project (the first Concorde passenger flight did not take off until 1976).

Let us here remind ourselves of Singer's basic premise: "If it is in our power to prevent something bad from happening, without thereby sacrificing anything of comparable moral importance, we ought, morally, to do it." Thus, "if I am walking past a shallow pond and see a child drowning in it, I ought to wade in and pull the child out. This will mean getting my clothes muddy, but this is insignificant, while the death of the child would presumably be a very bad thing."[20]

4

Bob's Bugatti

THE SHALLOW POND has something in common with The Invisible Hand. Everyone is familiar with Adam Smith's potent metaphor in *The Wealth of Nations*. Individuals, acting independently and selfishly, produce an outcome that's in the best interests of the economy as a whole—as though magically guided by an invisible hand. So effective is the metaphor in capturing the notion of benefits of the free market that it is now ubiquitous in debates about capitalism. Surprising, then, to discover that its appearance in *The Wealth of Nations* is so fleeting. Far from being the star of the show, it is barely granted a cameo. The individual "intends only his own gain; and he is in this, as in many other cases, led by an invisible hand to promote an end which was no part of his intention."[1] That's it.

Likewise, the Shallow Pond. Given how extensive the literature on the thought experiment has become, the oddest aspect of "Famine, Affluence, and Morality," at least in retrospect, is that the Shallow Pond merits merely two initial sentences, before popping up again later in the article in just one more.

Neither the Invisible Hand metaphor nor the Shallow Pond analogy were identified by their creators as imagery gold. The Shallow Pond is discarded as quickly in "Famine, Affluence, and

Morality" as an unwanted charity flyer. Singer can't pinpoint a particular moment when he realized it merited a more prominent role in the debate about rich and poor. It seems likely that this dawned on him gradually. In *Practical Ethics* (1979), a book that has chapters on various topics, including animals, abortion, and euthanasia, as well as the rich and poor, it receives more extended treatment, in a chapter on global poverty.[2] But it's only much later, with the publication of Singer's *The Life You Can Save* (2009), that it takes center-stage. The book opens with it.

As the Shallow Pond grew in prominence in Singer's philosophical case for charitable giving, it also changed in relatively trifling details. In *Practical Ethics,* Singer imagines that he is on his way to teach—so not only will he get his clothes muddy, but there will be the added inconvenience of being late or having to cancel a lecture.[3] In *The Life You Can Save,* the perspective moves back from the first to the second person singular (it's you, not Singer, walking past the pond) and now, in addition, "you will ruin the new shoes you bought only a few days ago."[4] The (relatively minor) financial cost is now made explicit.

But the basic argument is unaffected. Suppose that the cost of new shoes, and the tiresomeness of having to go to the launderette to clean your muddy clothes, as well as having to sort out problems arising from a late or canceled lecture, are at least as costly and time-consuming as arranging a money transfer to a charity like Oxfam. And suppose it is true that this money sent to Oxfam would save a life. Then, since we all agree that it would be wrong not to save the child in the Shallow Pond, we must also all agree that it is wrong of us not to send some of our own money to Oxfam or a similar organization to save a child in the Global South.

Mustn't we?

Distinctions and Differences

Is failing to send money to Oxfam really the moral equivalence of ignoring the child in the Shallow Pond? Or are there relevant differences between the thought experiment and the real world? The crucial word here is "relevant": between any two cases there will be some differences—the question is whether these are significant enough to justify dismissing the analogy, and carrying on with our lives much as before.

Already, in the original article, a few objections are anticipated and swatted away. Does it matter that the Shallow-Pond child is nearby, while the strangers that we might help by giving money to charity are far away? It may matter psychologically, concedes Singer. But distance per se is *morally* irrelevant. In the past, we were in a better position to know how to help those nearby—providing us with a rational reason to help those in close proximity first. But with swift travel and instant communication, the gap between our knowledge of how to assist locally and how to help abroad has shrunk: we can no longer justify discrimination on geographical grounds. And so, "[i]t makes no moral difference whether the person I can help is a neighbor's child ten yards from me or a Bengali whose name I shall never know, ten thousand miles way."[5]

Here Singer inadvertently conflates two points. Identity—whether you know the identity of the person you're in a position to help—is distinct from distance. In theory, one might carry moral weight, but not the other. By the time he wrote *Practical Ethics,* Singer had come to recognize this, and tackles the identity issue independently.

> Suppose that I am a travelling salesman, selling tinned food, and I learn that a batch of tins contains a contaminant, the

> known effect of which, when consumed, is to double the risk that the consumer will die of stomach cancer. Suppose I continue to sell the tins. My decision may have no identifiable victims. Some of those who eat the food will die of cancer. The proportion of consumers dying in this way will be twice that of the community at large, but which among the consumers died because they ate what I sold, and which would have contracted the disease anyway? It is impossible to tell; but surely the impossibility makes my decision no less reprehensible than it would have been had the contaminant had more readily detectable, though equally fatal, effects.[6]

There exists some empirical evidence (as we shall see) that knowing the identity of a victim makes us more inclined to help. But once again, according to Singer, it's *morally* insignificant.

Is a related disanalogy relevant? The child in the pond is one "of our own,"[7] and we have a greater obligation to look after one of our own than to look after other people. But what does it mean to label somebody "one of our own"? Presumably we can't be suggesting that the child's race or ethnicity has any bearing? That would obviously be objectionable; we shouldn't care whether the child is Black or White, Christian, Hindu, Jewish, or Muslim. A fellow citizen perhaps? Well, perhaps we do have some special obligations to our compatriots, but, again, it surely doesn't matter whether the drowning child has a British, American, or Bengali passport.

Singer addresses yet another disanalogy in "Famine, Affluence, and Morality." In the Shallow Pond, only one person can save the child. But millions of people could help provide resources for those starving in a famine. Singer repeats what is now becoming a familiar move. This might be relevant at the psychological level, but it is not morally pertinent. "Should I be less obliged to pull the drowning child out of the pond if on looking around I see other people, no further away than I am, who have also noticed the child but are doing nothing? One has only to ask this question to see the absurdity of the view that numbers lessen obligation."[8]

Living High and Letting Die

After his Oxford lectureship, Singer had a one-year spell at New York University (NYU), as a temporary assistant professor, a job he was offered on the back of his "Famine, Affluence, and Morality" article, as well as the *NYRB* review about animal liberation. The publication of *Animal Liberation* in 1975 made him—as philosophers go—famous. There was a book tour around the USA, and he appeared on the *Today* show, interviewed by the celebrated news anchor Barbara Walters.

Meanwhile, although "Famine, Affluence, and Morality" was quickly acknowledged as an exemplar of philosophical clarity and reasoning, and Singer spoke about it in lectures and seminars, there was initially surprisingly little engagement with it within academia. Or outside academia. It failed to breach the walls of the ivory tower. Nor was there any interest from the fourth estate: the media.

It was only in 1996, a quarter of a century after the article's publication, that an American philosopher, Peter Unger, analyzed it afresh. Unger was born and raised in the Bronx. All four of his grandparents were impoverished Jewish immigrants who arrived in the USA from eastern Europe at the turn of the twentieth century. His family moved out of the Bronx to an enormous house in Westchester after his father earned a small fortune making small electric parts. At Swarthmore College he studied alongside a remarkable set of contemporaries, including Gilbert

Harman and David Lewis (who became lifelong colleagues at Princeton). Unger, meanwhile, landed a job at NYU in the early 1970s, where he overlapped briefly with Singer. At the time he was interested in epistemology (the investigation of what we can know and how we can know it). It was only much later that he became fascinated by ethics—and when he taught a class in ethics, he assigned students Singer's *Practical Ethics* as a text.

Unger's own book, *Living High and Letting Die*, he declares, is built on Singer's "famous case," the Shallow Pond.[9] But the conclusion of Unger's book is a surprise. It is not that Singer went too far in his demands upon us; it is that he did not go far enough.

Living High and Letting Die begins by contrasting two cases, which Unger calls "The Vintage Sedan" and "Envelope." It's worth spelling them out in full.

> The Vintage Sedan: Not truly rich, your one luxury in life is a vintage Mercedes sedan that, with much time, attention and money, you've restored to mint condition. In particular, you're pleased by the auto's fine leather seating. One day, you stop at the intersection of two small country roads, both lightly travelled. Hearing a voice screaming for help, you get out and see a man who's wounded and covered with a lot of his blood. Assuring you that his wound's confined to one of his legs, the man also informs you that he was a medical student for two full years. And, despite his expulsion for cheating on his second year final exams, which explains his indigent status since, he's knowledgeably tied his shirt near the wound so as to stop the flow. So, there's no urgent danger of losing his life, you're informed, but there's great danger of losing his limb. This can be prevented, however, if you drive him to a rural hospital fifty miles away. "How did the wound occur?" you ask. An avid bird-watcher, he admits that he

trespassed on a nearby field and, in carelessly leaving, cut himself on rusty barbed wire. Now, if you'd aid this trespasser, you must lay him across your fine back seat. But, then, your fine upholstery will be soaked through with blood, and restoring the car will cost over five thousand dollars. So, you drive away. Picked up the next day by another driver, he survives but loses the wounded leg.[10]

The Envelope: In your mailbox, there's something from (the US Committee for) UNICEF. After reading it through, you correctly believe that, unless you soon send in a check for $100, then, instead of each living many more years, over thirty more children will die soon. But, you throw the material in your trash basket, including the convenient return envelope provided, you send nothing, and instead of living many years, over thirty more children soon die than would have had you sent in the requested $100.[11]

We routinely bin charitable appeals that arrive through the post without pausing to think about it. But Unger wants to undermine the intuition that you've only done something wrong in Vintage Sedan. In fact, in various ways, the moral deck is stacked against Envelope. After all, the financial burden of picking up the wounded man is $5,000, while the Envelope donation would cost a mere $100. Vintage Sedan involves one person, Envelope thirty kids. The wounded man is only in danger of losing a limb, whereas lives are at stake in Envelope. One assumes that the children in Envelope are blameless, but in Vintage Sedan the man has acted illegally and irresponsibly. Finally, Envelope is no effort, whereas Vintage Sedan entails a lengthy trip out of your way.

Unger searches for and fails to find any relevant distinctions between Vintage Sedan and Envelope that would justify our behavior in the latter, but not the former case. We can point to distinctions. In Vintage Sedan we are physically closer to the victim than in Envelope. We might also be socially closer; for example, we might assume in Vintage Sedan that the person needing help is, say, a compatriot. In Vintage Sedan we find out in a very direct way that a person needs help (we see the wounded and suffering man in front of us) while in Envelope we only hear about those in need indirectly, via a piece of paper. In Vintage Sedan, unlike in Envelope, we alone can save the wounded man. What's more, we're more likely to describe the Vintage Sedan scenario as an emergency. In Vintage Sedan, the good deed is what Unger calls "causally focused" on a particular person, whereas in Envelope there are many donors contributing together to save individuals in need. In Envelope, as distinct from Vintage Sedan, you would never know which individuals you've saved. Finally, in Vintage Sedan you would not just be sending money, but providing goods and services (i.e., the use of your car).

Singer had already addressed some of these dissimilarities. Unger was more systematic. His approach was to take each distinction in turn, modify or propose a new thought experiment to highlight the distinction, and then ask us to concur that it was a distinction without a difference. So far, so Singer-esque. Then things get wilder. Compare "The Yacht" and "The Account."

> The Yacht: You're employed on the waterfront estate of a billionaire. Through binoculars, you see a woman out in the waves, already in danger of drowning. And, in under an hour, a hurricane will pass through the area. So, there's this: If you go to aid her soon, she'll be saved; if not, she'll soon die. But, there's also this: To aid her, you must use a motor yacht worth many millions of dollars. And, if you go, then, on the

return trip, to avoid complete wreckage by the hurricane, you must pass through a channel where the yacht will suffer a few million dollars damage. Since the boat's the billionaire's and you don't have his permission to do this, it's against the law. And, being far from rich, you can't help much with the repair bill that, even after insurance, will be over a million bucks. Still, you take the yacht and save the woman.

The Account: You're one of many accountants who work in the large firm among whose clients is a certain billionaire. As you know, he gives a lot to several fashionable charities, but does hardly anything to aid the world's neediest people. Today, you've the rare chance to decrease, by only a million dollars, the billionaire's huge account. Partly because it can be done without ever being noticed, for the billionaire this won't ever mean even as much as mild annoyance. What's more, via a sequence of many small anonymous contributions, the million will all go to UNICEF and, as a result, ten thousand fewer children will die in the next few months. Now, largely because you've long been in the habit of giving most of your own money to UNICEF, you'll never be in a position to reimburse the magnate to any significant degree. Still, you shift the funds and, in consequence, ten thousand more children don't die soon but live long.

Unger assumes that most people will think that you've behaved badly in Account but not in Yacht. But he thinks that while our intuitions are right about Yacht, they're wrong about Account. Acting in Account is arguably more praiseworthy—the cost is only a million, and it saves many more lives. If that is right, we may be justified in stealing where lives are at stake.

There are of course many differences between Yacht and Account, but, as before, Unger argues that none of these is morally pertinent. This, then, stretches our obligations beyond those suggested by Singer in "Famine, Affluence, and Morality." Unger starts by writing that "on pain of living a life that is seriously immoral, a typical well-off person, like you and me, must give away most of her financially valuable assets, and much of her income, directing the fund to lessen efficiently the serious suffering of others";[12] he goes on to suggest that for the same purpose we should also demand, and if necessary steal, money and possessions owned by others.

In another thought experiment designed to illustrate the extent of our obligations, Unger gives us Bob the Bugatti owner.[13] Bob has used up all his savings (bar $3,000) to purchase a rare Bugatti, worth $3 million, a vehicle that can't be insured. Bob adores the car, but the aim is to sell it at some stage and retire on the proceeds. One day, Bob parks the Bugatti at the end of a train track and heads off for a walk. Suddenly (you've guessed it), he sees an out-of-control train barreling toward a fork in the line. If Bob does nothing, the train will proceed down a track on which a young child is trapped. The child will almost certainly be hit and killed. Bob could turn a switch sending the train down the other side of the fork. But that's where his Bugatti is parked, and the train would destroy it.

At stake here, then, is not a pair of expensive shoes, or a cleaning bill for some muddy clothes, but Bob's prized possession representing his entire livelihood. And yet, Unger assumes that we will all share his intuition that Bob should sacrifice his Bugatti and save the life.

Unger's book received a mixed reception. On page 1, to emphasize that his arguments were about practical action, not mere philosophical debate, he included the New York address of the United Nations Children's Fund and exhorted his readers to send checks.[14] Other charity contact details are dotted through the text. This was an unorthodox approach for a philosophy book and displeased the philosopher Martha Nussbaum, who repeatedly clobbered the book with a hatchet in a lengthy review.

> His implied reader is a moral imbecile. . . . Unger keeps giving us phone numbers and addresses of charities, on the apparent assumption that we don't know how to find them for ourselves. His sentences are full of slogans and capital letters. . . . He writes as if trying to speak to someone who is not only obtuse but deaf.[15]

Maybe so, but for the time being nobody seemed to be listening. Until. . . .

5

From the Pond to the World

> Either you decide to leave people to die or you decide to do something about it.
>
> —JEFFREY SACHS

THE YEAR WAS 2005. The BPhil at Oxford had changed since Singer's day, when candidates were assessed through a series of three-hour exams at the end of their second year. With so much riding on a few exams, the strain of the final few months had always been intense. The restructured BPhil replaced these exams with a requirement that in the second year students submit six essays over a fourteen-week period, that ran between term one (Michaelmas) and two (Hilary).

If part of the aim was to reduce the pressure, it had the opposite effect. The young philosophers retreated for this period into a feverish and lonely hibernation; some were driven to the brink of breakdown (and one or two to beyond the brink, dropping out or failing because of the stress).

Candidate number 35946 felt the heat, like everyone else. He had selected moral philosophy as one of his BPhil options, and given a range of possible essay questions within this area he chose Topic 4: "Ought I to forgo some luxury whenever I can thereby enable someone else's life to be saved?"

He wrote his answer between February 2 and February 22, 2005. Candidate 35946, aka Toby Ord, had never read "Famine, Affluence, and Morality" before, but to respond to this question he was obviously required to do so. His essay began with a slight variation of the Shallow Pond, in which saving the child would entail missing a concert you've been eagerly anticipating. The conclusion, however, was essentially Singer's: that no luxury was worth a life. For this, and his other ethics paper, he received an A–, not the highest mark, but straight As were almost unknown.

Having convinced himself that Singer's reasoning was sound, Ord felt that he, personally, had to act upon it. He had, to lift a phrase from his blog, "a moment of moral clarity."[1] The paper also triggered a practical idea which crystallized over the next few months. How about setting up an organization to encourage other people to join him in giving away money? His idea involved a second simple and, in hindsight, obvious component, that had not been paid the attention by Peter Singer that it merited. If money was given away, how could we assess how much good it could do?

Like Peter Singer, Toby Ord was raised in a comfortably-off family in Melbourne, though his father, an architect, had ascended into the middle class from a working-class background. His mother, Alexis, also trained as an architect and was briefly—during the bicentennial marking the two-hundredth year since the British arrival in Australia—the lord mayor of Melbourne, the first woman ever to hold the position. It was a politically engaged home; both domestic and international issues were regularly discussed round the dinner table.

Ord took two degrees at the University of Melbourne, in science (majoring in computer science), and afterward in arts (majoring in philosophy and mathematics). Then he was awarded a scholarship and, following the Singer route, moved from Melbourne to Oxford to study for the BPhil.

Already he'd begun to think about donating significant sums of money to charity but had yet to translate intention into action. At the time he came across "Famine, Affluence, and Morality" he was living contentedly on his graduate stipend of £12,000. Acting upon his moral convictions necessitated some long-term planning. He intended to remain in academia—there was no Plan B—and worked out that an average university salary would deliver lifetime earnings of at least £1.5 million. He could, he figured, satisfy all his basic needs on £18,000 a year, and donate any surplus over and above that level. As it happened, £18,000 was the then median income in the UK; few people earning this amount would consider themselves rich, but, as Ord also worked out, they were actually among the top 5 percent of earners worldwide.

If he executed his plan then, over his career, Ord's pot of savings would pile up to roughly £1 million—he'd need a big pot. He had married Bernadette (Dette) Young on Armistice Day, November 11, 2006. A doctor, she made a similar vow—pledging to donate any income exceeding £25,000 per annum. They were then childless, but were they to start a family they agreed that they would grant themselves additional financial wiggle room: £5,000 per annum per child. (Their daughter was born in 2014.)

On their joint salary, Ord reckoned they could still have a "pretty wonderful life. . . . How is this possible? Basically, because the best parts of it (listening to one's favorite music, cuddling on the sofa, reading *Jane Eyre*) don't really cost much money at all."[2] Throughout his time as an Oxford student, Ord spent an amount buying drinks in pubs equivalent to what most students manage over a single lunchtime. One of his low-cost hobbies was exploring every Oxford nook and cranny, quad, and public garden, capturing the city in photographs, especially in the late afternoon, when sunshine bathed the limestone.

While he didn't think he would have much success persuading others to make the same financial commitment as he and his wife had made, Ord was more confident that he could convince people to pledge a smaller percentage of their income. The amount he alighted on, 10 percent, was hardly original. Singer had proposed the same percentage in *Practical Ethics*,[3] and, of course, the practice of lay people contributing a tenth of their income to support their religious institutions went back to the Old Testament—so the figure had deep cultural roots.

It was an appealing number for two other reasons. The first was that it is a tough target. There would be little point signing people up for, say 0.2 percent, when many gave such an amount already. The second was that, though tough, it was not impossible or unrealistic. Indeed, the same balance of considerations applies to the Church: 10 percent is a large amount, but not enough to cause mutiny within the congregation. Making the pledge public, Ord figured, would deter people from changing their minds. Having given an open commitment, it would be embarrassing, shameful even, to renege on it.

So this was the vision. But Ord still couldn't be sure anybody else would be persuaded to share it.

Having completed the BPhil, Ord had enrolled for a doctorate—a DPhil, in Oxford-speak—beginning in the autumn of

2005; his thesis would be on how we should make moral decisions. He was particularly interested in cases like "Clare," discussed by Derek Parfit in *Reasons and Persons*.[4]

Clare has a decision to make. She "could either give her child some benefit, or give much greater benefits to some unfortunate stranger. Because she loves her child, she benefits him rather than the stranger."[5] Clare is a consequentialist. What matters to her is the overall consequences of her actions, judged impartially. Psychologically, however, she cannot bring herself to help the stranger rather than her child.

The puzzle is that at this particular moment Clare, as a consequentialist, should choose to help the stranger. But imagine a world in which parents did not have a special bond with their children and were not disposed to rank their child's well-being above that of strangers. The consequences would be catastrophic. Clare's decision to help her child seems simultaneously both right and wrong. So how should we assess it? Parfit categorized this as an example of blameless wrongdoing, and Ord agreed. Consequentialism implies that it is better that people have motives like Clare's, even if it leads them, on occasion, to act in ways that don't produce the best consequences.

A few months into his DPhil, on Saturday, February 25, 2006, Ord went to Balliol College to hear a paper by a well known, German-born Yale philosopher, Thomas Pogge, who was a leading scholar in "global justice"; in other words, fairness and distribution at the international level. Afterward, a few of those attending the talk moved on to the Balliol Middle Common Room (a room reserved for use by graduates). Ord had been chewing over his organization plans and it was here that he first publicly aired them. Expecting skepticism, he was surprised by the warm reception the idea received. He jotted down the names of those who were supportive. "It was after midnight when we dispersed," he wrote in a blog that he ran for three years, "and it became clear that things had begun."[6]

Ord decided he would call his organization "Giving What We Can." In seeking supporters, one convincing stratagem was to highlight what good a single person could do. Ord calculated, for example, how far his lifetime donations could go in the treatment of trachoma—an infectious disease that can cause pain and blindness and that affects millions of people, mostly in the developing world. A cheap and straightforward procedure restored sight—and £1 million could fund eighty thousand operations.

He floated some of his ideas in his blog. "Being able to restore sight to a single person would be quite amazing—it is the stuff of miracles. Being able to restore sight to tens of thousands is simply staggering."[7] Reading the blog in retrospect, one is struck by the optimism—the promise of adventure.

You can't change the world by shaking a charity tin and having a few people drop in some loose change. But if dozens or hundreds of people commit to donating substantial sums over decades, well then, reasoned Ord, there's the potential for real impact. Many lives could surely be saved. Three weeks after the Pogge event, Ord went on a walking trip with friends to the Lake District. One memory suggests that he must have been confident that his plans would come to fruition. He was scrambling up a path where there was a spectacular sixty-foot waterfall crashing into a ravine. "And half-way up I remember thinking that this was way too dangerous because I'd calculated how many people would die with me. And I then very carefully climbed the rest of the way."[8]

Counting What Counts

Toby Ord is a stats man, happiest when playing around with numbers and formulae. But his initial calculations about charity effectiveness were rudimentary. Charities are often compared in terms of how much of their income goes on overheads—on staff salaries, utility bills, stationery, marketing. Donors really care about this metric;[9] but it's a hopeless one. To cure patients and save as many lives as possible, overheads expenditure can be vital.

What Ord really wanted was an evaluation of what charities achieved for each pound or dollar they received. Individual charities themselves were not much help. "If they're distributing condoms, they'll want to distribute as many as possible as cheaply as possible. But they won't look into whether they would do better switching their focus completely—to, say, anti-malaria nets."[10]

So Ord set about researching charities himself. A lack of hard evidence impeded progress, but a breakthrough occurred in 2007. On January 1 that year, he was contacted by a research associate at the Future of Humanity Institute (FHI) at Oxford University. The FHI investigated what it deemed the vital issues facing the future of humanity (such as artificial intelligence, and global warming). The FHI researcher, Jason Matheny, having heard of Ord's interest in global poverty, emailed him the data from the Disease Control Priorities Project (DCPP), which contained detailed information on the multiple ways of helping mainly impoverished countries improve the health of their citizens. The second edition of the DCPP (DCP2)—1,400 pages—was released in 2006.

This provided many of the numbers Ord needed. He pored over them for weeks, translating them to the world of philanthropy, so as to better understand their moral consequences and to expose what he calls their "jewel-like results."[11] It was only to be expected that the cost-effectiveness of interventions varied from, say, disease to disease, but burrowing through the DCP2 data, the young philosopher was struck by a startling fact. The difference in the good that programs achieved per dollar spent was not marginal; it was not a matter of a few percentage points. Spending on overheads didn't vary dramatically between charities, but some interventions were literally a thousand times better than others. The best interventions were a hundred times better than middling ones. "It really woke me up to this fact: that where you give can be even more important than whether you give."[12]

Suppose one charity is estimated to save a life for every £500,000 and another for every £5,000. The person who donated £5,000 to the second charity would be doing more good than the person who gave £490,000 to the first. Ord realized, for example, that treating Kaposi's sarcoma, a type of cancer that causes skin lesions and is often associated with patients who are HIV positive, was hugely costly compared to the distribution of condoms that would prevent HIV and AIDS. His general approach was first to work out which of the many serious health challenges around the globe were most easily tackled, and then to seek out the charities through which the best results could be achieved.

At approximately the same time, two Americans were doing something similar, but from the opposite direction.

Give Well

Elie Hassenfeld is not a philosopher and to this day has never read "Famine, Affluence, and Morality." He did, however, read a 2006 *New York Times* magazine article by Singer, which mentions the Shallow Pond and offers a guide to how much rich Americans should be giving, depending on their wealth.[13] For Hassenfeld, the article appeared at an apposite moment, following several deeply frustrating months during which he and work colleagues had been trying to determine which worthy causes they themselves should support.

Hassenfeld had been raised in a Modern Orthodox Jewish household in a Boston suburb and recalls that at around age six, after watching a television charity appeal, he persuaded his lawyer father to donate—for which they received a copy of the New Testament. After high school, he spent a year in a Jerusalem yeshiva (seminary) and then studied religion at Columbia University. For a brief period, he considered becoming a Talmudic scholar, but instead was seduced by an industry that worshipped Mammon. On the first day at Bridgewater Associates, a Connecticut-based hedge fund—which traded liquid assets, such as currencies—he met his future collaborator, Holden Karnofsky.

That was 2004. In the summer of 2006, Hassenfeld, Karnofsky, and a few other coworkers decided that they should form a charity club and give some money away. Not mega-bucks—Hassenfeld was planning on around $2,000; but pooled with contributions from the others, the sum would be quite sizeable. The question was, which charity should benefit? The traders agreed that they would each undertake research on a different topic—deploying the kind of sophisticated data analysis that they applied to the day job—and report back. Then, at the end of the year, they would reach a consensus.

And that's when the trouble began. Hassenfeld, like Ord, couldn't source the necessary data. He was investigating water-related diseases in Africa. The organizations he approached would make various claims, such as "$20 will provide a person with clean water for life!"; but when he tried to delve into these

(What does "for life" actually mean? How is the outcome achieved? What is the evidence?—and so on), he found that the charities either didn't possess, or wouldn't share, the relevant information. "And they couldn't believe anybody would even put questions like this. It was shocking."[14]

He and Karnofsky concluded that there was a need for a body that would scrutinize and extract facts and figures from charities and thus enable potential donors to make an informed choice, armed with knowledge about which charities were most effective. Indeed, it turned out that wading into research on, for example, dysentery was both revelatory and something they excelled at. In 2007, after raising some money, they left their hedge fund, and set up GiveWell.

They were soon reaching conclusions broadly similar to Ord's. Overheads were a terrible metric. There were some extraordinarily effective charities. And the per-dollar gains from the developing world far outweighed those that were possible in the developed world.

They also carried out some detailed analysis on how much it costs to save a life. Peter Singer had implied in "Famine, Affluence, and Morality" that lifesaving was remarkably cheap—the price of some ruined clothes. But, according to the calculations of GiveWell, it is much costlier than this: even the most effective charities need "between $3,000 and $5,500" per life saved.[15] To contrast charities, GiveWell, like Toby Ord, exploited a relatively new statistical tool.

QALYs

If you want to buy a tin of kidney beans, and two adjacent supermarkets offer the same tin at different prices, it would be odd, all else being equal, to shop in the more expensive store.

You would need a reason to pay more for a product that you could purchase for less. But our shopping choices may not be straightforward. What if the tins are not the same—perhaps there is a brand of kidney bean that you prefer? What if a recipe doesn't specify what kind of bean is required, and you have to select between kidney, pinto, and cannellini?

Choosing between pulses is easy-peasy, compared to selecting a charity. Ord had researched the efficacy of anti-malaria nets and cures for trachoma-related blindness: one intervention saves lives, while the other has a massively beneficial impact on the quality of life. How should these interventions be compared?

That was one problem. There was also that misleading phrase, "saving lives." If you were to drag me from the path of a speeding car, you would save my life. Yet despite your welcome intervention, I would not be saved for eternity; you would "merely" have postponed my death.

Humans are on average living longer than in the past. Nevertheless, few of us will make it beyond a hundred, and the death of a nonagenarian is not typically felt to be a tragedy. A child dying of cancer or killed in a car accident is a tragedy—for the child had many more years to look forward to. Does that suggest that saving the life of a child should have priority over saving the life of a pensioner? And how should we think about a treatment that gains an extra year's life when this extra year is one of being bedridden, and full of indignity and pain?

In 1974, Joseph S. Pliskin was finishing his twelve-chapter Harvard PhD in mathematics. His chosen subject was decision making in patients with end-state renal failure. It provided some intriguing mathematical puzzles. Given constraints on resources, it was impossible to treat everyone. There were then, as now, two main medical options: dialysis and transplantation. Dialysis is grueling, requiring trips to hospital each week, with each visit lasting several hours. Patients who have transplants have a better, though typically shorter, life.

The cold-blooded objective of the thesis was to determine who should and shouldn't be offered treatment. Pliskin was by no means the first academic to attempt to capture ways of evaluating quality of life, but in his fifth chapter he dropped in a phrase that over the next few decades would become ubiquitous among health economists, policymakers, and medical practitioners around the world. He still has the typewritten pages to prove it: "[W]e must determine appropriate trade-offs between life years and quality of life. . . . Hereinafter we will refer to quality adjusted life years."[16]

Quality Adjusted Life Years. A subsequent paper by two economists introduced the acronym "QALY."[17] The basic idea is this: if a patient is about to die, and a treatment gives them an extra year of life with good health, that gets marked as a gain of 1 QALY. But if this extra year is burdened by a debilitating condition or illness, the score is scaled down, depending on the seriousness of the condition. It might, say, be a 0.75, or 0.5.

It's easy to see why the QALY has proved such a useful instrument for health professionals. If a hospital or health care system can afford either drug A or drug B, and wants to know which to fund, then QALYs can point to a solution. Does drug A produce more QALYs than drug B? In the UK's National Health Service (NHS), there is a cutoff point: if a new drug produces a QALY for below £30,000 it will usually be funded, but not it if costs more than that.[18]

Toby Ord found QALYs very helpful. Scouring multiple sources for health data, he became so absorbed in the calculations that he lost sight of some of the more humdrum logistical planning required to establish Giving What We Can. One important achievement, however, was his success in securing the backing of a key intellectual. Ord wrote to Peter Singer on May 28, 2007 outlining his plans. Singer was due in Oxford the following month to deliver the annual Uehiro Lectures in Practical Ethics. Ord explained that Giving What We Can was inspired by Singer's article "Famine, Affluence, and Morality," and that it would be ready to launch later that year. They met at noon on June 11, and Singer immediately expressed enthusiasm.

But 2007 came and went. And then another year passed. Perhaps Giving What We Can would never have materialized had it not been for another meeting that, in time, would radically alter how many people think about charity.

6

Turning Point in the Grave

THE APPOINTMENT, at 2 p.m. on Wednesday, April 23, 2009, between twenty-nine-year-old Ord and a twenty-two-year-old Scottish postgraduate led to what the younger man would later describe as "the most important conversation in my life."[1]

Will MacAskill and Toby Ord were both interested in the role of uncertainty in moral theorizing. Often we're uncertain about the outcomes of our initiatives: perhaps one course of action might be guaranteed to produce a decent outcome, while the alternative course could produce a far better result, but is risky, and things might go badly wrong. On what basis should we make a decision? That's one kind of uncertainty. But MacAskill was more interested in a deeper kind. What happens if we're not sure about our values? You continue to include meat in your diet, but have a nagging sense that you should go vegetarian. You are unsure whether to prioritize your family or your career. How should we proceed when we're not confident that our values are the right ones?

At this stage, Ord had just completed his doctorate and was now a junior research fellow (JRF), still at Balliol College, and on a salary of £25,000. A JRF is a highly sought after postgraduate award, providing funding for a fixed term, usually three years, with few conditions or obligations attached. The White's Professor of Moral Philosophy, John Broome, had supervised Ord's DPhil thesis, and was also supervising MacAskill, who was at St Edmund Hall, known informally as Teddy Hall, and studying for the BPhil. Knowing that the two young men shared a mutual interest in ethics under uncertainty, Broome suggested they meet.

The mise-en-scène for the encounter was a graveyard, once belonging to a church and now incorporated within the gardens of Teddy Hall. The mainly nineteenth-century gravestones, some of whose inscriptions are too worn to be legible, stick out of the lawn at irregular intervals like incisors in a gap-toothed mouth. The two young philosophers had intended simply to go for a quick coffee, but they immediately clicked, both emotionally and intellectually, and ended up in an intense five-hour conversation, almost none of which was about moral uncertainty.

Ord, on this occasion, did much of the talking, raising ideas that left MacAskill "completely blown away." He told him about QALYs. He mentioned how he'd researched animal welfare and what foodstuffs caused animals the most suffering. And he talked about "existential risks," the various hazards that threatened to bring an end to human existence. His apprehensions about these risks made MacAskill wonder whether his new Australian friend was "insane."[2]

But the most profound effect Ord had on the younger man resulted from telling him about his commitment to donate most of his income to charity, and in particular his ambitions to set up Giving What We Can. For MacAskill, this was a lightbulb moment. So taken was he with the scheme that he dropped all his other commitments, and he and Ord set about planning its launch.

William MacAskill was born William Crouch in Glasgow in 1987. (He changed his surname after getting married, MacAskill being the name of his wife's maternal grandmother. The long-standing tradition of wives adopting their husband's name had dubious connotations, he felt, and needed to be challenged.) Will was the youngest of three sons; his mother had earned a PhD in genetics and was employed by the NHS as an expert on gene abnormalities; his father worked in IT for a clothing company. Education was prioritized: all three boys were sent to private school, leaving not much to spare in the bank.

It was a loving family, but the emphatically right-wing *Daily Mail* was the parents' newspaper of choice, and their views on immigration and climate change led their left-wing inclined youngest son to conclude that, in the interests of harmony, political discussion was best avoided. Will was packed off to Sunday school each week, though can't remember ever believing in God. He discovered and fell in love with the novels of Dostoevsky. They suited his intermittent depressive moods, and he was preoccupied by their proto-existentialist themes: the idea that each of us is free to create meaning in our lives, to live authentically and not be beholden to societal norms. The adults in his life, he felt, barely reflected on their values, and lived unhappily and inauthentically. He was taken by the Christ-like figure of Prince Myshkin, in *The Idiot*: "I was attracted to a certain conception of Christian morality that involved intense forgiveness of others."[3]

Perhaps the most notable characteristic of the young MacAskill was his abnormally sensitive moral antenna. He volunteered at local charities, including in a care home for the elderly, and every Monday evening for six years (plus occasional weekends and summer camps) at a scout club for disabled children. Aged around fifteen he started a novel, about two Canadian teenagers running away from home, aiming to donate 50 percent of the royalties to support people dying of AIDS. The plan was abandoned, but not before he'd written thirty thousand words.

At school, co-ed Hutchesons' Grammar School, he excelled—becoming dux (a Scottish term meaning top pupil academically). In fact, he was not merely top overall, but in every subject, including philosophy. In his first philosophy essay he criticized a strand of utilitarianism and was awarded a "B." Philosophy must be difficult, he deduced, since his marked papers rarely featured Bs. That made him more, rather than less, interested in the subject, and when he decided to apply for Oxbridge, he chose Cambridge over Oxford because there he could take a degree in philosophy alone. The brightest students from Hutchesons' were supposed to become lawyers or doctors, and both his parents and teachers were dismayed at his preference for such an impractical subject that offered no guaranteed route to a stable income.

Toward the end of his final school year, he gave a talk to his fellow senior pupils, explaining that the scout group he helped needed more volunteers. An unintended but welcome consequence of such publicly expressed do-gooding turned out to be a sudden interest on the part of members of the opposite sex.

At home, a "proper" meal involved meat. MacAskill had once been an avid carnivore. "Three quarters of a kilogram of steak and a single slice of bread to mop up the blood was my favourite meal." But on the day he left home for university,

October 1, 2005, he became a vegetarian. "I thought all the arguments that defended meat eating could have equally justified slavery two centuries before."[4]

At Cambridge he was initially "freaked out." He'd been a star at school; now he was surrounded by other wiseacres. "I spent my first year partying and getting drunk."[5] A 2022 *New Yorker* profile of him recorded how as a student MacAskill would "frolic about in the nude, climbing pitched roofs by night for the life-affirming flush; he was the saxophonist in a campus funk band that played the May Balls, and was known as a hopeless romantic."[6]

There was, however, at least one important intellectual development in his first year. He attended a series of lectures designed to introduce undergraduates to ethics. Beginning with Plato, it went on to cover Singer's "Famine, Affluence, and Morality." The lecturer, Alex Oliver, used an adaptation of Singer's thought experiment to assess candidates applying to Cambridge: instead of buying Christmas presents for your family, should you give the money saved to charity? During his lectures Oliver made the point that Singer was returning to a long tradition in ethics, in which philosophers had not shied away from making ethical pronouncements. He also pointed out that in *Living High and Letting Die*, Peter Unger suggested we should try to earn more money in order that we could then give more of it away. "Everybody laughed."[7] Except, MacAskill, who thought it made perfect sense.

In the summer of 2006, MacAskill spent a formative two months working in a rehabilitation center for children with polio and clubfoot, close to the Ethiopian capital Addis Ababa. Although there was abject poverty in the region, he was struck by how much happier people were than he'd envisaged. The farmers lived in mud huts: perhaps he too should live in a mud hut, he mused. But he was appalled by how the traditional rugs the farmers wore had been replaced by "bright pink Disney-Princess" rugs, imported from China. "It was dystopian; it felt like these people were living off the dregs of consumer capitalism."[8]

He was awarded a "first" in the summer exams—his lowest mark being in ethics, so he dropped moral philosophy to focus on what he thought of as the "hardcore" areas of the discipline, logic, metaphysics, and philosophy of science. His specialism was the philosophy of language, in particular a claim by the American logician W.V.O. Quine that the basic unit of meaning is not the word, but the sentence.

The following summer he went with his then-girlfriend to Spain, and while there the two of them went to see a bullfight—an embedded cultural practice, celebrated by its devotees as half-sport, half-art. "I expected to be torn between the aesthetics and the cruelty. But there was this huge crowd watching these animals get tortured, and I remember crying my eyes out. It was a big hit to my belief in the essential goodness of humanity."[9]

He was not entirely set on a career in academia, and in his final year at Cambridge applied for various jobs, including at Goldman Sachs. The idea, following Unger, was to make money in order to give it away. J. P. Morgan brought him in for a day's assessment, but it did not go well. The interviewers and the interviewee mutually agreed that he was a poor fit for the financial world; he had no genuine interest in banking, and it turned out banks had no interest in him.

More happily, he applied for the Oxford BPhil, and was accepted. He was given a glowing reference from Cambridge: his tutors uniformly regarded him as exceptionally able, one writing that they would not be surprised if he swiftly gained an international reputation for excellence.

Before moving to Oxford, he spent a couple of days busking with his saxophone in Edinburgh, and then took an £8-per-hour job fundraising in the street for, first, the Samaritans, then Care International; the work of the latter reminded him of his experiences in Ethiopia. "I was OK with the Samaritans, but a bit intense for Care International."[10]

Arriving in Oxford, MacAskill became more politically active. He went on a pro-Palestinian demonstration, and the day after he finished reading Singer's *The Life You Can Save* traveled to London for a climate change protest. But he eventually distanced himself from environmental politics, in part because his pragmatic approach was at odds with some of his fellow activists. He supported carbon-trading—involving caps on carbon emissions and allowing countries and industries to trade their carbon quotas—condemned by many of his fellow environmentalists as being a capitalist, market-based, and insufficiently radical solution.

It was a period when MacAskill was feeling disoriented by what he would later call "moral vertigo," "the dizzying feeling when you realise that there are so many sources of suffering in the world, and you really can make a difference to many of them, but not to all."[11] He wondered how to reconcile his pursuit of academic philosophy with an inchoate but powerful sense that he should be engaged in something practical and of benefit to others. What shocked and disappointed him was that studying ethics for many Oxford ethicists was a purely intellectual exercise that made no difference to their lifestyles. Like Singer and Ord, MacAskill believed philosophy should be lived, not just studied. He was aghast that so many philosophers continued to eat meat even though they couldn't rationally justify it. He himself had now transitioned from vegetarianism to veganism.

He started donating 5 percent of his modest income—his parents were financing his living costs, while a couple of scholarships were paying for his accommodation and fees—to organizations such as Care International and Oxfam. He managed this by becoming increasingly frugal. If he met friends at a pub, he'd order water. At home he ate beans on toast.

Here was a man in search and in need of a cause—and with Ord, and Giving What We Can, he'd found it. He was enthusiastic about the public pledge; he understood the power of overt signaling as a way of constraining not just the choices of others, but also his own. "I was on board with the idea of binding my future self—I had a lot of youthful energy, and I was worried I'd become more conservative over time."[12]

As in most successful partnerships, MacAskill and Ord complemented each other. Ord has the command of detail, the moral earnestness, and the quiet but ardent conviction to persuade people of the intellectual case. But he's introverted: happiest at home with his wife and data crunching on his spreadsheets. The vision for Giving What We Can was his, but for several years little progress had been made; MacAskill has the energy, and the organizational and people skills to make things happen. The two philosophers would occasionally disagree, but never argue.

The frantic six months after MacAskill and Ord first met were spent building a website, cataloging interventions and relevant organizations, and linking to influential philosophical literature, most especially "Famine, Affluence, and Morality." A nifty function allowed potential pledge-makers to enter their income and calculate how rich they were compared to the rest of the world.

An early MacAskill impact was the discovery of Snail Man. Ord had already identified that the deaths and illnesses caused by intestinal parasites could be tackled relatively cheaply, but he had made a rare statistical error, which MacAskill spotted: combating these illnesses turned out to be even more cost-effective than Ord had appreciated. All that was left was for MacAskill to locate an organization focusing on the problem. His research led them to Snail Man, aka Alan Fenwick.

Snails and Beatles

You can tell a lot about society by the types of people who become famous within it. We live in a society in which someone can become a household name by eating worm-pizza on reality TV.[13] Meanwhile Alan Fenwick, whose snail research has helped improve the lives of millions of people, is unknown.

Born in 1942, Fenwick spent his first few years in the northeast of England, before his family moved across country to Liverpool where he attended school. A group of local friends, including one by the name of Lennon, regularly went to the local church youth club. Fenwick was there when, in June 1957, his pal John first met a certain Paul McCartney; these two are rumored to have formed a band and left school to pursue a musical career.[14] Fenwick, meanwhile, stayed on to take A-level exams for entry to Liverpool University to study chemistry, first as an undergraduate and then as a postgraduate at the School of Tropical Medicine. His laboratory-based PhD was never completed, however, because his experiments failed. His research was on how to kill snails with a copper sulphate solution. The snails dutifully perished in the lab, but treated with the same substance in the field, in muddy water with vegetation, they stubbornly survived.

What did the young student have against these innocent shelled gastropods? Well, they were not as innocent as they appeared. Even back in the 1960s there was a known link between certain species of snails and a devastating disease called schistosomiasis, which affected hundreds of millions of people, mainly in Africa.

In 1965 a position was advertised for a biologist and chemist with expertise in snails—a rare combination of qualifications. Fenwick duly applied for and was offered the post, based in northern Tanzania. It was the start of more than three decades living in and traveling around Africa, on the trail of the snail, researching schistosomiasis by inspecting water bodies, human blood, and feces.

The life cycle of schistosomiasis is complex, but it goes from aquatic snail to human host and back again. A human body swimming or bathing in snail-infested water can be invaded by parasites, which grow into one-centimeter long worms within a month. These make their home in the blood vessels. Male and female worms couple up, and the female worm lays as many as three hundred eggs a day. This egg tsunami rolls through the veins, bursting capillaries and emerging in human feces or urine. If, as is common in parts of Africa, urination or defecation takes place in, or along the banks of, freshwater lakes or rivers, the eggs hatch, and the emerging larvae penetrate snails who provide temporary safe housing for larval development and multiplication. New larvae then swim away from the snail in search of a human host.

What harm the worms and eggs do to the human body depends on the number of invading worms and the type of parasite. They can affect the cervix, uterus, and lower genital tract of young women and are a factor contributing to HIV/AIDS. They routinely damage the bladder, the intestines, and the liver.

Every day, tens of millions of people will see blood in their urine or stool. That's the most obvious early symptom. A later symptom is swollen bellies.

Since 1980 (and the discovery of a new drug, taken in pill form), it's been possible to treat schistosome worms in humans without having to kill off any snails. The pills have been made available by pharmaceutical companies at cost price, and then donated by NGOs. A person can be protected from the disease for as little as seventy cents a year. With a major grant from the Bill and Melinda Gates Foundation, Fenwick set up SCI (Schistosomiasis Control Initiative) at Imperial College London in 2002.[15]

Not so long after Ord and MacAskill met in the Oxford graveyard, the telephone rang in Fenwick's office. It was a short conversation; Ord and MacAskill wanted to meet him. A few weeks later, there was a knock on his door. The two earnest young men had arrived with a proposal. "They said they wanted to raise money for us. I assumed they would want to take a cut—maybe 10 percent—for themselves, not that that worried me. But I was wrong. They told me about their plans for Giving What We Can and asked me to come to the launch. I was amazed by their altruism and immediately asked to join their crusade."[16]

Fenwick was present on November 14, 2009, when MacAskill and Ord addressed those assembled in a small room (the Massey Room) in Balliol College.

There were barely two dozen present, most of them friends, but Ord was both nervous and exhausted, having spent the entire night getting the website ready to go live. He explained the Giving What We Can 10 percent pledge. There would also be "a further pledge" for those who wanted to give more, binding them to donate everything they earned above a fixed baseline. Ord and MacAskill themselves both took the further pledge. Ord had been putting money aside since starting to save in 2006. And at the end of his talk, he called Alan Fenwick up and, to Fenwick's astonishment, presented him with a personal cheque for £10,000.

The movement was underway.

7

Growing Pains

OVER THE NEXT FEW YEARS, the original organization, Giving What We Can, would divide and multiply as if by mitosis. The process began in 2011, led by MacAskill and the first non-founding member of Giving What We Can, Ben Todd, a long-haired physics and philosophy undergraduate at Balliol College. Bowled over by a talk he heard from Toby Ord in 2009, Todd had signed the Giving What We Can pledge within a week.

Giving What We Can was set up to research the greatest good we can do with our money, specifically. But money is not our only or even our major resource. MacAskill and Todd concluded that there was a need for another organization, offering advice on how we can maximize good with our time, and, in particular, with our working lives. This was initially called "High Impact Careers," then "70,000 Hours," and finally, after a quick back-of-the-envelope recalculation, the name that stuck: "80,000 Hours." Eighty thousand was the number of hours that a typical person might work in a career lasting forty years.

It was a catchy title. Although comprised mainly of bright young scholars at the most nerdish end of the nerd spectrum, the crusade begun by Ord and MacAskill has always had an uncanny commercial instinct for publicity, MacAskill being the more PR savvy. Their organization 80,000 Hours went on to promote an attention-grabbing idea: they called it "earning to give." Typically, philanthropically minded individuals might be tempted by a career in NGOs, such as Oxfam or Save the Children. But even if they went on to make valuable contributions to such organizations, the chances were that others could perform these roles nearly or just as well. Could the philanthropically inclined instead not do more good, perhaps, by working for a hedge fund and donating a chunky percentage of their telephone-number salary and bonus to good causes? Even "[b]y donating 50% of those earnings . . . a banker could pay for several charity workers—thereby doing several times as much good as if he or she had instead worked in the charity sector."[1] Such a career might not suit everyone. Some might not have the skills required to succeed in the financial sector. Others might be qualified, but detest the work, and thus be unable to stick with it. But for a subset of individuals, it could be the most effective route to making a difference.

It was not an entirely original notion. As we've seen, it was briefly touched upon in Peter Unger's *Living High and Letting Die*. Unger assumed philosophers constituted the majority of his readers and urged budding academics to instead "seek employment in fields where there's markedly more money to be made."[2] But it was 80,000 Hours that popularized the idea.

This apparently rational yet counterintuitive twist to the traditional conception of a pious life immediately attracted media interest. Our image of a moral saint tends to be Gandhiesque—loincloth and abstinence—not a man or woman in an expensive suit behind a desk in a gleaming glass skyscraper. MacAskill was interviewed on the UK's most influential news program, *Today*, on BBC Radio 4, on November 22, 2011. The *Today* program has millions of listeners; in the course of a short conversation with an unusually jaunty John Humphrys (better known for his grumpy, intemperate exchanges with politicians), MacAskill sneaked in five mentions of 80,000 Hours, including details of the website: further evidence of his marketing acumen.

Neither MacAskill nor Todd pursued a career in finance. Ben Todd reckons he would have enjoyed it, but in his case the numbers didn't stack up. Even if he donated a high portion of his income, it was still only a percentage of a single salary. Operating within 80,000 Hours, his impact could cascade through many others and redirect many salaries—reasoning that led him to become the organization's chief executive.

These days, it's becoming more unusual to work for the same company throughout a career, and increasingly common even to switch careers entirely. Still, as 80,000 Hours likes to emphasize, since work occupies so much of our lives, it is worth young people investing at least a tiny amount of this time up front, to reflect seriously about their future. And while the organization does often encourage advisees to seek work in potentially impactful and less highly remunerated areas (such as pandemic preparedness) in both the public and the private realms, it remains best known for its advocacy of earning lots to give away.

Giving What We Can and 80,000 Hours were sibling organizations, and the legal advice was that a structure should be established to incorporate both of them. Among other things, this would facilitate the employment of staff and their movement from one organization to another; economies of scale would also tamp down the cost of back-room requirements, such as accountancy.

Choosing the name for this umbrella organization took a couple of months, and several votes—taking up energy that a few members of the movement moaned was misdirected. "Do-Gooders Alliance" was apt, but no good. More serious candidates included the "High Impact Alliance," the "Alliance for Rational Compassion," and the "Effective Utilitarian Community." The rejection of the last of these is interesting, for reasons we shall come to. In the end "Centre for Effective Altruism" (CEA) won out. It was established in 2012.

The protracted naming process proved to be time well spent. Although CEA was designed merely as the title of a legal entity, the phrase "effective altruism" (EA) immediately took off, and within a year was an established ideological label. The intellectual godfather of EA, Peter Singer, used the term "effective altruism" in a TED talk in 2013.[3]

The next decade was one of rapid growth. While 80,000 Hours moved to London initially, the Giving What We Can "office" was in Exeter College, Oxford, on a narrow mezzanine floor overlooking a medieval hall. It had tables and plug sockets, and most importantly was free. But it was impossible to use this space during term time, so there was a brief decampment to another free Oxford University space, the social science library common room, before Giving What We Can rented a small room at the back of an estate agency, a few minutes' cycle ride from the town center. It was so crowded, recalls one of the founding members, Michelle Hutchinson, that "in order for me to get out I needed two other people to move."[4] The low ceiling meant anybody tall had to hunch. The storage room doubled up as the meeting area. In the summer it was insufferably hot; the staff would take lunch outside: bread, hummus, and a few raw vegetables was all they could afford. There was a rota to wash the dishes. Peter Singer paid a visit in May 2013 and performed this task.

By the summer of 2012, there was enough money to pay staff. The initial donors to the organization were also the early signatories to Giving What We Can. They included Julia Wise, an American social worker. For those on the payroll, being financed by the likes of Julia Wise, people who didn't themselves have much spare cash, "felt like a lot of responsibility."[5] But more money flowed in, and about a year later the skeletal organization moved back into Oxford city center, renting rooms not far from Christ Church. That was home for a few years, until the official headquarters were upgraded to swankier offices close to the railway station.

Throughout this period, the movement grew steadily. By 2024 nearly ten thousand had taken the pledge, from over a hundred countries. Effective Altruism chapters had sprouted up all over the world, mostly in universities. Meanwhile, there were large-scale gatherings, initially called "EA Summits" and then, from 2015, "EA Global Conferences," which were billed as a chance for like-minded people to network and learn; they were organized in the UK and United States, but also many other countries, from Kenya and the Philippines to Australia and India. An EA logo was commissioned—a lightbulb in which there was a heart-shaped filament, representing an ingenious idea powered by love.

The speed of expansion surprised everyone. The Centre for Effective Altruism took on several dozen employees and grew to become one of the top one hundred charities in the UK. "I've been shocked," says Michelle Hutchinson, "but I think my original [lower] expectations were calibrated correctly."[6] It would surely have been irrational to predict the charity's success.

The impact of the Shallow Pond had taken four decades to be felt. Why so long? News from far-flung places was already traveling quickly in 1971, but the communications revolution—the internet, mobile phones—had yet to arrive. Individual citizens were not able to film events on a smartphone and instantly send them around the world. The capacity to do this has made distant shallow ponds feel closer. Dramatic footage of the terrible tsunami on Boxing Day (December 26), 2004 was captured on mobile phone cameras by multiple eyewitnesses. Satellite technology brings live images of famines and natural disasters.

Today's world is data-rich. The internet facilitates the dissemination of information about the efficacy (or otherwise) of various charities; in 1971, it was virtually impossible for potential donors to discover which organizations delivered the biggest bang for the buck. The internet moreover enables like-minded altruists to interact with each other. Although effective altruists are widely dispersed, there are blogs and forums through which individuals can communicate in ways that were inconceivable in 1971—giving a sense of community and reinforcing norms of both values and beliefs.

More important than the technological advances, however, is the messaging. In "Famine, Affluence, and Morality" Singer writes that we must redraw the boundary between duty and charity. When we give money to a charity we're thanked for our generosity. The commonsense view is that we're not required to make such a gift, and shouldn't be condemned if we don't. But Singer insists that we have an obligation to donate to prevent bad things from happening. "The way Peter presents this," says MacAskill, "is . . . you're this asshole if you don't do this, and people are like, well, fuck you. And that's a natural human reaction. Whereas actually most people really want to do good with their lives. If you could be that person rescuing that drowning child or if you could knock down the door to a burning building and save someone from inside, you'd feel like a hero, you'd feel great about yourself. And that's the situation that we're in."[7]

Effective altruism began with the language of obligation. But sometime around 2010, Ord noticed "that we were able to give very good talks, that were substantially more motivational, focusing on how amazing it is to be able to make such a difference to people's lives."[8] Since then, both Ord and MacAskill have tried not to induce guilt. Think of a moral hero like Oskar Schindler, they would say. The German industrialist saved twelve hundred Jewish lives during World War II, putting his own life in peril, and by the end of the war he'd used up all his money bribing Nazi officials. His heroics are known the world over thanks to the blockbuster Steven Spielberg movie *Schindler's List* (based on a book by the Australian writer Thomas Keneally). The Israeli government honored Schindler posthumously as one of the Righteous Among the Nations.[9] Yet, at no risk, and for much less personal sacrifice, any reasonably well-off person was also in a position to save many lives. "We might not get books or films written about us, but we can each do an astonishing amount of good, just as Schindler did."[10]

Ord had what MacAskill describes as "an incredible nerdiness" in his analysis of charities.[11] There was none of this in Singer's original article. Singer's case was pitched purely at the level of ideas. It took the details, along with activism—including all the tedious and time-consuming organizational work—to turn an idea into action.

Success brought growing pains. When the movement was tiny, it made sense for individual members to reflect on what they, individually, could do—marginal though this impact might be. But with membership numbers expanding exponentially, and with pledged funding expanding faster still, the movement was becoming a serious force in the development sector. This led to a shift in thinking from the individual to the organization: from "How should I act?" to "How should we, collectively, act?"

We may see this as an instance of an "I–We" problem. The philosopher Derek Parfit described individual–group dilemmas. Suppose a hundred people are in danger. "These people can be saved if I and three other people join in a rescue mission. We four are the only people who could join this mission. If any of us fails to join, all of the hundred will die. If I fail to join, I could go elsewhere and save, single-handedly, 50 other lives."[12]

Clearly, in this situation I should join the other three, even though my share of the total benefit would be only twenty-five lives, whereas acting alone I could save double that number. Parfit's point—in this and many other stylized examples—was that in deciding what to do, we shouldn't just consider our individual acts in isolation; we should do what is best overall, taking into account the actions of others.

There were various I–We coordination issues. Suppose an extremely effective charity was identified. It might make sense for a few people to donate to this charity, but not necessarily for everyone to do so. After, say, ninety-nine people have supported it, the charity might be reasonably funded, and funds from the hundredth donor might do little more to help. That hundredth donor might do far more good donating money elsewhere. The same was true of careers: individuals should be thinking about how they could contribute to the optimum result overall, which might involve, for example, some individuals working directly for charities, with others earning to give.

Beyond I–We moral concern, there was also the more mundane but very real matter of image. Ord and MacAskill had neither sought nor procured an effective altruism trademark, so anybody could set up a group and call themselves effective altruists. The founders perceived EA not as a specific organization, but "as an idea, like feminism."[13] It was an approach that carried reputational risk.

A handful of people announcing that they were pledging to give away 10 percent of their income, or deciding they were going to "earn to give" was a quirky, "and finally"-type current affairs news item. A movement of thousands of people with billions at its disposal warranted more intense scrutiny. Journalists' interest in effective altruism was in some ways helpful—it spread the message—but it was also discomfiting.

Effective altruism was used to operating like a philosophy seminar. From 2014, it had an active online forum, in which ideas were freely traded, and opinions proffered, including those critical of aspects of EA. As in a philosophy seminar, someone might conjure up a bizarre thought experiment, or push an outlandish idea—this is what philosophers do (and it's what gets them noticed within the profession). Do insects feel pain; how can we reduce insect pain; how do we weigh up the significance of insect pain; is the pain of a million insects more significant than the pain of one human? There was a lively discussion of insect matters on the online EA Forum, of interest to philosophers but likely to annoy (or bug) readers on the Clapham omnibus.[14]

What happens in Vegas stays in Vegas, goes the slogan, and what's said in a philosophy seminar stays in the seminar (a philosophy seminar in Vegas is a black hole). At least, that's been the cultural norm. The philosophy seminar is a space where arguments can be tested. It's a space where, within limits, unusual opinions can be expressed without offense being taken. It's understood that the seminar is less like a factory, in which products are manufactured and distributed around the world, than like a laboratory, where they are prodded and probed, analyzed and scrutinized, discarded or retained or improved.

But with expansion came attention, and some EA members began to worry that remarks and proposals could be taken out of context. For the first time, they had to attend to how comments would be perceived, about how effective altruism would be viewed by the outside world; this was bound to inhibit expression. There was an erosion of innocence, a loss of naïveté: internally there had never been much doubt that effective altruism was on the side of the Right and the Good. It was a shock to discover that not everyone agreed.

Laid bare was a tension between the twin functions of the movement. On the one hand, it retained its academic and research remit—to investigate and weigh up global issues and threats. On the other hand, it was an advocacy group, recommending projects and causes. The first function called for openness, debate, nuance, and a tolerance for unusual, even bizarre, ideas. The second required consensus coupled with discipline and straightforward, simple messaging. This was not a harmonious marriage.

Inflows of funds produced suspicion. The first few jobs at Giving What We Can were poorly remunerated. Nobody would take them unless they believed passionately in the mission. With more resources, salaries rose. That led to a worry about motivation. Far from wanting to help the poor, might the new recruits be rather more interested in helping themselves?

But it was not just the money and number of supporters that expanded; so too did effective altruism's intellectual landscape.

8

Longtermism

THE SHALLOW POND WAS for many years taken as an injunction to the relatively well-off to help those in need. That was the message that the early effective altruists internalized. Although demanding, it was narrowly focused. It was specifically about charity and how to assist people alive today who were in desperate straits.

But along the way, the radius of effective altruism concern was extended. Firstly, to animals (hence the insect chat)—unsurprisingly, especially given that Peter Singer's other major contribution, beyond the Shallow Pond and arguments for helping the global poor, was to put the case for taking seriously the interests of nonhuman animals. It was deemed legitimate to direct charitable money to organizations that sought to improve animal lives. Secondly, and far more controversially, to future people: people not yet born.

The inspiration behind this intellectual move came from the Oxford philosopher Derek Parfit. At All Souls College, Parfit spent the last quarter of his life determined to demonstrate that there were moral facts: that morality was objective. Morality can't just be a matter of opinion, or relative to a particular culture, he thought: if it was, his life, and all our lives, would be meaningless. For Parfit, the task of demonstrating the objectivity of morality became all-consuming: almost nothing else mattered to him. It was to this mission that he needed to devote all his energies. He wore the same clothes every day—gray trousers, white shirt, red tie—so that he didn't waste time selecting between outfits. He read while exercising and brushing his teeth. He made instant coffee from a hot water tap (and sometimes the cold tap), so that he didn't waste time boiling a kettle.[1]

His writings on the topic eventually coalesced in the monumental three-volume *On What Matters*. Its core thesis convinced Peter Singer. For much of his career Singer had been a subjectivist—asserting that our ultimate values are based on our desires, which are neither rational nor irrational, and therefore reasoning cannot lead us to agreed moral conclusions. Now, persuaded by Parfit, he came to believe that if you were walking past the Shallow Pond there was a moral imperative to help the drowning child, irrespective of your own beliefs and desires. If you thought that there was no reason to help, you were in error.

But it was Parfit's rich and inventive first book, *Reasons and Persons*, published in 1984, that contained the most comprehensive account of his thoughts about future people. And *Reasons and Persons* had a more profound influence than *On What Matters* on EA. Some early effective altruists apparently owned two copies of *Reasons and Persons*: one for home, one to refer to at work.

Reasons and Persons identified some genuinely puzzling puzzles about our obligations to future people, most of which need not concern us. But Parfit's central intuition was this. While Singer believed that it should make no moral difference whether a person in need is on the other side of the world, as opposed to standing (or drowning) right in front of us (space is irrelevant),

Parfit held that it should equally make no moral difference whether a person we help or harm is alive today, as opposed, say, to being alive a hundred years from now (time is irrelevant).

This is not as far-fetched as it might initially appear. Take one of Parfit's examples: if I leave broken glass in the undergrowth of a wood, it's possible that tomorrow a child may step on it and cut her foot. That would be bad. But it would surely be no better if the glass stayed hidden for a week, or a month, or a year, or a hundred years, and was only then stepped on by a child. A cut foot is a cut foot, today, tomorrow, and in a century.

This contrasts with how some economists deal with the future. Economists refer to a discount rate. Suppose you have a choice between using £100 to buy twenty bottles of wine today or depositing the money in an interest-bearing bank account so that in a year's time you could purchase twenty-one bottles. If you're indifferent as to these two options, your discount rate is 5 percent.[2] Revealed in your savings and investment decisions, the discount rate is the current benefit you're willing to give up for a future benefit.

Although discount rates are vital for the functioning of market economies, Parfit condemned *moral* discounting as a wicked idea with consequences that no decent person could reasonably endorse. If, for example, we discounted the value of a life at 5 percent a year, then a life today would be the equivalent of 39 billion lives in five hundred years' time.[3] To proceed on such a basis would clearly be unacceptable. But another, seemingly absurd, conclusion followed from Parfit's work: the suggestion that saving the life of the drowning child should be relatively low down on the list of our priorities.

Parfit makes two claims that together have been hugely influential in what has been called "Longtermism"—the idea that an attempt to improve humanity's long-term prospects should be of key moral significance. One appears in *Reasons and Persons,* the other in *On What Matters.* In *Reasons and Persons,* Parfit writes that given a choice between

> (1) Peace.
> (2) A nuclear war that kills 99% of the world's existing population.
> (3) A nuclear war that kills 100%.
>
> (2) would be worse than (1), and (3) would be worse than (2). Which is the greater of these two differences? Most people believe that the greater difference is between (1) and (2). I believe that the difference between (2) and (3) is *very much* greater.[4]

Interestingly, there is some evidence that Parfit was right about most people's intuitions. This has been tested, and the majority do indeed believe that the difference in badness between nobody dying and almost everyone dying is larger than the difference between almost everybody dying and extinction.[5] But Parfit's reasoning was that, if we don't wipe out humanity, civilization might regenerate and then could continue for hundreds of thousands of years. The civilization that has existed to date would then prove to have been only a tiny fraction of the whole.

It is not at all obvious, Parfit claimed, that the pluses of human existence had so far outweighed the negatives. Until now, humans' existence had often been short and miserable, blighted by poverty and disease. But he was optimistic that, given social, economic, and scientific progress, future lives would be a vast improvement on past ones. It would be tragic if the potential for a lengthy and flourishing human existence was snuffed out.

A rosy human future is by no means guaranteed. Indeed, later, in *On What Matters*, Parfit makes his second important claim about Longtermism. He writes that we are living "during the hinge of history":

> Given the scientific and technological discoveries of the last two centuries, the world has never changed as fast. We shall soon have even greater powers to transform, not only our surroundings, but ourselves and our successors. If we act wisely in the next few centuries, humanity will survive its most dangerous and decisive period. Our descendants could, if necessary, go elsewhere, spreading through this galaxy.[6]

Things might go right, but they could pivot in the opposite direction and go wrong. Humanity now faces catastrophic threats. Besides nuclear and biological weapons, there is climate change and the collapse of biodiversity, the possibility of devastating pandemics (a risk exacerbated by globalization and our interconnected world), and the danger, perceived by many experts, that we may be destroyed or enslaved by artificial intelligence.

Do we live in a unique period? Are we at the hinge of history? We are not the first generation to regard ourselves as special. Certainly, however, the threats are real, and we should not be fatalistic: we have the power to shape our destiny. This was on Parfit's mind when he was approached to sign the Giving What We Can pledge.

He was eager to do so, he said, but the problem was the phrasing. He tended to take language literally, and pointed out that it wasn't true that donating 10 percent was "giving what we can," since many people could in fact give more—as Singer, Ord, MacAskill, and others had proved. The word "giving" caused him disquiet too; it suggested we had a right to what we owned and a right not to share it with others if we chose not to do so; our wealth was, in other words, morally ours to disburse or to keep. But Parfit believed that, essentially, those of us born in the developed world into comfortably well-off families are lottery winners; it is not that we deserve our wealth, and we have no moral claim to it.

However, most importantly, Parfit encouraged Giving What We Can to widen its altruistic lens, so as to encompass future people. It ought to be acceptable, he said, for Giving What We Can money to be directed at people who do not yet exist. He met with no resistance. Through reading *Reasons and Persons,* the leaders of the effective altruism movement had reached much the same conclusion; the wording of the pledge was modified in January 2015 to accommodate future-facing causes.[7]

In 1981, Peter Singer published *The Expanding Circle*—the circle being the boundary within which creatures were worthy of full moral concern.[8] Over time, we had used our reasoning powers to expand the circle and thus embrace beings that were once completely or partially excluded: other communities, other races, women, nonhuman animals. Often this expansion occurred after a struggle, such as that of the civil rights movement. A notable absence in *The Expanding Circle* is future people (Singer says that at the time the book was published, climate change was not yet an issue). But Parfit's basic insight was picked up and amplified by Will MacAskill. In his 2022 book *What We Owe the Future,* he writes that the next phase in this struggle is to encompass those who will, but don't yet, exist.

Longtermists like MacAskill point out that mammalian species typically survive for a million years. If the human species lasts that long, trillions and trillions more people will come to exist who don't yet exist. But we may last even longer; spacecraft are now probing the outer reaches of our solar system, and it's not a preposterous dream that one day we may populate other planets.

The Shallow Pond thought experiment reproaches us for walking on by. We have a moral duty to help the destitute when we can do so at trivial cost. Longtermism asks us to imagine hearing the cries from the Shallow Pond not just today, but on every day stretching toward an infinite future.

The most controversial aspect of Longtermism runs as follows. There are approximately eight billion people in the world today. There could be quadrillions to come. In the light of this, the eight billion come to seem much less important. They constitute a tiny fraction of the people who matter. Some Longtermists have even suggested that since citizens in the rich West are more likely to contribute toward scientific innovation that helps save the planet than those in poor countries, their lives should be valued more highly.[9] Resources are limited. The priority should not be to save today's drowning child, but rather to build a fence around the pond to ensure that the area is safe for the countless children who could be endangered in the future.

That seems heartless and cruel. But in practice, the Longtermist responds, the interests of the near future and the far future are likely to be aligned: improving the lives of my children will probably improve the lives of their children, and so on, down the generations. And one study suggests that those who care about the long-term future are also more likely than others to care about the present.[10]

Nonetheless, the turn to Longtermism has led to a shift in focus. Many effective altruists see research as the route to making the most positive impact, and more of this research is now devoted to existential threats to humanity, and how these can best be parried.[11]

The real species-endangering risks are not those we're typically accustomed to confronting. The Swedish-born philosopher and founder of Oxford's (now defunct) Future of Humanity Institute, Nick Bostrom, has put this point coldly and bluntly:

> Our intuitions and coping strategies have been shaped by our long experience with risks such as dangerous animals, hostile individuals or tribes, poisonous foods, automobile accidents, Chernobyl, Bhopal, volcano eruptions, earthquakes, droughts, World War I, World War II, epidemics of influenza, smallpox, black plague, and AIDS. These types of disasters have occurred many times and our cultural attitudes towards risk have been shaped by trial-and-error in managing such hazards. But tragic as such events are to the people immediately affected, in the big picture of things—from the perspective of humankind as a whole—even the worst of these catastrophes are mere ripples on the surface of the great sea of life.[12]

Among the panoply of species-endangering challenges, Bostrom has stressed artificial intelligence and in particular, the problem of value alignment and how to ensure that human and AI values don't diverge. With an ever increasing number of decisions being subcontracted to AI, we want to ensure that the technology does what we want it to, and does not reach the goals we set it through objectionable means that we failed to foresee. The notorious paper-clip problem is surprisingly hard to solve: Bostrom imagined that we set AI the apparently innocuous task of manufacturing paper clips. A superintelligent AI will find ingenious ways of doing this, building more and more factories. It may never stop—causing paper-clip Armageddon, as Planet Earth is quickly submerged under fleximetal wire contraptions.[13]

A plethora of Longtermist organizations has sprung up, including, in Oxford, one devoted to issues surrounding artificial intelligence governance, and another to global priorities, with a research remit to examine how best we could use our limited resources to do the most good. Meanwhile, in the United States, GiveWell and a foundation set up by the multibillionaire couple Cari Tuna and Dustin Moskovitz (the latter a cofounder of Facebook),[14] spawned Open Philanthropy, which hands out grants on the basis of effective altruism methodology. It too has become much more interested in catastrophic threats, such as that posed by AI.

Naturally, Peter Singer has welcomed the burgeoning of the movement grounded in his ideas—and that nonhuman animals have become a core concern. But he has repeatedly expressed misgivings over the emphasis on future lives and about "how dominant longtermism should become in the movement."[15] Although the majority of effective altruist funds continue to be directed toward development—the focus of "Famine, Affluence, and Morality"—Singer laments the way existential risks now capture much of the attention and so many of the headlines. He questions whether work on AI done today is of much use, given how rapidly it is evolving, and worries that Longtermism puts off potential recruits. More Mali, less Mars is his preference.

PART II

Charity and Its Discontents

SO FAR THIS BOOK has covered the story of the Shallow Pond; its origins and its impact, chiefly felt through the rise of effective altruism.

Part II covers criticisms. The Shallow Pond analogy was compelling enough to spark a movement. But is failure to contribute to effective charities really analogous to allowing a child to drown? We've already described some objections anticipated by Singer: that while the Shallow Pond involves helping somebody close, donating to charity often involves helping someone far away; that the Shallow Pond involves a particular identifiable person, whereas we can't be sure who's helped through charity; and so on. Singer, and later Peter Unger, dismissed these disanalogies as morally irrelevant.

But many more objections have been made. Here I've identified the major ones. We might label them: the Utilitarian Critique; the Numbers Critique; the Demandingness Critique; the Institutional Critique; the Billionaire Critique; the Historical Critique; the Power Critique; the Effectiveness Critique; and the Psychological Critique. Some of the objections overlap, but they also have distinct elements that make it worthwhile to keep them apart. Not all the objections are strictly philosophical: a few of them are about the practical application of the Shallow Pond argument.

We begin with skepticism about the very form the Shallow Pond argument takes, however: the Thought Experiment Critique.

9

Laboratory in the Mind

THE THOUGHT EXPERIMENT CRITIQUE

AT 2 P.M. ON JUNE 19, 1889, twenty-one-year-old Edgar George Wilson, son of the Reverend George Wilson, was walking along a footpath by the Isis tributary in Oxford on his way to his job as an assistant at the chemist's in Cornmarket Street, when he saw two little boys struggling in the river, after falling in while fishing. Edgar immediately jumped in fully clothed and managed, with difficulty, to rescue them both. He himself then became caught up in the fishing tackle. His lifeless body was found half an hour later. The Rev. Wilson later said that though his grief about his son's death was deep, "he felt that he would rather have had him drowned than for him to have passed by and allowed the little ones to suffer."[1]

This real-life case is quite different from most imaginary philosophical examples.

The Ring of Gyges; The Missing Shade of Blue; The Prince and the Cobbler; The Beetle in the Box; The Trolley Problem; Twin Earth; The Chinese Room; What Mary Knew. Like the Shallow Pond, these are all delightfully titled thought experiments. I love them. Not every philosopher feels the same way.

Thought experiments are among the philosopher's basic tools; they need them as carpenters need saws. In a thought experiment, the philosopher conjures up a scenario, and then seeks to learn something from the intuitive response it elicits. Although often implausible, they're not logically incoherent. They're seen as particularly useful for testing theories or hypotheses. Often that's because the real world is too complex and messy to isolate a specific feature that the philosopher wishes to scrutinize.

Take one of the thought experiments mentioned above, Mary's Room. Mary is a woman who has spent all her life in an entirely black-and-white room. The walls are black-and-white, the furniture is black-and-white, television channels only broadcast programs in black-and-white, there are black-and-white books lining the black-and-white shelves. Mary has never seen anything that isn't either black or white. However, through studying she has become a renowned neuroscientist, physicist, and chemist. She knows everything that there is to know about the properties of color, about wavelengths, about how vision works, about brain-states, and so on. One day, the black-and-white door to the outside opens, Mary leaves the room, and for the first-time encounters color—in the form of a red tomato. Here's the question. Has Mary learnt something new? Frank Jackson, a friend of Singer's and the originator of this experiment argued that she has[2]—it's only when Mary sees the red tomato that she discovers what "redness" actually looks like. But if that's right, it suggests that a purely scientific and physical description of the world doesn't capture everything that there is to know about it.

It's easy to see why reflecting on Mary's Room is philosophically fruitful, but I mention it to illustrate a more general point. Thought experiments are often associated with the modern study of applied ethics. But in fact they've existed since the dawn of philosophy and crop up in every area of it. In *The Republic,* Plato discussed how humans would behave if they wore the ring of Gyges, which granted them the power of invisibility. In the eighteenth century, the Scottish philosopher David Hume imagined there being multiple shades of blue, from light to dark, except in one spot along the continuum, where there was a missing shade. According to Hume, in such a situation we'd be able to picture how the missing shade would look. This posed a puzzle for Hume, and for empiricists generally, for it suggested that we could gain knowledge of at least some part of the world without direct experience of it.

The twentieth century spawned many classics of the genre, such as the Beetle in the Box (devised by Ludwig Wittgenstein), the Chinese Room (John Searle) and Twin Earth (Hilary Putnam). It's true, however, that no area of philosophy is as rich in thought experiments as ethics. In fact, one that is relevant for the Shallow Pond is ancient, appearing half a century after Plato. The Chinese philosopher Mencius believed that all humans were basically altruistic, and as evidence for this position asked what our reaction would be if we witnessed a child falling, not into a shallow pond, but down a deep well: all of us, he supposed, would experience a sense of shock and sympathy.

So the Shallow Pond sits within a long tradition. It followed close behind two thought experiments that have already made an appearance in this book, Thomson's sick violinist, and Foot's runaway train. One way in which thought experiments have been used is to reach what John Rawls called "reflective equilibrium." To be consistent, we need to reconcile a general theory (e.g., that we should always act so as to maximize happiness or well-being) with particular judgments in particular cases (in such-and-such a situation we should behave in such-and-such a way). Now, sometimes the theory and a particular judgment will be compatible, while at other times there will be a conflict—the theory will suggest one course of action, say, and the judgment another. In these cases, we might either want to tinker with the general theory, or else we might decide we should overrule our individual judgment, dismissing it in this instance as unreliable. If we go through an iterative process, with a variety of other cases, then the hope is that we will reach a point where the general theory and the particular judgments are in balance.

Thus, suppose we postulate (as Singer in fact does, though not in "Famine, Affluence, and Morality") the general theory that we should maximize happiness or well-being. We are then presented with Foot's runaway train: the train that will kill five people tied to the track, unless you turn a switch, sending it down a spur, where it will kill just one. The judgment of most people aligns with the general theory—we should redirect the train. There's no tension. But if we're offered a variation on this scenario, in which the only way to save the five people is to push a large man off a high footbridge, so that his bulky and now lifeless body blocks the train, the intuitive response of most people ("Surely it can't be right to push the big man to his death") is at odds with utilitarianism. In this case, we can choose to adjust the theory, or else reject the intuition.

There are parallels here with another hoary case in the literature, which asks us to imagine that two people need lung transplants, two others need kidney transplants, and a fifth needs a heart transplant. All are close to death. An unhappy and friendless tramp—let's call him Walter—wanders into a hospital; by bashing him on the head, and then removing his organs, a surgeon could save these five lives. Should the surgeon do so?

Singer has no use for reflective equilibrium. He is a utilitarian for whom no bullet is too unpalatable to bite. True, he'll point out that in practice utilitarianism doesn't have the wildly counterintuitive implications that thought experiments imply.[3] After all, the utilitarian will want to take into account the broadest considerations of consequences, and it's almost inconceivable that a crude utilitarian response would in fact produce the best consequences. If hospital staff in real life seized individuals and extracted their organs without their permission, it would cause widespread panic and anxiety. You might be reluctant to visit Aunt Beryl after her operation, for fear that it might happen to you.

Nonetheless, suppose Walter could be killed in a one-off murder carried out by a surgeon, who would suffer no ill psychological effects and who could be a hundred percent certain that nobody would ever find out what she had done: well then, claims Singer, sinking his teeth deep into another bullet, if we accept this far-fetched set-up it would be the right thing for the surgeon to do. Singer is highly unusual in this response. Most people believe that if the consequence of your theory is that in such cases you should push the large man off the footbridge, or wallop Walter on the head in order to harvest his organs, then the theory has run into a reductio ad absurdum.

Thought experiments have their detractors. Outside of moral philosophy in particular, the gripe is rarely one of unreality. Few object to Mary's Room on the grounds that it could never exist. However, within ethics the most common complaint is that the hypothetical scenario is weird, even surreal. Underpinning this criticism is the notion that our moral intuitions are formed by and respond to real-world situations. They can't be relied upon in bizarre cases.

Scores of articles have been devoted to the issue of whether we should push the large man off the footbridge to save five lives. But nobody has ever been, or will ever be, in such a predicament. If we were on that footbridge we couldn't be sure that the brakes had failed on the train, we couldn't be certain that the five really were helpless and unable to free themselves from their manacles, and we wouldn't assume that a man, even a bulky one, could stop a fast-moving train; we would worry too that we might lack the strength to shove him over the rails, and would be terrified that he might retaliate (perhaps throw us over instead?), and that even if all went to plan, and by killing the large man we saved five others, we would open ourselves up to arrest and imprisonment for murder. These, and numerous other complexities, would color our judgment.

"Don't worry," the philosopher reassures us, "take it as a given that none of these uncertainties apply." The philosopher has an enviable superpower—that of stipulation. The philosopher simply stipulates that if you do nothing, the five will inevitably die, that you are physically powerful enough to push the large man, that the large man will stop the train, and so on. The problem is, says the critic, that we can't make all these preposterous assumptions and still trust our intuitive reactions. Our intuitions are set to respond to ordinary, not outlandish, situations.

The difficulties may run even deeper than that. It's not just that we can't trust our intuitions in bizarre circumstances. It's that moral judgments are appropriately made within a unique, intricate, and interconnected setting, and to airlift one single factor out of this setting, plonk it on a piece of separate ground, and then ask people to examine it in isolation is in effect to ask them to adjudicate on a different issue altogether—like trying to make sense of a single jigsaw piece without seeing how it slots in with the surrounding pieces.

Even putting this contentious last point aside—for if valid it would make it almost impossible to extend any conclusions drawn from one scenario to any other, since every state of affairs is unique—many ethical thought experiments are indeed wildly improbable. While there have been a few rare cases of a person dying after being tied to a railway track, none of these deaths, as far as I know, was preventable by toppling a bulky stranger from a footbridge.

The literature on the Shallow Pond has its fair share of unlikely scenarios. A typical thought experiment from Peter Unger, supposed to demonstrate that theft is justifiable when it can save lives, runs as follows:

> Key: A tycoon owns a valuable antique key. In a nearby town, a bomb's set to explode in a few hours and, if it does, dozens of people will die. But, if the key is used, then a certain door will be opened and the bomb, which is behind it, will be defused. Now, even though the tycoon is aware of this, he's so greatly concerned about the great prospective damage to, and devaluation of, his antique that he won't part with the key. A gifted pickpocket, you can take the key from him and, thus, make sure the bomb's soon defused. Though the ensuing damage to the uninsurable antique will lessen its value by over a million dollars, you take his key, use it as needed, and, in consequence, dozens are saved from dying soon.[4]

Ingenious though this is, it's evidently ridiculous in multiple ways. And if the thought-experiment critic is right, our intuitive response to it cannot be relied upon. The next section describes another case from the Shallow Pond literature, designed to undermine Singer's reasoning by suggesting it leads to an absurd conclusion. This was put to Singer directly in 2015 in a public forum.[5] Moral philosopher Larry Temkin came up with a more baroque version, though the point is essentially the same.[6] Temkin's version involves Mark and his watch.

The Rolex and the Deep Pond

Mark owns only one real luxury: "a non-waterproof Rolex watch given to him by a favorite uncle." The Rolex has "an elaborate set of safety clasps," so it can only be put on and removed with help from his partner. He passes a deep-water pond in which, of course, a child is drowning: "Mark's first thought is that he must dive into the pond and save the child. Mark's second thought is that if he does so, his Rolex will certainly be ruined. . . . Mark's third thought is that as much as he loves owning, and wearing, his favorite uncle's watch, that is of no significance in comparison with the life of a child."[7]

So far, so more or less familiar. But then Mark has a fourth thought. "He realizes that he could sell his Rolex, raise $5,000," give the proceeds to a charity, and "save three children, who are no less deserving than the drowning child." This is what he decides to do. The drowning child dies, and "[s]ometime later, three innocent, desperately ill children on the other side of the world are saved."[8]

Temkin believes that the fourth thought is what Bernard Williams describes in an arresting phrase as "one thought too many."[9] Brilliant and quick-witted, handsome and urbane, funny but caustic, Williams was a public intellectual as well as a renowned philosopher: he served on several royal commissions, including those on drug abuse, gambling, and pornography:

"I did all the major vices,"[10] he said. But what did he mean by "one thought too many"? If a man can save only one of two lives, Williams writes, one life being that of a stranger, the other being his wife's, he does not need a complex (or indeed a simple) calculation to justify saving his wife—merely regarding this as a dilemma worthy of a nanosecond's reflection shows that he has gone awry. It is enough for him to act instinctively and later say, "She's my wife."

There are no data on this, but I suspect that the Temkin/Williams intuition would be widely shared: most people would believe it reflected very poorly on Rolex Mark to have the fourth thought, and it would be even worse to act upon it. Singer and the effective altruists disagree. Although Singer is a utilitarian, it is worth pointing out that no harm is inflicted by selling the Rolex: no murder is committed, no lie is told, no promise is broken. In other words, there is no violation of what philosophers call "deontological constraints." The choice that is most effective is indeed to ignore the drowning child and sell the watch.

In public debate with a philosophically trained, combative vicar, Will MacAskill was interrogated about what he would do in the following scenario.[11] A building is on fire, and when you run into it to check if anybody needs help, you see a room on your left, in which there is a child, and a room on your right in which hangs a Picasso painting. You could save the child, or the painting, but not both. If you save the Picasso, you can sell it, and with the proceeds—millions of dollars—save many lives. It is self-evident, thought the bellicose vicar, that you should save the child, and in a show of hands, the large audience expressed their assent. This was a moral error, argued MacAskill. Our intuitions were letting us down. If the choice is between a room with one person, and a room with a thousand, we can all agree that we should save the thousand. In real life, "there are many, many people out there who are effectively in that burning building," and the Picasso case was merely a more indirect route to reach them. That it was indirect was morally irrelevant. And while the vicar insisted that "[t]he technical term for the person who saves the Picasso is 'a heartless bastard,'" actually, responded MacAskill, saving the painting reveals "a more cultivated sense of sympathy." The saver of the Picasso shows an ability to sympathize with people on the other side of the world, not just with a single person in front of them.

Again, the implausibility of these cases might lead us to question our initial response. In Rolex, we are told that if Mark doesn't save the child he will definitely sell the watch, definitely raise a large amount of money, and definitely donate the money that will definitely save three children. But consciously or unconsciously we're likely to feel skeptical about every bit of this. What an odd thought for Mark to have! How come he'd never thought of selling his watch before? Could we really be sure that proceeds from the Rolex would be sent to a charity and that this would guarantee the saving of lives? Contrast this uncertainty with what we can see with our very eyes—that in front of us a child is drowning and needs help.

We are right, then, to be cautious about thought experiments. Still, it's difficult to see how the "too wacky" objection lands a blow on the Shallow Pond itself. One adjustment to the thought experiment is required, on account of an underlying, far-fetched assumption. In the early days of the Shallow Pond it was assumed that saving a life was cheap—the cost of a pair of shoes. But as we saw in chapter 5 above, the organization GiveWell estimates that the cost is considerably higher than this—up to

$5,500. But insofar as this is an objection to the Shallow Pond, it is easily met, just by adding in a ruined suit and expensive watch to the side effects of rescue. That won't affect anybody's intuition: nobody will say, "Oh, I'd willingly have sacrificed my expensive shoes alone, but I won't wade into the pond if both my suit and watch are at risk of ruin too."

Even with this slight modification, the Shallow Pond has no very peculiar features. It is not at all like Judith Jarvis Thomson's concert violinist—who, you'll recall, was wired up to you overnight (remarkably, you didn't wake up, even though the Society of Music Lovers was plugging the violinist's circulatory system into your own). On the contrary, drownings, such as that of Edgar George Wilson, in Oxford in 1889, are depressingly common: around three hundred thousand people die by drowning every year,[12] many of them young children, and of course thousands of others are rescued before they drown. It requires no contortions of the imagination to envisage a Shallow Pond scenario.

There are, then, legitimate criticisms of many moral philosophy thought experiments, on account of their zaniness; but these don't apply to the Shallow Pond.

10

Shallow Ponds in Deep Waters

THE UTILITARIAN CRITIQUE

> You are never going to be able to quantify the world perfectly, but you can try to turn everything into a number.
>
> —SAM BANKMAN-FRIED

ON APRIL 28, 2022, two gray-haired men sporting jackets and open-necked shirts sat on a stage next to a much younger man with a mop of unkempt black hair, wearing cargo shorts, a white T-shirt, and sneakers, who looked like he'd just popped in following tennis and cocktails at his club. The two older men were ex-leaders of their respective countries. Former British prime minister Tony Blair and former US president Bill Clinton were attending the Crypto Bahamas conference, billed as "an invitation-only event featuring collaboration and networking among leading players in the crypto and traditional finance industry."[1] The Tony Blair Institute failed to respond to my inquiry about how much they were paid. Maybe Blair didn't demand recompense, being inspired by nothing but a pure and altruistic urge to spread the crypto gospel. . . .

Whatever the fee, the shorts-wearing man could apparently afford it. He had just turned thirty and was chairing the session. The shorts were revealing in more ways than one. Yes, it was a casual dress event, dressing-down was the norm for his tribe, and it was his standard attire (the Bahamas was now his home); but if you were preparing to take part in an event in front of an audience and with world-famous politicians, wouldn't you scrub up? If not a tie, then at least a shirt? A comb through the hair? What did this flouting of convention imply? Was the young man so geeky and unworldly as not to notice? Or was he trying to convey a message? Perhaps he meant to stress how radically changed social norms were in the futuristic realm of crypto currency. Ties, combs, and personal hygiene belonged to a bygone era. Perhaps he intended to demean his guests, indicating that he didn't care what they thought: in this sphere, he was the guru, the visionary, the big shot, not them. Perhaps, in other words, he was arrogant and overconfident. Tony Blair commented drily that he felt "a little overdressed."[2]

The shorts-wearing man, Sam Bankman-Fried, known in financial circles by the moniker SBF, had a peak wealth of $26.5 billion. This was based largely on his ownership of half of the crypto currency exchange FTX, which he'd set up just a few years earlier. Crypto currency was the hot new thing: investors were terrified of losing out, and SBF was supposedly a genius. Money poured into FTX in various fundraising rounds. Crypto acquired a sheen of glamour: the singer Katy Perry was among those at the Crypto Bahamas conference afterparty. Few people understood how FTX made its money, but what did that matter while its value kept rising? The company's renown spread way beyond the opaque crypto community. Miami Heat's basketball stadium became the FTX Arena. The racing driver Lewis Hamilton had the FTX logo on his Formula One car. Tom Brady appeared in promotional advertisements. There were ongoing talks to have a Taylor Swift endorsement.

For Bankman-Fried, the ascent to the billionaire summit had been rapid. Nobody had ever become quite so rich quite so quickly. And then, virtually overnight, in November 2022, SBF's wealth vanished, from billions to zero. Rumors that there was a black hole on FTX's balance sheet prompted panicked traders to try to withdraw their money—money FTX didn't have. The king of crypto was dethroned. "I fucked up," he wrote on Twitter on November 10, 2022. The following day, FTX was put under bankruptcy protection. A month later, SBF was arrested and subsequently extradited to the United States. It turned out his activities had been criminal, not merely incompetent. On November 2, 2023, a New York jury found him guilty of fraud and money laundering, for which he received a lengthy prison sentence (ending up sharing a dorm with rapper and music mogul Sean "Diddy" Combs, arrested in September 2024 on sex abuse and trafficking charges).

The rise and fall of SBF is relevant to our tale for many reasons. SBF was the wealthiest supporter of effective altruism. More than that, he was its creature. There is even a creation-myth, one that used to be enthusiastically promoted by EA leaders. SBF's future was fixed, the story goes, during a pivotal meeting over lunch with Will MacAskill in Cambridge, Massachusetts, where SBF was a math and physics student at MIT. First, MacAskill persuaded him of the merits of effective altruism. Then he convinced him that before committing himself to a life working for a charitable organization, and spotting his mathematical aptitude and potential to make big bucks as a quant (applying statistical analysis to investment), he should approach various charities and ask them what they wanted from him—in essence, either his time or his money. SBF followed this advice. "Money," the unanimous response bounced back.

And so, he set out to make as much as possible. Many billionaires after becoming rich choose to donate a portion of their wealth to charitable causes. But SBF told us that he was a billionaire with a difference. He sought wealth precisely in order to give it away. Given his family upbringing this was not as bizarre a choice as it appeared: his Stanford academic father strongly self-identified as utilitarian, his Stanford academic mother was sympathetic to utilitarianism, and SBF himself soon became a "take-no-prisoners utilitarian."[3] He described himself as a "fairly pure Benthamite utilitarian,"[4] and was convinced by the arguments of Peter Singer. "Ultimately," he said to the BBC, "what I, in theory, wanted to do forever was maximize the ultimate happiness, maximize the amount of good in the universe."[5] He didn't care much for crypto—it was a mere means to an end, a means to money. He'd happily have switched to trading orange juice futures, he admitted to another journalist, if he believed that was more lucrative.[6]

He claimed to take "expected value" extremely seriously. We can never be certain what the effects of our actions will be, but we can assign probabilities. We can compare two options by multiplying the predicted value of each by the probability of its occurrence. Suppose Option A has a 90 percent chance of saving ten lives (and a 10 percent chance of saving none), while Option B has a 10 percent chance of saving a hundred lives (and a 90 percent chance of saving none). We should prefer B over A, since the expected value of B is ten lives, and the expected value of A only nine.

Expected value theory struggles with a paradox—the so-called St. Petersburg paradox,[7] the preposterousness of which SBF was willing to embrace. Suppose you were offered an unusual bet that promised a better than even chance of increasing total happiness/well-being: you could either double life—say, create another Earth (51 percent chance)—or annihilate all life (49 percent chance). Would you take this bet? Yes, said SBF. What about if the bet were then offered again, and again, and again? Yes, and yes, and yes, said SBF, though the chance of extinction would then become extremely high.

His utilitarianism was linked to the scale of his ambition, he said. Becoming a millionaire might make a young worker happy; making a second million is unlikely to produce as big a jump in happiness. Driving a second Bugatti won't be as thrilling as driving the first. But "doing good" doesn't suffer from such precipitous marginal decline. The world is so replete with misery that the second million can be almost as effective as the first. As SBF put it, "If you really are trying to maximize your impact, then at what point do you start hitting decreasing marginal returns? Well, in terms of doing good, there's no such thing: more good is more good."[8]

SBF's stated mission made him an intriguing and appealing figure. He was lucky, he said, that "I don't happen to have a whole lot of desire for a yacht."[9] Instead, the media reported how he spent his spare time playing League of Legends, a multiplayer online strategy game involving battles, enemies, death, and the accumulation of gold. He seemed distracted during interviews, jiggling his legs furiously whether from nerves, impatience, or boredom. Those who wrote about him, or included contributions from him in broadcasts (and a mea culpa has to be inserted here),[10] regurgitated accounts of his abstemious lifestyle. He was a vegan and teetotaler, drove an unassuming car—a Toyota Corolla—and routinely slept on a beanbag in his office. He shared an apartment with nine other people. This was all more or less true. But it wasn't the whole truth. What most journalists chose to overlook was that the apartment was a penthouse in an exclusive residential block within a gated community, next to a marina sprinkled with luxury yachts.

Although most of his wealth was tied up in his FTX shares, and not liquid, SBF was a major donor to effective altruist causes and had set up a Future Fund, which aimed to award grants to individuals and not-for-profit organizations working on projects likely to affect future generations. He had been an important funder of the Democratic Party, and financially supported Joe Biden's successful presidential bid in 2020. It subsequently transpired that he'd also backed some Republican candidates, but secretly, "because reporters freak the fuck out if you donate to Republicans."[11] Shortly before his wealth evaporated, he explained that so far he'd given away "a few hundred million," but was optimistic that during the course of his life he'd be able to donate "certainly in the billions, hopefully higher than the low billions."[12] Other senior figures in his company were also dedicated effective altruists. According to the author Michael Lewis, who trailed SBF for many months, effective altruism "was extremely serious to them . . . it was what drew them together in the first place."[13]

This was a riches-to-rags tale—and when SBF's wealth imploded, effective altruism was caught in the fallout. MacAskill had just published a book on Longtermism, *What We Owe the Future,* and it had been extensively reviewed, scaling the bestseller lists. MacAskill himself drove the book's marketing effort. Not many philosophers develop a public presence beyond the academy, but he was the subject of sympathetic profiles in prestigious newspapers and periodicals, such as the *New Yorker*;[14] he even made the cover of *Time* magazine. He went swimming with reporters and was interviewed ("Lunch with the *FT*") over meals. He was invited onto popular podcasts and TV shows, including the cult late-night satirical program *The Daily Show*. It was obvious why producers liked him: he was young (for a professor), quietly charismatic, telegenic, with a soft Glaswegian burr ("devastatingly Scottish," according to an early article about him)[15] and the inexhaustible patience to engage in cheery badinage with presenters and to repeat ad infinitum the book's key arguments and messages.

Suddenly, however, the effective altruism brand was tainted. The Oxford effective altruists were accused of being naive about SBF, even of ignoring warnings. The account of how MacAskill had convinced SBF to earn to give became an acute embarrassment. Aspects of effective altruism, never hidden, began to be questioned. These included the links it had, and the support it received, from some mega-wealthy people, many based in Silicon Valley, and the increasing focus within EA on Longtermism. As well as being a utilitarian, SBF was a self-declared Longtermist; Longtermism had links to some of the zanier fringes of philosophy, such as transhumanism, which explores the possibility that technology might allow humans to transgress their current biological limitations. Critics of EA delighted in highlighting these connections.

The main question for effective altruism, however, was whether SBF was a bug or a feature. Was he a one-off, a rogue operator, who should not blot an entire movement? Or was there something inherent in effective altruism that produced bad-faith actors, rotten apples? Numerous articles in the press referred in particular to the utilitarian ideology of EA, implying that this alone sufficed to explain the debacle.

Utilitarianism

Peter Singer is a utilitarian, and utilitarianism has a couple of salient components. First, it is an impartial philosophy—all other things being equal, one life is as valuable as another. My life is no more valuable than yours. My child's life is no more valuable than your child's life.[16] Second it is maximizing—it wants to maximize the good and minimize the bad. This in turn means that utilitarianism has no side-constraints: in theory it is sometimes acceptable to harm one or more individuals for the greater good—for example, framing an innocent man to avoid a catastrophic riot. It also means that if the consequences are identical, there is no moral distinction between an act and an omission. Failing to save a life is no more intrinsically excusable than taking one.

The details of Sam Bankman-Fried's crimes need not concern us, but as a utilitarian, had he convinced himself that it was legitimate to commit fraud for the greater good—that dishonesty and deceit were justified by all the benefits he could confer with his money? True, this would have been a daft moral calculation. The probability of his illegal activities going undetected was low; the probability of FTX clients losing money was high. However, as his approach to the so-called St. Petersburg paradox revealed, he was notoriously untroubled by risk, and he might have felt that the risks were worth the expected gain.

"He thought that the only moral rule that mattered was doing whatever would maximize utility," said Caroline Ellison, a business partner and former girlfriend of SBF.[17] Most of us do not have such utilitarian instincts; we do not believe that fraud is morally acceptable even when it is committed for the greater good. But the pure, or naive, utilitarian is willing to override typical intuitions. In the philosophical literature there are many thought experiments designed to test our reactions to cases in which acting to secure the greater good conflicts with ordinary moral constraints ("Don't lie," "Keep your promises," "Don't torture the elderly mother of a terrorist to extract the code to defuse a bomb that's about to destroy New York," etc.). The Trolley Problem is the most famous (or notorious) one: only a few people think that it is right to send a large man plunging from a footbridge to his death to save five lives. Indeed, there is some evidence of a correlation between individuals willing to harm in these types of dilemmas and psychopathy.[18]

Sam Bankman-Fried's opulent apartment, along with a few other instances of lavish private expenditure, suggest that we should not necessarily take his self-identification as a utilitarian at face value. Still, even if he was a naive utilitarian, most utilitarians are not of this naive type. Why not? Because, as many philosophers have pointed out, utilitarianism can be self-defeating.[19] If, at each and every moment of our lives, we attempted to maximize happiness or well-being, the results would spectacularly backfire. Overall, we would do far better to have emotional and behavioral dispositions that were not focused purely on maximizing utility. If people felt they could break a promise each time the utilitarian calculation suggested that they should do so, trust would quickly collapse, and our social world would become almost impossible to navigate. The character traits promoted by a more sophisticated utilitarianism will tend to be closely aligned with our ordinary, commonsense moral norms.[20]

Something similar is also true for institutional rules. In theory, utilitarianism might dictate that a court deliberately find an innocent defendant guilty in order to prevent a riot. But were this approach to justice to be widely adopted it would undermine faith in the entire legal system. Far better to insist that all citizens have the right to due process and a fair trial.

SBF comes across as a semi-tragic figure: a man, according to Michael Lewis, incapable of much emotion who "had committed his life to maximizing happiness on earth without feeling any of his own."[21] The point, however, is this. Insofar as Sam Bankman-Fried was a utilitarian, he was a very bad one. He's caused much harm, as, given his instincts and business ethics, was almost inevitable.

Alienation and Integrity

The most famous critic of utilitarianism is Bernard Williams. Williams argued that since utilitarianism is only interested in an impartial measure of consequences—which act produces the most happiness or well-being—it ignores the question of who is responsible for these consequences. And he insisted that this mattered a great deal. His oft-cited example involved George, who has a PhD in chemistry. George could take up an opening in a laboratory researching chemical and biological warfare, work that he would find repugnant. On the other hand, his family needs the money, and if he doesn't do the job, someone else will, and will pursue the research with far greater zeal than George ever would.[22]

From a utilitarian point of view, it seems that George should go and work in the lab. But this is to miss a vital point. For the utilitarian it's irrelevant who does the research. For George, however, it matters a great deal whether or not it would be *him* doing it.

> It is absurd to demand of such a man, when the sums come in from the utility network which the projects of others have in part determined, that he should just step aside from his own project and decision and acknowledge the decision which utilitarian calculation requires. It is to alienate him in a real sense from his actions and the source of his action in his own convictions.[23]

This is pertinent to the Sam Bankman-Fried story. SBF was told that EA promotes the option of earn-to-give. But is the hedge fund trader who believes that ultimately the work itself is merely a means to another end not alienated in much the same way as George? Perhaps. The parallel with George, however, is imperfect. First, so long as the trader does not believe trading is in itself evil, they would be no more alienated than any number of people who do a job they don't particularly enjoy purely so that they can provide for their needs and those of their family. Second, earn-to-give would clearly not be suitable for everyone—and would be less suitable for those who detest the work (since this would probably damage their earning potential). Peter Singer has also made the point that for those whose ultimate objective is to give away their money, then, by earning to give, they are "to a greater extent than most people, living in accord with their values."[24]

The charge that utilitarianism leads to a form of alienation crops up again in deciding which charitable causes to back. Take, as an example, one cause—charities working to fight breast cancer. Suppose breast cancer charity B1 is more effective on every metric than breast cancer charity B2. It helps twice as many patients per dollar, it spends less on overheads, its marketing and lobbying campaigns are more successful. If you have no personal connection to either charity, and are aware of the gulf in their operational performance, it would be baffling to give money to B2 rather than B1. But there might be another cancer charity, let's say a prostate cancer charity, P, that is more effective than B1. Money given to P is likely, let's say, to save more lives than the same amount donated to B1. If we wish to donate, are we obliged to favor P over B1?

A fundamental tenet of effective altruism is that we should be altruistic *effectively*. Setting aside the fact that effectiveness is not the sole, or even the primary, criterion by which most people do actually give,[25] is it really the basis on which people *should* give?

Return to the example of charities B1 (for breast cancer) and P (for prostate cancer) and let us imagine Georgina. Georgina's mother died young from breast cancer, an event that, naturally, has cast a shadow over Georgina's life. Georgina herself is thought by oncologists to be at risk of breast cancer. After leaving university, Georgina found a job in a charity that aims to fund research into the disease. Although her work is not particularly well remunerated, Georgina believes that she can easily give away 10 percent of her income and still have a comfortable lifestyle. She also has plans to run the London marathon, and to ask people to sponsor her in a charitable cause.

What if an effective altruist were to drop a "logic bomb" on Georgina,[26] demonstrating that she could do more good, overall, by donating her time and money to prostate charity P? Would it not be ludicrous, à la Williams, to expect Georgina to shift her priorities accordingly? Georgina's identity is bound up with a particular worthy cause. Her life takes on meaning because of its association with this cause. This association cannot be irrelevant for Georgina and brushed aside on the grounds of effectiveness. Effective altruist logic bombs are unlikely to move her.

The effective altruist could respond as follows. What motivates Georgina? Isn't her worry that lives are at risk and families potentially devastated? Isn't her underlying motive to help those affected by breast cancer because they suffer? It is not that they suffer from a particular disease. And, if that's right, then she should really aim to minimize the number of people who suffer.

The effective altruist need not be too critical of Georgina. After all, she's still doing something good, even if, from an EA perspective, it's not the most good she could do. But it's this claim—that her actions would be even more morally admirable if she switched causes—that's at the heart of the dispute between effective altruists and their critics. MacAskill has shown himself to be true to his philosophy. When he lived in Ethiopia, he visited the Fistula Foundation and met patients suffering from a fistula and doctors treating them. So, he had made some personal relationships. But back in the UK, he determined that his donations would be put to better use elsewhere. A commendable, impartial bird's-eye view of the moral world—or, in the words of one author, "a little chilling"?[27]

This chapter has been predicated on the idea that effective altruism is an offshoot of utilitarianism. But the effective altruist rebuttal to the SBF scandal was not to deny that SBF was a utilitarian. Nor was it to point out that, even from a utilitarian perspective, it was important to stick to commonly accepted norms of behavior (to be honest, do no harm, act with integrity, and not to steal, commit fraud, or torture old ladies). No; what the effective altruists instead emphasized was that effective altruism and utilitarianism are not one and the same.

So what, if any, is the link between effective altruism and utilitarianism? It is unquestionably true that many effective altruists are utilitarian. Recall that one canvassed name for the Centre for Effective Altruism was the Effective Utilitarian Community. But long before SBF became a story there were many instances of leading effective altruists distancing themselves from utilitarianism. The clearest expression of this came in a speech Toby Ord delivered in San Francisco at an EA Global event: "Effective Altruism is not utilitarianism. It's a much broader church than that. It allows for many diverse views about what makes someone's life go well, it doesn't have to be just happiness. And also about many other things mattering as well, such as equality between people, or rights."[28]

Although Peter Singer himself is a utilitarian, "Famine, Affluence, and Morality" makes no mention of utilitarianism. Nor does

Peter Unger's *Living High and Letting Die*. The aim in both publications is to persuade us that we are morally required to do far more than in fact we do, but the thought experiments and arguments deployed are not grounded in any particular moral theory.

As has already been reiterated, Singer states that "[i]f it is in our power to prevent something bad from happening, without thereby sacrificing anything of comparable moral importance, we ought, morally, to do it." What is to count as of "comparable moral importance"? Singer remains deliberately vague on this point. But it certainly leaves open the possibility of there being moral constraints that were violated by Bankman-Fried.

As for SBF himself, he was a disaster on the witness stand in court: evasive and dishonest. Just before he was sentenced, his mother sent a letter to the court appealing for a degree of clemency: her son was an unusual kid, who'd been intellectually drawn to utilitarianism as a boy, she explained. Aged fourteen, he'd even read some of the intricate philosophical writings of Derek Parfit. Inexplicably, the judge was unpersuaded that this fact mitigated the crime. On March 28, 2024, SBF was sentenced to twenty-five years in prison.

11

Moral Math, Play Pumps, and Microloans

THE NUMBERS CRITIQUE

Mathematics is the music of reason.

—[ATTRIBUTED TO] JAMES JOSEPH SYLVESTER (MATHEMATICIAN)

One accurate measurement is worth a thousand expert opinions.

—GRACE M. HOPPER (COMPUTER PIONEER)

THERE WERE VARIOUS beneficiaries of the will of Leona Helmsley, a real-estate and hotel magnate and convicted tax dodger, who died in 2007. They included an eight-year-old, who inherited $12 million. The eight-year-old was called Trouble, though others called her "the Rich Bitch," for Trouble was a white Maltese dog.[1] The money, to be held in trust, was enough to keep the multimillionaire canine in the lifestyle to which she had become accustomed.[2] Although her windfall was subsequently reduced by a judge to $2 million, this still sufficed to finance a retirement in Florida, as well as to attract death and kidnap threats. When Trouble died in 2011, at the age of twelve, newspapers awarded her an obituary. Without casting aspersions on Trouble herself, the general view was that this was a barking mad use of Ms. Helmsley's resources.

Americans give away a staggering $500 billion a year, two thirds of which is accounted for by individuals.[3] In one survey, roughly half of all households claim that they made some sort of donation during the year.[4] Richer households are more likely to give, but as a percentage of their income, they give less.[5]

In 2015, two similar books were published: *The Most Good You Can Do* (Singer) and *Doing Good Better* (MacAskill), the latter outselling the former, but both extolling the benefits of effective altruism and making similar points. You, they assured the reader, can make a big difference to the world if you donate, and more importantly if you donate—unlike Ms. Helmsley—with your head rather than your heart.

Even if there is no necessary link between utilitarianism and effective altruism, effective altruists believe utilitarianism gets one important thing right. There might be constraints on how we should act, but part of living an ethical life involves caring about the welfare/well-being/happiness of strangers—and this means caring about them impartially. One stranger's life is no more important than another's, and it is better to help more strangers than fewer. If you run into a burning building where you can either turn left and save one person, or turn right and save a hundred, it's obvious which direction you should go.

To put it another way, that part of our life (be it time or money) that we devote to doing good should be devoted to doing good in the most efficient way. We need, therefore, to come up with ways of measuring efficiency. It's for that reason that data become woven into effective altruism—and that charities are assessed by Giving What We Can, The Life You Can Save, and GiveWell using the equivalent of an effective altruist abacus.

Certain charities regularly come out highly placed in effective altruism recommendation leagues, including some specific organizations tackling malaria. Charities offering supplements to stop vitamin deficiency, and one providing cash incentives for parents to bring their babies to be vaccinated, feature too. GiveWell has downgraded its confidence that deworming has a major impact. It has been supportive in the past of GiveDirectly, a charity in which donors can pass money, no strings attached, to the desperately poor in several African countries; now it claims that the other charities on its "Top Charities" list are at least twice as effective.

The GiveWell calculation, that the most effective charities can save a life for around $5,000, is complicated; but think, for example, of insecticide-treated nets. Although the nets themselves are extremely cheap, there are challenging logistics. They need to be packed, loaded, and transported. All this requires monitoring. They might be stolen. There is the cost of employing people to demonstrate how they should be used. It's estimated that around 20 percent of nets will never be used and, in any case, malaria is the cause of death of only a relatively small number of those who die in malaria-infected areas each year. Five thousand dollars purchases a thousand nets. A thousand nets end up protecting around 1,400 people and, according to GiveWell, "protecting 1,400 people for the two-year lifespan of a net leads to around one less death."[6] If these are among the top recommendations, what kinds of causes and charities languish near the bottom? Several categories of philanthropy are ruled out by effective altruists from the start—categories that fail even to attempt to address basic health and economic needs.

These include religion. Religion receives about 30 percent of total US charitable giving, more than any other area.[7] Some of this goes toward paying for the upkeep of churches, mosques, and synagogues, including the stipends of clergy, imams, and rabbis. Religion frames the lives of a high (if declining) number of Americans; for many, a life without close ties to the local religious community is unthinkable. Still, from an effective altruist point of view, it's not a cause that can compete with disease or malnutrition.

Most spending on education will fail the test too. Education is a popular cause in the United States, accounting for around 13 percent of total charitable giving,[8] and yet—with a few exceptions—spending on education is not considered an effective altruist priority. The university at which Singer taught is already staggeringly wealthy but, mysteriously, each year Princetonians continue to top up its funds, lavishly donating more and more to their alma mater. "You need an anthropologist to make sense of it," says the historian of education Bruce Leslie. "In the US, college is an important part of your identity. For some, the most important part."[9] At the time of writing, Princeton's endowment is worth a staggering $34 billion, enough to wipe out the national debt of Niger three times over.

Then there are donations to cultural programs, accounting in the United States for around 5 percent of total giving.[10] Once again, compared to other charities, arts charities can't compete in EA terms. We don't need a calculator to work out that nobody dies from being unable to watch a subsidized production of *Measure for Measure*. On the Effective Altruism Forum, contributor

Scott Alexander lamented the "Buy a Brushstroke" campaign, in which eleven thousand donors were persuaded to give a combined total of over half a million pounds to ensure that J.M.W. Turner's painting *Blue Rigi* stayed in the UK. If the money had been spent "to buy better sanitation systems in African villages instead, the latest statistics suggest it would have saved the lives of about 1,200 people from disease."[11]

In the United States the amount of charitable donations going to "culture" is roughly equal to the amount that goes to international causes. By no means all international charities pass an effective altruist test, however. Among the charities to be avoided are the flashy and ineffective: projects that grab attention but produce little benefit. The stand-out (or sit-down) example with which MacAskill opens *Doing Good Better*, is PlayPumps—water pumps that were built as children's merry-go-rounds.[12] While some kids sat on them, others would rotate them, and while the youngsters were enjoying themselves, water would simultaneously be pumped into a storage tank. Brilliant—award-winning, in fact.[13] Funding for PlayPumps flowed in; by 2009 nearly two thousand had been installed across southern Africa. Nelson Mandela was present for the opening of one pump; rapper Jay-Z visited another.

What was not to like? Well, plenty, so it transpired. Typically, there was almost no consultation with the local community—and the pumps proved disastrously ineffective at their core function, extracting water, requiring far more hours of "play" than children could manage. That meant much of the burden of pushing the merry-go-rounds fell on women, who found it awkward and demeaning. The merry-go-rounds were poorly maintained, left rusty and unrepaired when they broke down.

Nonetheless, say the effective altruists, in general, sums of money that are modest in the rich world can have an outsized impact in the developing world. This makes some charities seem like a bargain; hence the comparison that effective altruists often make between funding guide dogs in the developed world (costing tens of thousands of dollars per dog) and funding cheap and straightforward operations (costing only a few tens of dollars) to tackle trachoma in the developing world.

Extreme poverty is defined as having an income below that on which a person's minimal nutritional, clothing, and shelter needs can be met. It is adjusted, as prices change, from a figure established in 2017, and as of 2024 stood at $2.15 a day.[14] With hundreds of millions of people still living on less than this amount,[15] it is not surprising that there are lots of (apparently) successful, low-cost interventions. According to the effective altruists, many people can be helped in the developing world for the cost of helping one person in the developed world. Likewise, the per-dollar impact differential highlights the contrast between what money can do for us, and what it can do for distant others. "Imagine a happy hour," writes MacAskill, "where you could either buy yourself a beer for $5 or buy someone else a beer for five cents. If that were the case, we'd probably be pretty generous—next round's on me!"[16]

EA calculations about which charities produce the best outcomes give a sense of impressive precision. But evidence is hard to come by and tough to interpret. Programs are constantly being reevaluated. Deworming was all the philanthropic rage, until it wasn't. Nobody doubts that those with parasitic worms can be quickly and easily treated with a tablet. The controversy—part of the so-called Worm Wars—is whether it is worth funding a mass program in which everyone in affected areas receives a tablet. GiveWell maintains that deworming has strong potential benefit, but it now restricts its Top Charities recommendations to those organizations for which confidence of success is very high: so deworming no longer makes the cut. That's contributed to a dramatic change in income for the SCI Foundation (now renamed Unlimit Health), which has plummeted from £20 million to £250,000.

As politicians and social scientists have discovered, intervening in human affairs is not like throwing dice. We can more or less assume that the chance of dice showing a five is one in six. And the probabilities of dice throwing are independent: the fact that I get a five with one throw doesn't affect whether I'll get a five on the next. Human life, by contrast, is messy and one effect can cascade into infinitely more. Preventing people dying from malaria will affect population size, and this in turn will impact almost every aspect of life. Human actions can be massively consequential, even if the consequences are largely unforeseeable. From an effective altruist perspective, mosquito nets in the developing world trump education scholarships in the developed world; but Singer, Ord, and MacAskill were all awarded scholarships, and had they not been, effective altruism itself would not exist.

There is a more fundamental problem, however, and that is the difficulty, if not impossibility, of assigning numbers to outcomes. How do we balance saving a human being from premature death against improved conditions for five thousand chickens on a factory farm? Can we really measure the significance of reducing suffering against other things we value in life? As the novelist and art critic John Berger put it, "How does the cure of a serious illness compare in value with one of the better poems of a minor poet?"[17]

If health and poetry are incommensurable—apples and pears—QALYs, Quality Adjusted Life Years, which have already made an appearance in this book (see chapter 5), are at least supposed to provide a way of comparing different health outcomes.

But even QALYs are problematic. A QALY requires us to judge the seriousness of an illness or disability. How? Think of a "disability"—blindness, say. Should we assess illnesses and disabilities by objective criteria, or should we rely on subjective evidence: polls and surveys, for example, about how people regard a particular condition? We might ask people, "Would you rather have an extra one year of healthy life, or two years of a life with Condition X?"[18] If the response is that it would be preferable to have an extra year of perfectly healthy life, we could repeat the question, but this time offering the option, say, of three years with Condition X. The process could continue until an equilibrium is reached: a point at which people express no preference. In theory, that would reveal what fraction of a QALY most people judge a year with condition X to be worth.

Yet the whole process is fraught with complexity. Ask people how debilitating it would be to go blind, and no strong consensus will emerge. Sighted people might assume that going blind would have a terrible effect on their lives, not just because of the practical problems of navigating the world, but because of the inability to fully appreciate a Netflix miniseries, a stunning sunset, a lover's face. In fact, there's overwhelming empirical evidence that when a previously healthy person becomes disabled, they tend to report, following a period of adjustment, that the impact on their well-being is not nearly as pronounced as nondisabled people imagine. Nonetheless, the iron logic of QALYs dictates that if you can only rescue one person from a burning building (there are lots of burning buildings in EA philosophy) you should, other things being equal, save a sighted person ahead of someone who's blind—a conclusion that will strike many people as unacceptable.

Besides the QALY, another statistical tool boasting an acronym, the RCT, is beloved of effective altruists.[19] RCTs—randomized control trials—are the "gold standard" for assessing interventions. Following an intervention in the world (let's say the purchase of mosquito nets by a charity), there may appear to be an immediate effect (let's say a fall in the number of people catching malaria). But we can't be sure that the intervention caused the effect. Perhaps the fall in the number of those with malaria is the result of something else (maybe it was hotter that season, leading to there being fewer infected mosquitoes around).

RCTs try to tease causation and correlation apart. Separate people into two sets, Set A and Set B, that are the same in all relevant respects, then try an intervention in Set A (buying mosquito nets, or handing out free textbooks, or incentivizing parents to have their children immunized), but not in Set B. If Set A then experiences a statistically significant decline in deaths due to malaria, or an improvement in education standards, or an uptake in childhood inoculation, you can have some confidence that this is due to the intervention.

RCTs have been used to debunk some high-profile initiatives, such as microfinance, in which small sums are loaned to the desperately poor—to people, in other words, who would typically be unable to access banking facilities. Microfinance took off after the perceived success of minuscule loans by a Bangladeshi economist Mohammed Yunus to forty-two people in the Chittagong District—a mere $27 divided among them. That was in 1976. Heralded as a rocket-booster for entrepreneurship and a miracle cure for poverty, microfinance earned Yunus acclaim and a Nobel peace prize; similar initiatives were rolled out in several other parts of the world. When Yunus wrote his memoir, the Prince of Wales (now King Charles III) provided the foreword, describing Yunus as "a remarkable man."[20] It took RCTs run by some American economists to show that insofar as microfinance has any impact at all, it is a very modest one.[21]

Effective altruists love a well-designed RCT, because like QALYs they provide—or seem to provide, at least—solid, meaty data. They can be revelatory. Out of the statistical cacophony, an RCT can extract the "melody of the logic of behaviour."[22] But while it would be churlish to deny their value, RCTs can't measure everything. They work best when the intervention is straightforward. Do free textbooks improve educational results? What about smaller class sizes? Does offering a small incentive—like a bag of lentils—encourage parents to inoculate their children?

By contrast, RCTs can't deal with complex institutional comparisons, or broad interventions. It would be hard to arrange an RCT, for example, to assess the efficacy of an insurance-based against a publicly funded health system, or to compare effects in a single nation where interest rates are raised in one local region and not another. Large-scale interventions, major institutional changes, and so on are inevitably more difficult to pull off, inevitably longer-term, and inevitably tougher to measure, and so are frowned upon by some effective altruists. One can see why interventions with more speculative outcomes arouse misgivings; but perhaps this reflects a kind of measurement bias. (A marvelous cartoon is quoted by the philanthropy expert Beth Breeze: the bureaucrats are talking to Mahatma Gandhi.

"We won't fund you," they say, "because we can't see the link between spinning and bringing down the Empire.")[23]

So that's one drawback. But even when RCTs are deployed in the narrower areas in which they are most illuminating, caution is advisable. Recall the PlayPumps fiasco: RCTs would probably not have picked up the problem of how undignified women found them.

There are issues with RCTs in medicine, but if you want to know whether a Covid vaccine is effective, you can be reasonably confident that the results of an RCT in the UK will apply in the USA. Social science is not medicine. We cannot always assume that the result of a social science RCT, even one that includes a medical element, is relevant for a different time and in a different place. An RCT in Togo might not replicate in Laos. Indeed, we can't guarantee that an RCT in one village will necessarily tell us something about the neighboring village. And conditions change over time. An RCT in 2026 might not replicate in the same location in 2036.

Thus RCTs can easily generate a level of confidence that is unwarranted. In any case, they only make sense within a wider scientific context. Why would you fund an RCT on class sizes unless you had a hunch that this factor was playing some important causal role? Why would you think that, unlike in parts of Africa, deworming was not the solution to low educational standards in, say, Toledo, Ohio? A randomized control trial does not generate answers in a vacuum; it tests a preexisting hypothesis.

One final point on RCTs. When they're used in Western medical studies they tend not to be contentious. But in the developing world, RCTs "are almost always carried out by light skinned people on dark skinned people,"[24] and, partly as a result, can arouse resentment among both those included in and those excluded from an intervention—who can feel as if they're being used like laboratory rats.[25]

Suppose we park these statistical and methodological concerns, and we manage to reach consensus on a quantifiable measure of the costs and benefits of our actions. Still, many detractors of moral mathematics will remain dissatisfied. For them, the problem with moral mathematics is not that it can't be done. It's not that they believe numbers can't, in practice, be applied to moral decisions. It's rather that they think they shouldn't be applied, as a matter of principle. These people have an almost aesthetic objection to effective altruism. Math and morality, they think, apply to, and should operate in, separate realms. This is the impulse that leads to the critics accusing effective altruists of being "infused with logic so cold that even Mr. Spock would cringe upon hearing it."[26]

Is turning aspects of morality into formulae evidence of a sort of hyperrational psychopathy? That they're driven by logic, as well as emotion, is an accusation the effective altruists are happy to embrace. While MacAskill starts his book with the playground pump, Singer's first chapter in *The Life You Can Save* targets the Make-A-Wish Foundation, which grants a wish—"I wish to fly in a Spitfire"; "I wish to have a Nintendo Switch"; "I wish to go to a Taylor Swift concert"—to critically ill children. Satisfying these wishes is heartwarming, writes Singer, but the average cost per case is enough to save several lives in the developing world.

Indeed, the (math) apple and (morality) pears incommensurability objection is not easy to deconstruct. Quantitative or qualitative tasks carried out by the apparatchik with a clipboard or an Excel spread sheet might not, on the surface, appear ethical in nature but government bodies routinely base their decisions on a cost–benefit analysis. We should be thankful that they do so—that they (at least sometimes) determine policy on the basis of evidence, not emotion or whim. A local council wanting to reduce traffic accidents should site new traffic lights, speed bumps, and pedestrian crossings where the data suggest that they are most needed to prevent or mitigate collisions. "How dare you apply numbers to policy!," in such a case, would be a ludicrous complaint.[27]

How, then, can we get a grip on the objection to mixing morality with numbers? The revulsion is strongest at a very personal level; it's here that moral mathematics really jars. Other things being equal, governments should obviously choose more rather than less effective policies in pursuit of valid goals. And if we have no connection to any particular charity, deciding which to support on the basis of effectiveness also seems uncontentious. But we would be aghast at the parent whose choice between paying for violin lessons for their musically talented child and sending money to a charity that helped strangers far away was determined by plugging numbers into an equation to see what produced the highest expected value. We shall see below (in chapter 18) that the intuition that such a parent is a flawed, callous, calculating machine is widely shared.

One final point. As already explained, moral mathematics has pretensions to objectivity; but in fact it's as vulnerable to motivated reasoning as any other approach to ethical questions. Motivated reasoning is the biased assessment of information to justify a position that one is disposed to support, or already supports. Much of this takes place at a subconscious level, and the flabbier the metrics, the more leeway there is to get away with it. The future of AI, for instance, is clearly of fundamental importance. But those especially fascinated by it can easily employ a few perhaps spurious assumptions to "prove" that addressing the threats posed by the technology deserves the highest priority.

There is a trivial yet illuminating example of the same phenomenon in the *New Yorker* profile of Will MacAskill. MacAskill told friends that he was thinking of getting braces to improve the appearance of his teeth, on the grounds that the more handsome a person was perceived to be, the more money they would be able to make. One friend is quoted: "We were, like, 'Dude, if you want to have the gap closed, it's O.K.' It felt like he had subsumed his own humanity to become a vehicle for the saving of humanity."[28]

Motivated reasoning can generate results that at best are self-interested and at worst appear to outsiders to have a whiff of corruption. In April 2022, the Effective Ventures Foundation (at that time the umbrella organization for the growing number of effective altruism offshoots) purchased a stunning fifteenth-century manor house near Oxford, Wytham Abbey, for close to £15 million. That could have paid for around 5 million mosquito bed-nets. On the other hand—or so it was argued—it could turn out to be cost-saving, since money would no longer have to be spent on renting venues. Moreover, it would encourage EA affiliated groups to hold extra workshops, and this could seed valuable ideas. On the EA Forum, a distinguished academic argued that "the aesthetics, antiquity and uniqueness of the venue can have a significant effect on the seriousness with which people take ideas and conversations, and the creativity of their thinking."[29]

Who knows? Maybe this last assertion was true. What can be stated for certain, however, is that the plucking of vague numbers from the air was a long way from the detailed stats and calculations that Ord had pored over in the embryonic days of EA. And, as several contributors to the online Forum pointed out, it was not a good look. The optics were left out of the cost–benefit equation. Yet the reputational threat from ostentatious expenditure was surely more predictable than any possible creativity boost from an aesthetically agreeable milieu; and reputational damage can have a knock-on impact on all manner of things, including donations.

For all these reasons, then, there is reasonable suspicion about the data-driven approach of effective altruists. The search for numerical precision is a venture into fantasy. On the other hand, exact precision is not required to validate their basic point. There may well be some fuzziness about the numbers—and possibly the treatment of one disease may not be, as they claim, a hundred times more effective than the treatment of another, but only seventy or eighty times. Still, even such a gulf as that between two treatments is surely useful information when it comes to individuals choosing which charities they should fund.

12

Mrs. Jellyby and Groundhog Day

THE DEMANDINGNESS CRITIQUE

MUDDYING A PAIR of trousers is a trivial price to pay for the life of a child. But suppose you act as morality commands. The child is saved. You retire to bed that evening, with a warm glow, knowing that you've done the right thing. You've dropped your sodden, soiled trousers off at the dry cleaner's. The following morning, you rise bright and early, pull on a fresh pair of chinos, and with a righteous bounce in your step, head to work, via the scene of yesterday's emergency. And . . . oh no! An almost identical scenario is playing out in front of you. A different child is in distress, struggling in the water. Well, just as yesterday you can't stand by for fear of destroying your fancy clothes—and so in you wade. Day Three, the same scene plays out. And Day Four. It's Groundhog Day at the Shallow Pond.

Even if Singer's principle—if it is in our power to prevent something bad from happening, without thereby sacrificing anything of comparable moral importance, we ought, morally, to do it—is not utilitarianism, it seems open to the following objection: it demands too much.

There is more than one person living in dire poverty. Indeed, there are millions. Translate Groundhog Day at the Shallow Pond into our obligations to those in need in the developing world. You're about to trade in your fifteen-year-old car for a new model. Hang on—is this purchase really necessary? It wouldn't be a significant sacrifice to stick with the beat-up jalopy, and the money you thereby save could be redirected to the saving of lives. Maybe you could dispense with a car altogether. That evening, you're intending to drive to a celebratory birthday meal with friends at the local Italian bistro. But wait: why not cook pasta for them at home, and donate the saving to charity? Expensive bottle of wine? How about purchasing instead some perfectly potable plonk? Or just drink water from the tap?

The inexorable logic seems to require sacrifice after sacrifice—morality mission-creep. We must eschew most of our worldly goods; instead, we should live our lives in a heightened state of harm-reduction vigilance. MacAskill captured the spirit of this when he wrote that "[e]very day, newspapers lie to you by telling you, 'This is what is the most important of what is going on right now.'"[1] He would call his own paper the *Reality Times,* he said: it would tell readers in each edition how many people had died that day from malaria and how many animals had been killed that day on intensive farms. But the critic asserts that to have our moral antennae permanently attuned to global suffering represents too radical a departure from the usual way that we think about ourselves; this is not reasonable, moderate, ordinary ethics. This is ethics on steroids.

In response to the claim that Singer's morality is overly demanding, a legitimate reply might be, "Tough!" If the argument is sound, we are obliged to swallow its implications. We have to revise our ordinary standards of conduct.

Singer himself adopts this position. But over the years, he has softened his original message, as set out in "Famine, Affluence, and Morality." Even though he still maintains that reasonably well-off people should indeed give away much of what they earn, he now acknowledges that it is more effective in raising money to propose a level of giving within normal psychological reach. Ideally, Singer believes, we should give most of our wealth away, but pragmatically it's fine to set the bar at a lower, more realistic level. If we tell people that they're morally required to give away almost all their wealth, the sheer scale of their obligations might put them off: they might be deterred from giving any. Or they might start off donating, with the genuine intention to persist, but come to suffer from philanthropic burnout, and turn their backs on charity.

But, to be clear, setting a lower bar means falling short of what morality requires. Mrs. Jellyby would agree.

"Mrs. Jellyby had very good hair but was too much occupied with her African duties to brush it."[2] A minor, if unforgettable, character in Charles Dickens's *Bleak House*, Mrs. Jellyby is obsessed with the (fictionalized) African village of Borrioboola-Gha, on the left bank of the Niger. Her plan is that poor families should move there, cultivate coffee beans, and educate the natives. In pursuing the plan, it's not only her hair that she neglects. Her home is filthy, as are her children, whom she ignores even when they fall down the stairs. She ignores her crushed, browbeaten husband too.

The heading for chapter 4 of *Bleak House* sums up Mrs. Jellyby's operational zeal: "Telescopic Philanthropy." Mrs. Jellyby is an absurd figure. She "devotes herself entirely to the public."[3] When her pet project collapses, she simply moves on to the next cause, all the while blind to the needs of those around her. Charity, Dickens is telling us, begins at home—or at least it should.

The utilitarian might concede that we should prioritize our own kids. If we were all inclined to act like Mrs. Jellyby, the results would be catastrophic. From a consequentialist perspective, it is useful that parents love and value their own children more than others'. But the nonutilitarian would say that this still gets things the wrong way around. Even if Mrs. Jellyby's do-gooding produced more good than harm, she would still be open to criticism. Special obligations to our children are morally foundational, of an entirely different order from our obligations to needy strangers. They're not based on any calculus of utilitarian efficiency.

So might the moral relationships we have with particular individuals offer an escape route from the demandingness objection?

The Green Button

Let's grant that you do indeed have a special obligation to your children. Unlike Mrs. Jellyby's offspring, your kids are properly fed, clothed, and sheltered. At home they have a broadband internet connection, books, and a smattering of toys. For Christmas you can afford to buy them FIFA 2026, the soccer video game. But now they're pestering you for the latest update, FIFA 2027.[4] Should you capitulate? It's hard to see how rejecting this filial plea—and donating to charity any money saved from not indulging a demand for an almost identical gaming experience with marginally improved graphics—would require much of a sacrifice. Certainly the gaming update is not of "comparable moral importance" to saving a life.

So we still seem to be left with demands that we should do far more than we actually do. But how much more? To put it in the terms with which we began this chapter, if each day you save a drowning child, does there ever come a point at which it is acceptable to think, "I've done my bit, I've saved enough lives, I need to prioritize my own kids, I'll let the next child I see struggling in the water go under?"

One proposal is that we would always have an obligation to save the drowning child, but the same obligation does not arise with regard to a person in abject poverty, since the former is an emergency, whereas the latter situation is chronic.[5] Coming to the assistance of individuals in emergencies, in this reading, is a sort of insurance scheme—I help others in an emergency, and if I was in a similar predicament, the implicit deal is that other people would help me. But these scenarios are very infrequent, so they would not impinge much on the rest of my life.

There are various problems with this view, but essentially it implies that the fundamental rationale for coming to the assistance of someone drowning in a pond, or made destitute by an earthquake, is self-interest; whereas presumably we want rather to insist that I should save the drowning child even if there was no possibility of reciprocity.

Philosopher Liam Murphy tries another approach. He claims that our obligations don't extend beyond those that we would have if everybody did their share. For example, suppose it could be established beyond serious doubt that the problem of world hunger could be solved if all those who could afford it donated $1,000 to the effort—and suppose that nonetheless there were many people who failed to pull their moral weight. That wouldn't, according to Murphy, increase the obligation on what he calls "the complying person."[6] It is unfair, writes Murphy, to expect people to make up for the failings of others.

"I've done my bit" is a common and commonsense thought. "Why should I do more than others?" Those who take on a disproportionate burden can end up feeling like suckers, resentful toward those who free-ride on their efforts. But when it comes to matters of life and death, this hardly seems like a legitimate reason to opt out. On Monday you pass the pond, and a stranger strolls past in the other direction, apparently indifferent to the unfolding disaster. One of you has to save the child—and it may as well be you. It would be absurd to think that you are not obliged to save the drowning child just because another person is failing to do so. And why is this any less absurd if the scene recurs? Imagine the same scenario playing out on Tuesday. The child is once more in danger, the stranger is again present, but it becomes evident that again they have no intention of coming to the child's assistance. They take a seat on a park bench and look on nonchalantly. Is their coldness an acceptable excuse for you to leave the child to its fate? It hardly seems so.

The philosopher Theron Pummer believes a kind of logical subterfuge is at play here. It's true that each time we pass a drowning child we have a compelling reason to wade into the water. But that is to look at each pond incident as separate and distinct. We should, instead, consider our obligations over a lifetime. To illustrate the point, Pummer presents the following evocative example.[7]

Suppose that at every minute over the course of the rest of your life you could press a green button that would save a different distant stranger. Would you be required to stay by the green button forever? Certainly, if you slice time up into small, discrete chunks, you seem morally compelled to do so. If you fail to press the button at 7.43 a.m. someone will needlessly perish. The same is true at 9.17 p.m., and all other times. At no time will you have anything else to do that could be of comparable moral significance to pressing the green button. But look at what this demands of a life as a whole, rather than of any specific instant. It seems absurd to insist that you must be a perennial slave to the green button and forsake all personal plans and projects of your own. Surely, at some (admittedly difficult to pinpoint) moment, you will have discharged your green-button pressing duty and should feel free to strike out into the wider world in pursuit of a richer existence?

True, a moral saint might be happy to be tied to the green button—or if not exactly happy, then at least prepared to remain on green button service out of a sense of duty. But whether motivated by desire or obligation, the "saint" is not necessarily a role model, a person one should aspire to emulate. In her much-cited article "Moral Saints," the American philosopher Susan Wolf discusses a hypothetical person whose every action is as morally good as possible.[8] That type of person, she contends, would be a crashing bore: they would lack a decent sense of humor, for example, because some types of humor rest on the capacity for minor cruelty (such as excluding or denigrating others). More importantly, there is a whole bunch of nonmoral activities and virtues that make up what we think is a good life.

It's not just the special relationships we have with family and friends. Think of a eulogy at a funeral. Uncle Brian or Aunty Brenda has died. A tribute might mention their moral character. But it will also reference their passions—their work, maybe, but perhaps too their devotion to Aston Villa football club, or hill climbing, or jogging in the park, or walking the dog, their love of contemporary jazz, or Italian cuisine, or photography, or DIY, their devotion to learning Mandarin or mastering the didgeridoo, or tending to the allotment, or building model railways. We may not regard their pursuits as especially worthwhile, but recalling the fact that they resolutely watched every episode of a particularly dreadful soap opera might bring a smile to our faces. None of this would be possible without time off from doing good. A life slavishly devoted to being good would be "strangely barren."[9]

If this is right—and Mrs. Jellyby is thereby wrong—then we shouldn't need to maintain perpetual lifesaving vigilance; we are not required to be ever present for green button–pressing, or to save each drowning child.

13

The New White Man's Burden

THE INSTITUTIONAL CRITIQUE

> The philanthropy of the rich is a rain-drop in the ocean, lost in the moment of falling.
>
> —FRIEDRICH ENGELS

KARL MARX was no fan of philanthropy. He belongs to a tradition that regards charity as a mere sticking plaster that at best leaves the wound underneath unaffected and might even impede it from healing properly, or actually make it worse. According to the *Communist Manifesto,* "A part of the bourgeoisie is desirous of redressing social grievances in order to ensure the continued existence of bourgeois society."[1]

This chimes with the most common charge against effective altruism: what's known as the institutional critique.

The Institutional Critique

Roughly put, the institutional critique states that to solve global problems we need to overturn the system, not tinker around within it. The related empirical claim—that effective altruism simply doesn't achieve its goals—will be dealt with in chapter 17 below. But underpinning the institutional critique is a philosophical position. There is more to justice than the distribution (or redistribution) of money or material possessions. There are systemic issues, involving power imbalances. Conceiving of the world as merely a set of individuals, capable of being good, bad, or indifferent, misses this point. "Effective altruism doesn't try to understand how power works," runs the critique, "except to better align itself with it. In this sense it leaves everything just as it is."[2]

Martha Nussbaum's long (and unedifying) rant about Peter Unger's *Living High and Letting Die* contained a similar analysis. Unger, she wrote, focused on what individuals should do, and offered no wider exploration of global justice, and how politics and institutions could be reimagined such that the chasm between differing levels of opportunity and wealth internationally might not exist in the first place.[3]

Indeed, the stress on the individual ("you") is evident simply from some of the titles of books linked to or expounding effective altruism: *The Life You Can Save*; *The Most Good You Can Do*; *Doing Good Better: Effective Altruism and How You Can Make a Difference*. Where there's a "we" in the title, it refers to us as individuals, not as a collective: *Giving What We Can*. And the failure to address "power," goes the objection, might be explained by the socioeconomic background of many of its intellectual leaders.

"Mind-Blowingly White"

"Plainly stated, EA is mind-blowingly white,"[4] observes one effective altruism cynic. Not just white, but male, bourgeois, and Western. The four new horsemen of the apocalypse. The predominance of middle-class white men, wrote Amia Srinivasan, is "no doubt comforting to those who enjoy the status quo—and may in part account for the movement's success."[5] "To the extent that EA can be described as a social movement," writes another detractor, "it is in fact a movement not of struggling social workers, English teachers, or iron workers, but of wealthy (mostly white and male) capitalists, analytic moral philosophers at elite institutions, and, significantly, technologists."[6] Visit the Centre for Effective Altruism's website and there are photographs of past retreats and a sea of smiling white faces. The Centre for Effective Altruism's own data confirm the homogeneity: there are internal surveys of those who consider themselves part of the effective altruism movement that can be cited in support of the contention that it is an overwhelmingly White phenomenon.

The demographic statistics are shifting, however. Although the percentage of non-White supporters has remained fairly constant (about 25 percent), the movement is becoming less male (women now make up around 30 percent), and older: the average age at which people tend to get involved in effective altruism (twenty-six) continues to rise, and the percentage of students involved is falling. Just over one in eight respondents to a recent survey studied at one of the top ten universities in the world, such as Oxford or Cambridge, Harvard or MIT.[7] The vast majority consider themselves left-wing (remarkably, less than 3 percent report that they are right-wing), and the vast majority—80 percent—self-identify as atheists.[8] As for those who actually take the Giving What We Can pledge, the largest numbers are from the USA, the UK, Australia, Canada, and Germany, though there are active pledges from about a hundred countries.

But why does any of this matter? Shouldn't we just assess ideas on their merits?

If scientists around the world measured the temperature at which water boils at a certain altitude, you would expect them to report the same results, whether the experiment was conducted in London or Tokyo, by a man or a woman. And effective altruism has scientific aspirations: it aims to use objective methodologies to analyze interventions. But this involves complex assumptions and calculations—far more complex than gauging the temperature of H^2O; and one suspicion is that these calculations are influenced by the type of person doing the calculating.

This is not an absurd conjecture. If in the past more engineers had been female, perhaps the safety equipment that was initially deemed adequate for automobiles would have been reimagined and redesigned. Notoriously, crash-test dummies failed to take into account the fact that on average women are shorter and lighter than men.[9] Is it conceivable that the judgments and recommendations of effective altruists are shaped by their favored status within (in the words of yet another skeptic) "a white supremacist patriarchy"?[10] Are the skewed demographics of the movement what give rise to gaps in knowledge, flawed methodologies, subconscious or blatant bias?

As an example, one charge is that community-organizing in the animal rights movement and elsewhere is insufficiently valued because few effective altruists have any experience of how to engage non-White groups. Something similar is said to be true of poverty. "We sit and talk about poverty for days without 99% of the community having any experience of it," wrote one contributor to the EA Forum. "That's not only morally wrong, it opens us up to huge research blunders due to assumptions that are rarely correct."[11] The general claim is that the people responsible for the ideological framing of effective altruism, primarily those from comfortable backgrounds, lack the perspective, or imagination, to appreciate the structural injustices that underpin poverty and so doom it to persist. In some ways this is an ironic allegation. Most citizens of the developed world barely grant a fleeting thought to distant lives. They're the opposite of Mrs. Jellyby—microscopic, not telescopic, in their concerns. What marks out effective altruists is that they have reflected hard about the suffering of total strangers, and have a radical take on how individuals should respond to relieve it.

But it is true that the philosophical leadership of effective altruism tends to be cautious in inclination. They are moderate radicals, and proudly so. "I assume that, like it or not, capitalism will be the dominant economic system for the foreseeable future," writes Peter Singer:

> To challenge that assumption, opponents of capitalism would have to establish two claims. First, they would need to show that there is an alternative economic system that will, in a world like ours and given what we have learned about human nature, do a better job of providing people with food, clothing, shelter, health care, education, and the other things that are central to our well-being. Second, they need to tell a believable story about how that alternative economic system could come to replace contemporary capitalism. I've yet to be convinced by any attempt to persuade me of the truth of either of these claims.[12]

A similar mindset is evident in MacAskill's *Doing Good Better*, when he rejects the idea that we should boycott clothes produced in sweatshops. That, his argument runs, would only make those who currently work in sweatshops worse off.[13] "If you asked me for my top-20 list of changes I want to see in the world," he said in an interview with the *Financial Times*, "then overthrowing capitalism is not one of them."[14]

Although most effective altruists self-identify as being on the political left, their pragmatism inflames others who share their political leanings. The latter see the endorsement of capitalism as too pessimistic, and proclaim that there are alternative systems of arranging affairs that would do better at meeting our aspirations of fairness without sacrificing liberty—and that would turn out to be equally, if not indeed more, productive.

The label "capitalism," of course, covers a multitude of sins. The Danish and US economies, for example, are broadly capitalist, but differ in significant ways: Denmark has higher tax, more generous welfare provision, less poverty, less inequality, and lower crime. But it seems unlikely—it's usually unclear, at least—that those who make the institutional critique would be satisfied if effective altruism simply advocated for the world to be a little more like Denmark and a little less like America: a tinkering at the edges, a touch of reform to the World Trade Organization here, a fine-tuning of the tax system there. This sounds exactly like the same restrained agenda for which effective altruists are routinely condemned.

How alternative systems to capitalism would function and what they would achieve is at least in part an empirical matter. In any case, insofar as EA demographic patterns—too White, too male, and so forth—have warped judgments, and dampened ambition, an obvious corrective suggests itself: make effective altruism more diverse. And some within the EA movement itself have come to accept that if you view the world from one vantage point, you may be blind to issues that seem vital from another.[15]

But there are other points to be made in response to the institutional critique.

First, it's just not plausible that all episodes of large-scale human misery are the product of power asymmetries and institutional failures. Earthquakes will claim more lives when buildings are badly built, and poor construction is often linked to corruption, but this wasn't the case with the 1995 Kobe earthquake in Japan which killed thousands. Equally, a drought is likely to have a far more devastating effect under a despotic regime than in a democracy,[16] but poor democracies can be overwhelmed by natural disasters nonetheless. Something similar can be said of pandemics.

Second, even if misgovernance and/or institutional or trading structures are the nub of much of the suffering in the world, is the alternative proposal that in the short term we simply overlook the suffering? Are we justified in ignoring short-term pain because alleviating the worst effects of poverty today does nothing to fix poverty in the future? Are we justified in ignoring short-term pain, because by doing so we will force countries to sort their own problems out, thus improving long-term prospects? Not only is such an approach heartless, but it's also predicated on a nakedly utilitarian rationale (it's acceptable to harm, or allow harm to occur, for the long-term greater good), and as we have seen, utilitarianism is precisely the philosophical ideology that so many critics of effective altruism profess to abhor.

Third, while it is true that the effective altruist proposes that individuals should decide what to do on the basis that the world is likely to persist in its current state, it's not obvious why this should be considered an objection. Amia Srinivasan condemns the lurking assumption that "the world is a given, in which one can make careful, piecemeal interventions."[17] But in choosing how to act it is sensible for each of us to take into account how others will act. If it's implausible that others will act in a certain way—collectively to bring about radical institutional change, for example—why would one act on the assumption that such change will occur?

Fourthly, and finally, let us grant the institutional critics their basic premise. Maybe the only way to tackle poverty in a lasting way is through institutional change. If so, the effective altruist can happily accommodate this point. If, rather than donating money to charity, it really would be more effective to engage in the political process, to stand for election, to sign petitions and participate in protest movements, to advocate and lobby, to expose bad practice, to coordinate with others in order to bring about reforms: well, that is precisely what the effective altruist would recommend.

Indeed, when it comes to animal welfare, institutional change is where the efforts of the effective altruist movement have been largely concentrated. Not sending money to dog homes or pet sanctuaries. Not trying to change practice, for example, farm by farm, but by campaigning at the macro-level, putting pressure on giant retailers such as Cosco, MacDonalds, Nestlé, and Walmart, and supporting legislation to reduce the suffering of animals in the food production process. A whole plethora of groups—such as the Humane League[18]—has sprung up in this regard, many of them funded by effective altruist–linked organizations. There have been concrete results. Take, for example, how chickens are reared for eggs and meat. Those working for animal rights organizations have secured pledges from almost all the major retailers, food manufacturers, and food and hotel chains not to use products from caged birds—of which there are about seven billion. The European Union has banned the battery cages in which hens were kept in the industrialized egg production process. In California, Proposition 12 set minimum space standards for egg-laying hens, breeding pigs, and veal calves, and in 2023 the Supreme Court upheld the right of that state to prohibit the import of products from animals not kept in accordance with the standards.[19]

In any case, presumably there's worthwhile work to be done at both individual and collective levels. Why should donating money to charity preclude political engagement? Imagine rebuking someone who jumps into a pond to save the child on the grounds that instead they should have orchestrated or engaged in a campaign to ensure that all ponds are fenced off to prevent similar tragedies occurring in the future. It may well be true that fences need to be built; in the meantime, a child is drowning.

14

The Mega-Rich and the Pearly Gates

THE BILLIONAIRE CRITIQUE

The man who dies thus rich dies disgraced.

—ANDREW CARNEGIE

Who builds a church to God and not to fame / Will never mark the marble with his name.

—ALEXANDER POPE

ALTHOUGH THE VAST MAJORITY OF effective altruists have been ordinary people earning ordinary salaries, there have also been a few supporters—such as Sam Bankman-Fried—who've been mega-rich.

The proportion of charitable donations coming from the run-of-the-mill rich—those earning over $200,000 a year—has risen quite dramatically in the United States. But there's a particularly pronounced trend among the mega-rich.[1] Because the mega-rich—the multimillionaires and billionaires—now play an outsized role in philanthropy, they are worthy here of a short chapter to themselves.

The basic reason for their increasing significance is the growing gap over the past few decades between the mega-rich and everyone else—the poorest, the average, and the comfortably well-off. Staggeringly, the richest 1 percent now own almost 50 percent of global wealth.[2]

Suspicion of effective altruism has arisen because of its links with the mega-rich. Bankrupt former billionaire Sam Bankman-Fried was once the most high-profile mega-rich supporter of effective altruism. But there have been other mega-rich individuals who've expressed support for effective altruists' aims and, above all, their methods—which are not as new as they may seem. There's a tradition, more than a century old, of a minority of mega-rich individuals, having made their fortunes in the private sector, then turning to an empirically based philanthropy.

Billionaire Buddies

Dress smartly. Wear spotless linen. Brush your shoes. "See also that your hands are kept clean."[3] This is just some of the advice delivered by an expert on how to extract charity gifts from donors. He also suggested that the begging process would seem more dignified if donors were visited by two people, rather than one. Mind you, only one person should do the talking; the other should remain largely silent. When persuading potential donors to part with their money, the best strategy for the talker was to appeal only to the nobler motives, since the donor's "own mind will suggest to him the lower and selfish ones."[4]

The expert was Frederick T. Gates. Gates was not himself an entrepreneur, but he became the aide to the world's richest man at the time, John D. Rockefeller Sr., whose almost unfathomable wealth gushed from oil. Gates, an ex-Baptist priest, was a tall man with a paintbrush moustache and boundless energy that occasionally boiled over into histrionics. He had first impressed Rockefeller when plans were afoot to fund what became the University of Chicago. His clear and detailed report on the project demonstrated exceptional analytical skills and grasp of detail. In 1891, Rockefeller persuaded him to move to the East Coast to run his philanthropic office.[5]

Gates turned gatekeeper. Rockefeller was inundated with begging letters, "constantly hunted, stalked, and hounded almost like a wild animal."[6] As a one-time experiment, Gates counted these letters over a thirty-day period: there were fifty thousand of them. They poured in from all around the world, usually requesting a small sum and helpfully pointing out that Rockefeller wouldn't miss it. Sometimes they came from people in dire need, at other times payment was requested for luxuries—money for a piano, or for a bride's trousseau. The snobbish Gates was unimpressed by the quality of solicitations. "They were generally illiterate, often written in pencil, frequently in a foreign language and generally disclosed very limited intelligence."[7]

Notwithstanding his philanthropy, Rockefeller's wealth continued to snowball. In June 1905 Gates wrote to his boss urging him to dispense with more of his fortune—not on the grounds that there was so much pressing need in the world, but rather because of the inflating value of his assets. "Your wealth is rolling up, rolling up like an avalanche! You must keep up with it! You must distribute it faster than it grows! If you do not, it will crush you and your children and your children's children."[8]

As for his own children, he sent them to private schools, because of the type of kids that they'd encountered in public ones: "some of the colored and of the foreign-born children were ill mannered, filthy, and unsanitary. Very little children had no protection from them at all."[9]

Frederick Gates was born a century before Bill Gates (no relation), who like Rockefeller, became the richest man in the world (from selling computer software). But perhaps the most notable link between Gates I and Gates II, was their approach to charity. Gates II modeled some of his charitable practices on Rockefeller's philanthropy—largely shaped by Gates I. Gates I was an enthusiastic supporter of the early twentieth-century Efficiency Movement—which promoted the elimination of waste and inefficiency—and was also a proponent of what he called "the principles of scientific giving."[10] His boss concurred that charity should be more like business.

Power, influence, and status in the philanthropic sector are not procured with cents and pennies. Although many people in the Global North can afford to give away small sums, very few have the resources to single-handedly transform the prospects for millions. Charities will welcome your cents and pennies, but for small change they won't fawn over you, wine and dine you, or even shift their priorities or agenda to accommodate your interests.

The nonrevolutionary, pragmatic agenda of the effective altruists may be one reason why they've received support from among the mega-rich. The effective altruists pose a challenging question to them—"Should you not be using your mega-wealth to do good?"—but hardly a threat. There are other appeals too. The logic of 80,000 Hours is that earning big bucks is not immoral: quite the contrary, provided you then give away a sufficient amount. That's a refreshing and convenient message for the Silicon Valley set. No doubt, too, they approve of EA's scientific approach. Moreover, the way the effective altruists weigh up options feels comfortingly familiar to the investor. The only difference is that the investor spreadsheet itemizes profit and loss, while the effective altruist spreadsheet lists malaria nets and cases of diarrhea. After reading MacAskill's *Doing Good Better,* Bill Gates called the author "a data nerd after my own heart."[11]

Cynicism about the philanthropic activities of the mega-rich is understandable. Only the rich are capable of giving amounts that will burnish their reputation, purchasing a kind of gratitude-immortality. Their names adorn the swanky edifices constructed with their funds: Rockefeller's aide Frederick Gates grumbled that Andrew Carnegie donated "for the sake of having his name written in stone all over the country."[12] Significant but smaller sums will buy you a plaque as one of many on a corridor—as a wander through the buildings surrounding leafy quadrangles in elite US colleges will reveal. "Graffiti of the rich," it's been called.

It's not just the vanity pay-off that arouses distrust. Charity can buy concrete benefits. The mega-rich are often at their most generous when they or their enterprises are in trouble. Rockefeller's giving coincided with the passage of antitrust legislation that was designed to undermine the dominant market position of Standard Oil. Teddy Roosevelt thought Rockefeller was "alms-washing" but that "[n]o amount of charities [*sic*] in spending such fortunes can compensate in any way for the misconduct in acquiring them."[13]

Rare are the billionaires who hollow out their bank accounts with such vigor that they cease to be mega-rich. While sharing their income, they tend to hang on to its source. The Mexican multibillionaire Carlos Slim captured this approach when he compared wealth to an orchard: "You have to share the fruit not the trees."[14]

Meanwhile, in various jurisdictions, philanthropy is tax-deductible. Arguably—and many critics of the philanthropy industry argue the point forcefully—it would be better if governments did away with this incentive, even if it led, as it inevitably would, to a decline in charitable giving. Why? Because the state would then receive more tax receipts, and because billionaire benevolence erodes democracy. The foundations through which most of the mega-rich channel their funds are often opaque about their decision-making processes, and are not accountable to the wider public. Yet they can have enormous influence in shaping policy.

One example is education. Powerful foundations like the Gates Foundation, for example, have championed charter schools—public schools, publicly funded, but operating independently (not run by local school boards). Putting aside the merits of these schools, you might think that the complexion of the educational landscape should be broadly settled by democratically elected politicians, not by unelected plutocrats, however well-intentioned. Because most of the mega-rich have made their money in the private sector, they are naturally inclined to believe that markets, competition, and the price mechanism are the principal drivers of excellence—thus downplaying and possibly degrading the motives and values that inspire people to work in many professions (such as teaching and nursing). Do we really want billionaires setting the agenda in essential services such as education or health? Shouldn't that be left to government?

In fact, few billionaires have shown much interest in involving themselves in the core functions of the state. Perhaps repairing potholes, collecting rubbish, or doling out welfare payments is not sexy enough. Nevertheless, the mega-rich and their philanthropic foundations can be useful at the edge of these activities, and they have certain advantages over the state. Their decision-making process might be more nimble and less bureaucratic. And since they are not beholden to shareholders or voters, they can be more experimental, risk-taking, and long-term oriented. The combined oral contraceptive pill ("the pill") was funded in its early development by the feminist philanthropist Katharine McCormick, who had married the heir to a manufacturing industry fortune.[15] "Most importantly," according to one billionaire philanthropist, "we can work in the interest of those who are structurally underrepresented in terms of their political power, such as incarcerated people, potential immigrants, the global poor, animals and future generations."[16] In the charitable sector more generally, there are numerous examples of organizations identifying vital causes that politicians have overlooked—and sometimes, as in the case of the UK's National Society for the Prevention of Cruelty to Children, campaigning on an issue will lead to legislation (the first UK law to protect children from neglect and abuse was passed by parliament in 1889, five years after the precursor to the NSPCC was founded).

As for international aid in particular, leaving it to the government alone will probably mean a precipitous fall in quantity. Governments are very stingy (giving away less than 1 percent of GDP) and the "aid" they give is often tied to their own nations' political and economic interests, rather than allocated according to where it is most needed.

Dustin Moskovitz was not the first to tread the path from Harvard dropout to billionaire. A Harvard roommate of Mark Zuckerberg and a founding partner of Facebook, he moved to the West Coast where his Facebook shares were soon valued in their billions. Then he launched another wildly successful Silicon

Valley company, Asana, specializing in software to assist in the organization of work projects. He and Cari Tuna were once the second-wealthiest backers of EA. The Bankman-Fried debacle promoted them to the number one slot.

Cari Tuna read Singer's *The Life You Can Save* in 2010, on the cusp of leaving her *Wall Street Journal* reporter's job to focus full time on philanthropy. The book, she says, "introduced me to the idea of trying to do not just some good but as much good as we could with our giving, and I became quite passionate about that idea. At the time, most of the advice we were hearing was along the lines of 'follow your heart' and 'give to what you are passionate about.' But . . . Singer's advice resonated more deeply."[17]

Another Harvard dropout and his wife were also inspired by Singer. In June 2010, Bill and Melinda Gates, along with Warren Buffett, America's least flamboyant yet most successful investor (the so-called "Sage of Omaha"), launched the "Giving Pledge." The idea was to persuade other members of the billionaires' club (there are around three thousand billionaires around the world) to donate at least half of their wealth, either during their lifetime or in their will. Discussing the pledge on TV shortly after the launch of the initiative, Melinda Gates invoked *The Life You Can Save*.[18]

There are no doubt many reasons why the Gateses established the Giving Pledge. Singer is part of the explanation. As of 2024, there were two hundred and forty signatories to the Pledge from thirty different countries.[19] If all those who sign up to the Giving Pledge are as good as their word, that's hundreds of billions of dollars going to charity—quite some impact for a philosophy professor. In a lengthy *New York Times* article Singer welcomed the Giving Pledge initiative and lauded the billionaires, pointing out that, even adjusting for inflation, Buffett alone was pledging to give away much more than Carnegie and

Rockefeller combined. This was a "Golden Age of philanthropy." Attacks on their motives he dismissed as "sniping," that revealed "more about the attackers than the attacked." Besides, parents of children who would get lifesaving vaccines, funded by the billionaires, didn't care about their motives.[20]

True, Bill Gates was hardly living on the poverty line (Singer pointed out that Gates had paid over $30 million for a book handwritten by Leonardo da Vinci). But he was doing more good than most. Others should follow his example. In fact, Singer proposed a rough target for how much the mega-rich and the not-quite-so-rich should give away—a tapered schedule, in which the top 0.01 percent of US taxpayers should donate a third of their income, and the top 1 percent (of those outside the top 0.1 percent), should donate 20 percent, with a 10 percent target for the top 10 percent.

To critics, the hobnobbing with billionaires is further evidence that effective altruism is morally broken, and irredeemably so. Within the effective altruism movement, too, there are misgivings about the influence of a few mega-rich individuals. Singer himself fears that the movement has gravitated toward a few "high net worth sophisticated individuals" and thinks "that's a mistake."[21] Others are suspicious of how neatly aligned Longtermism is with the interests of the Silicon Valley investor community.[22] Even if well-intentioned, Longtermism "risks becoming a Trojan horse for the vested interests of a select few."[23]

An alignment of interest in future-gazing is one reason why effective altruists and the tech crowd rub along so well. "This is a close match for my philosophy,"[24] Elon Musk wrote about Will MacAskill's Longtermist book. Musk, who donated money to Bostrom's Future of Humanity Institute, has declared his ambition to build a rocket that can take passengers to Mars, with the ultimate objective of creating a permanent settlement there.

There's a heavy overlap of EA supporters and those in the so-called rationalist movement. The rationalists (amusingly if unfairly ridiculed as "Mensa with orgies")[25] are primarily based around Silicon Valley. Among other elements, their project involves trying to identify and then eliminate various biases that afflict many humans (race and gender bias, of course, but also an alphabet soup of less familiar biases such as "anchoring bias," "belief bias," "confirmation bias," etc.). Their mission is to be "LessWrong"—the name of the website where much of the rationalist debate takes place. They are particularly preoccupied with the transformative power and dangers of technology, especially artificial intelligence. But perceived (and real) links between the rationalists and the effective altruists have not been helpful, says Toby Ord. "The rationalists give off a certain vibe. They are often people interested in protecting the world from AI. But if it turned out there was no AI risk, and the thing you had to care about was global poverty, they would go off and do something else."[26]

There are, then, sound reasons to be distrustful of the close ties between EA and the mega-rich. But such ties don't represent an argument for not giving 10 percent of one's income to effective charities, nor do they justify the casting of aspersions on the vast majority of EA supporters, who have no connection to the mega-rich. Buffett says that when he dies, his remaining wealth will go into a charitable trust run by his children, and it's unclear how the money will then be used. However, what is the alternative to trying to co-opt the mega-rich into effective philanthropy? One day, the economy might be reimagined, such that nobody earns the mind-boggling income of a Gates—or, more plausibly, that they earn it, but keep much less, because far more is funneled into the government exchequer through taxation. In the meantime, there are people swimming in money. For Will MacAskill, as for Peter Singer, trying to liberate and redirect a percentage of this wealth to those who are metaphorically drowning is a worthwhile activity. "If I can help encourage people who do have enormous resources to not buy yachts and instead put that money toward pandemic preparedness and AI safety and bed nets and animal welfare that's just like a really good thing to do."[27]

15

Righting Past Wrongs

THE HISTORICAL INJUSTICE CRITIQUE

I know it was you Fredo. You broke my heart. You broke my heart.

—MICHAEL CORLEONE TO FREDO CORLEONE (*THE GODFATHER, PART II*)

ANOTHER WATER SCENE—from possibly the finest movie ever made. It's sunset, and two men are fishing from a small boat in a vast and beautiful and empty lake, the man in front, wearing a fishing hat, facing forward while quietly intoning Hail Marys. A cut away to another man who is standing and observing events from his house. We hear a gun shot, and when the camera returns to the lake scene, the praying man is gone.

Philosophers often talk of the divide between Analytic and Continental philosophy. The Englishman Bertrand Russell (1872–1970) and the German Martin Heidegger (1889–1976) are seen as canonical figures in the Analytic and Continental traditions respectively. The Analytic–Continental demarcation is contested—it's difficult, if not impossible, to identify a single characteristic shared by all Analytical philosophers and no Continental philosophers, and vice versa. But one rough division is this: Continental philosophers tend to be more interested in situating philosophical puzzles and problems within history. Analytic philosophers, as a crude generalization, pursue philosophical questions using methods similar to those in logic and mathematics, and these can be, as it were, lifted out of space and time.

The scene described above, from *The Godfather, Part II*, in which Frederico (Fredo) Corleone is executed by order of his ruthless younger brother, is the culmination of a complex moral drama, impossible to grasp or adjudicate upon without the context of the broader narrative, the character development of the protagonists, and Mafia norms around honor and status, revenge and retribution.

There is an analogy here: we need context to understand a death in the Shallow Pond just as we do to understand this assassination in the deep lake.

When you walked past the Shallow Pond it was a particular time and day in history. It was morning or afternoon. It was a weekday or a weekend. It was rainy, cloudy, or sunny. The Shallow Pond was in a particular place too. But where? Was it in Oxford or New York, or Tokyo, or Kuwait City?

The institutional critique of the Shallow Pond is that any real future fix for poverty requires institutional and structural change: a transfer of power, not merely the transfer by individuals of income or resources. The institutional critique faces forward. The historical critique, by contrast, complains that the Shallow Pond doesn't look back. It is described to us ahistorically; it has no past, no narrative. It is a catastrophe that is presented as occurring only at a particular moment. We know nothing about the child's background, nor why she has been abandoned. We don't know how long the pond has been there. Was it man-made? If it was, who made it, or ordered it to be made? We don't know anything about the man walking past the pond. What's his history?

Let's invent some details. It turns out that the man is not entirely innocent in relation to the unfolding events. He campaigned for the pond to be built, but also, on aesthetic grounds, vehemently opposed a protective fence—using his influence as a wealthy local resident to ride roughshod over the concerns of parents.

This seems morally relevant. In the absence of this background information, we only have a partial ethical understanding of our duties and obligations in this instance. We have a snapshot, a single scene; we need the whole film for the moral subtleties of a situation to emerge.

In theory, we could frame philanthropy in an ahistorical way. There are impoverished people, today, in the developing world, and people in the developed world with the means to help them. But this situation did not just spontaneously or randomly occur; there's a context.

The causes of poverty are, naturally, multifarious and complex. Colonialism and Western exploitation are there in the mix. In the late nineteenth and early twentieth centuries, the nation now called the Democratic Republic of Congo (DRC) was terrorized by its Belgian colonizers, while being systematically looted. Locals were enslaved and forced to hunt elephants for their tusks. When the ivory began to run out, attention turned to lucrative rubber, extracted from rubber vines. Female villagers and children were kept hostage until the soldiers' rubber quotas were met. Opposition to the plundering was snuffed out by massacres, rape, and mutilations. The numbers are disputed, but millions are thought to have died at the colonizers' hands.[1]

Today the DRC is one of the most deprived countries in the world. There are multiple reasons for this; but few would dispute a connection with its brutal colonial past, even if almost everyone in the DRC today was born after independence (achieved in 1960). And even had the DRC entirely overcome its colonial past, and become wealthier than its former Belgian master, this wouldn't erase the historical fact that its resources had once been stolen.

This matters. Suppose that once in your wilder, younger, troubled days, you smashed in your neighbors' front door, forcibly entered, and then removed the contents of their house—the sofa, the fridge, the Nintendo Switch. The police paid no attention and you escaped unpunished. A few years later you (or perhaps your children), are still occupying your home when your neighbors (or perhaps their children) wander past your window. You notice that they appear thin and drawn, and are dressed in rags. Taking pity on them, you go next door to offer them a wad of cash, and some secondhand garments that you no longer wear.

Your sympathy might be genuine. But we would not, I think, characterize what you do here as "charity." The distinction between compensation and reparations, on the one hand, and charity on the other, is not merely a matter of semantics. You have wronged your neighbors, or perhaps your neighbors' children, and you are required to offer redress or make some kind of amends. What's more, if you have acquired benefits illegally, and you then transfer them back to their rightful owner, it would be wholly inappropriate to attempt to impose conditions on how they are used. It is usually presumed that it is within the donors' rights to identify the causes to which donated money is directed. That only makes sense in the context of a charitable rather than a reparative relationship.

This was something acknowledged by the philosopher Philippa Foot, who urged the charity she was heavily involved in, Oxfam, to reimagine its core mission as one of justice, not charity. "Fundamentally, it means that the help that is given to those who need it is seen as something *to which they have a right* rather than solely as something which, from compassion, we want them to have."[2] Foot was a critic of utilitarianism. Looking in the rearview mirror at the causes of extreme poverty is not, as Singer concedes, "a utilitarian way of thinking about it."[3] For nonutilitarians that's an additional reason why utilitarianism is flawed. It's not that the particulars of the past affect *how* we think we should respond to the child drowning in the Shallow Pond—of course we should save the child—but they do affect *why* we think we should act.

That is to say, even if Singer and the effective altruists are right about what we should do, they might be right for the wrong reason.

16

Distance and Dignity

THE POWER CRITIQUE

SO, THE previous chapter suggests, the Shallow Pond analogy with our obligations in the real world is flawed because it lacks history. It is flawed too, some say, because it lacks any analysis of power dynamics. What does this mean?

When Jean-Jacques Rousseau thought friendship was only achievable between equals, he was onto something. Most readers will know that it is nigh impossible to be friends with your boss, when they have the license to order you around, allocate you tasks, promote or demote you, determine your income. It is far worse to be in the subservient position in an asymmetrical power relationship, but the asymmetry has costs even for the dominant party. The boss who wants to be friends with their underlings is usually an embarrassment.

The awkwardness of the boss–employee relationship is predicated on the fact that's it ongoing. You don't let your guard down when chatting to the boss over a glass of wine at the Christmas party, because they'll still be the boss the following morning when you're both sober.

The Shallow Pond is a one-off jeopardy. In the Shallow Pond, there's a potential victim and a potential savior; one person is powerless, while the other has the power to help. But beyond this incident, there is no assumption that the potential savior is from a privileged group while the victim is, for example, economically deprived. Philanthropy is typically not like this, however. The givers are rich, the receivers are poor, and whatever the benefits of philanthropy, this asymmetrical power balance is uncomfortable, making almost inevitable condescension on the part of the rich, and feelings of helplessness, shame, and humiliation on the part of the poor. Historically in Britain, benefactors have often seen the poor as morally deficient, and charity as a means to improve their character.[1]

Although here I'm mainly interested in the relationship between the distant donor and the recipient, this imbalance in power and status can be even more conspicuous at the point of aid-delivery. In her book *Spaces of Aid,* Lisa Smirl names the areas in which donors and receivers interact "Aid Land": "Aid workers visit project sites in air-conditioned Land Cruisers while the intended project beneficiaries walk barefoot through the heat. The aid workers check their emails from within gated communities, while the surrounding communities have no running water."[2] As to life for aid workers within the compound,

> Clothing is Western, the language is usually that of the previous colonial power, the electricity, water and sanitation systems, and communications networks, are self-contained. Certain exceptional behavior is also permitted within the confine. This applies not only to the ability to drink alcohol in Muslim countries, for women and men to work together or for women to bare their heads, but also to the categorization

> of workers into pay scales and privilege according to their place of birth. Within the UN system, those workers categorized as local will earn a fraction of what their international colleagues earn.[3]

In the world of effective altruism philanthropy, the aid donors don't typically know the aid receiver; they hit a few buttons, click a few links on their computer or phone, and transfer money from their bank account to an intermediary: a charity or NGO. There are charities in which a sponsor is encouraged to form a connection with an individual child, and the child is expected in return to write or send drawings to the sponsor. No doubt there are tremendous benefits from these relationships, not least building solidarity and keeping the sponsor engaged in the charity. But it is intrinsically one-sided. However well-intentioned the sponsor, the child and the child's family are likely to be motivated to sustain the relationship by a different set of motives—gratitude, perhaps fear that the flow of money will dry up. There's nothing wrong with gratitude of course. But this is merely to point out that the relationship between the sponsor and the sponsored is not an equal one. Being dependent on others, as Rousseau understood, is belittling. In the case of effective altruism, the people in need are reliant on the calculations of those who crunch the numbers in Oxford or San Francisco.

When national and racial identities are layered over this asymmetry, it becomes more problematic still. The 1971 concert for Bangladesh co-organized by George Harrison (see chapter 3 above) would prove to be the template and inspiration for other charity-raising concerts, most notably Live Aid in 1985, when a forceful and garrulous Bob Geldof metaphorically bludgeoned many musical celebrities into performing on stage (in one of two venues, London and Philadelphia) in front of a mass TV audience, in aid of starving Ethiopians.

In retrospect, one cannot help but cringe a little at this "glamour aid."[4] In October 1984 the BBC journalist Michael Buerk had traveled to the town of Korem, in Tigray, Ethiopia. His trip was facilitated by Oxfam. "Dawn, and as the sun breaks through the piercing chill of night on the plain outside Korem it lights up a biblical famine, now, in the twentieth century."[5] The language implied that this was akin to an act of God, a tragedy beyond human control. His famous report flew around the world, and moved Geldof to action. "Do they know it's Christmas?" asked the patronizing Christmas charity song released at the end of 1984. "They" probably did have some inkling, since the majority of the nation's population was Christian. (As a thought experiment, one might wonder how Americans would react if the Nigerian pop star Burna Boy held a fundraising concert in Lagos for the hundreds of thousands of homeless Americans.)

Social identities are contingent. There's no necessary reason why ethnicity should be a powerful aspect of identity; one can imagine a world in which it was irrelevant. Still, that is not our world, and in our world, if the donors are White and the recipients brown or Black, there's an added layer of discomfort and humiliation in the donor–benefactor relationship. This relationship has to be understood within the historical context of colonialism and that of existing national and racial inequalities. It is not as simple as some humans wanting to help others.

The Shallow Pond is blind to all these subtle and sometimes belittling dynamics. One response to this worry is that such sensitivities are an irrelevance, or at the very least of marginal concern. An empty stomach matters more than hurt feelings, which are a luxury the indigent can ill afford. But this is to ignore evidence that suggests the very poor are indeed as mortified by the shame that accompanies their condition, and their perception of powerlessness, as by their material deprivations.[6] When an NGO decides that it's going to fund this well, or that school, it acts paternalistically, as though the local people can't determine what to do for themselves. As one political theorist puts it, "[i]n treating adult persons in this way their moral status is demeaned or diminished."[7]

If relationships of domination and subordination are more significant than Peter Singer or the effective altruist movement have conceded, the question is, what can be done? Might there be ways of donating that treat the recipient with dignity and avoid or diminish the sense of humiliation that accompanies charity?

There's a passage in *A Passover Haggadah* by Elie Wiesel that describes such a world: "In some towns, before Passover, Jews would raise funds discreetly: One by one, they would enter a room in the community house. There they would find a dish filled with money. Those who had money left some; those who needed money took some. No one knew how much was given or how much was taken. Thus, the needy were taken care of with dignity."[8]

It's hard to see how to replicate this model in international charity. Nevertheless, in recent years, charities have become increasingly sensitized to power asymmetries. There's now a widely accepted notion that they should have at least some staff from the communities that they purport to serve. Most could go much further. Ideally, the local communities would articulate their needs (rather than these being identified by outsiders), would set out the solutions for how these needs are to be met, and would be the principal players in the implementation of these solutions. A host of organizations is trying to move toward this ideal. A British charity, One World Together, for example, aims to give money to reputable community organizations, with no strings attached.

Technology can help. GiveDirectly (mentioned in chapter 11 above) avoids many of the pitfalls, by arranging for donated money to be sent directly to very poor households, who can then use the money as they wish. This has only been made possible by the telecommunications revolution, allowing money to be transferred digitally through mobile phones. There were (and still are) paternalistic qualms about recipients blowing all the gifted money away; in fact, the evidence from a fascinating study in Kenya, where in some villages all the inhabitants were sent a lump sum of money, is that the economic benefits, particularly in terms of entrepreneurial activity, are substantial.[9]

There are, then, examples of NGOs and philanthropic organizations reflecting carefully about power and control. But Nobel Prize winner and aid skeptic Angus Deaton (who'll be introduced more fully in the next chapter) is doubtful that any real feeling of equality can be achieved between donor and recipient. "You can't do that when you've got all the money and they don't have any. It's a fake."[10]

17

The Harm You Do

THE EFFECTIVENESS CRITIQUE

Poverty Is No Pond.

—LEIF WENAR

The greatest harm done by the humanitarian international is to create delusion. Western governments and donating publics are deluded into believing the fairy tale that their aid can solve profound political problems, when it cannot.

—ALEX DE WAAL

I'm a normal person. I have a girlfriend. I watch football. I like driving a fancy sports car.

—RICHARD ARMITAGE

MEET DR. RICHARD ARMITAGE.

What might you hope of a philosophy paper? To appear in a "prestigious" journal? To be read by two hundred other philosophers? To be the focus of a workshop? It's rare for a philosophy paper to hurdle the discipline's wall and make an impact beyond philosophy. You wouldn't expect a philosophy paper to inspire nonphilosophers such as Richard Armitage.

Heavily influenced by Singer, Armitage lighted upon an unusual means to do good. He had just turned thirty-four when he decided to give away one of his kidneys. A UK National Health Service scheme allows donors to donate to an unknown stranger. That stranger may have a willing but incompatible donor, who then donates their kidney to another stranger, who in turn has a willing but incompatible donor. In this way, it is possible to trigger a chain in which three lives are radically transformed.[1]

The surgical procedure did not hold the same terrors for Armitage as it might do for others. From a working-class family in Yorkshire, he had made it to university and qualified as a doctor. He was not squeamish about blood and needles and was familiar with hospital procedures. When he first proposed donating a kidney, his family expressed concern about the medical risks—but he had researched the topic and knew these were low. In fact, the second kidney began to feel like a burden to him.

Dr. Armitage signed the EA pledge in 2019. Before taking his kidney decision, he'd crunched the numbers in a characteristically EA way; not only could he transform the lives of three patients, but over a ten-year period he could save the NHS around a million pounds (the cost of three patients on dialysis). Plugged into this equation too went the prospect that, through example, he might encourage others to follow suit.

He admits that his actions were partially generated by motivations that the ideal effective altruist—the effective altruist in Platonic form—would not possess. Although the NHS scheme operates anonymously, to reduce the recipients' sense that they owe donors a debt, it allows for the recipient to find out who the donor is, and to make contact, if both parties agree. This happened in Richard's case. Knowing the identity of the specific individual he's helped produced a warmer glow of satisfaction than the more tepid feeling that kicks in when donating to distant, more "abstract" causes, such as the provision of insecticide-treated bed-nets.

Kidney donation is not an outcome that could have been predicted when "Famine, Affluence, and Morality" was first published. There are much more obvious connections between the Shallow Pond thought experiment and organizations such as Giving What We Can, and GiveWell. Compared to an organ transplant, the impact of these organizations is hard to assess. Still, the charities have come up with a few tentative numbers. Giving What We Can has raised around £400 million, though that figure is misleading in both a negative and positive direction. Many people, inspired by Giving What We Can, will have donated to recommended charities directly, and these donations are not included in the data. On the other hand, many people who did donate, being naturally altruistically minded, would probably have donated at least some money anyway, even without a nudge from Giving What We Can.

GiveWell, in the United States, channels much more money still. They have logged donations to their suggested organizations totaling more than $2 billion. They claim that these donations "will save over 200,000 lives."[2] The private charity run by Cari Tuna and Facebook cofounder Dustin Moskovitz has given at least $1 billion to GiveWell's top charities, and estimates that its giving will have "saved hundreds of thousands of lives."[3] More specifically, deaths per year from malaria fell by three hundred thousand between 2000 and 2020, and effective altruism charities assert that they deserve at least some credit for this.

Have these effective altruists really made such an amazing contribution? That turns out to be contested.

Clearly not all aid donors are well-intentioned, and not all have the relief of poverty as their primary objective. The motivation for much government-to-government aid is driven, for example, by geopolitical considerations and to further the interests of the donor.

The effective altruist may, by contrast, have good intentions. But good intentions are not enough. What we need to know is whether charity and aid work. Take the case of how one well-intentioned $56 million program to combat the impact of HIV in Kenya went wrong. Many Kenyan children had lost their parents to AIDS, and it was estimated that around 150,000 Kenyan children were themselves infected with HIV.[4] But "because grant money went to bribe officials rather than being spent on orphans' school fees, many children dropped out of education and resorted to prostitution. A project intended to reduce HIV infection helped, instead, to spread the virus."[5]

This tragic counterproductivity was exposed by the World Bank's own Department of Institutional Integrity, in a leaked report of 2007, and described by the writer Michela Wrong in her devastating account of Kenyan corruption, *It's Our Turn to Eat*. The report "cited almost every imaginable stratagem for ripping off an externally funded aid project, from the bribing of public officials to abuse of office, inflated expenses, fraudulent claims, conflicts of interest, the concerted rigging of bids, failure to carry out allotted tasks, and blatant nepotism by MPs."[6]

This program was unrelated to the effective altruism movement, but within the aid world there's a plethora of similar stories. Each one reflects in microcosm the most fundamental objection to the Shallow Pond analogy. While wading into the pond saves a life, giving money to charity does not necessarily have any such effect. There's an even stronger version of this: aid "is not benign—it's malignant";[7] not just ineffective, but actually harmful.

Can giving money to countries in need really make the lives of their citizens worse? This claim seems, on the face of it, preposterous. However, it's really no stranger than the familiar admonition that when you pass the local drug addict in the street you should not feed their addiction by acceding to their request for a fiver.

The view that aid can be harmful is not new. In fact, in the year "Famine, Affluence, and Morality" appeared, a Hungarian-born British economist, Peter Bauer, published a book, *Dissent on Development*, making this very argument.[8] Bauer noted that money rarely reached its intended recipients, describing aid as the process by which poor people in rich countries subsidize rich people in poor countries.

Bauer was initially regarded as a maverick. But since his early pioneering research, a raft of books has followed, with titles like *The White Man's Burden* (by Bill Easterly) and *Dead Aid*.[9] Most of these attacks on charity focus specifically on government aid. Each makes a similar point: however well-meaning the donors, their efforts backfire. In particular, they are liable to exacerbate poor governance in the countries they are designed to help.

Does the evidence back this up? Beyond the multiple individual instances of failure, such as the Kenyan HIV project, do the macro-statistics indicate that the problems of aid are endemic and that aid is, on balance, damaging? Any settled verdict on this remains elusive: the world is complex, and trying to pick apart the causal mechanisms that contribute to poverty is notoriously tricky. For this reason, there is room for developmental economists to disagree. Alongside the aid skeptics are the aid evangelists such as Jeffrey Sachs, who insists that "much is known about how to help the poor,"[10] and whose book *The End of Poverty* claims that aid could eliminate poverty.[11] One (contested) analysis of a range of studies gives credence to this position: it suggests that the impact of aid has been broadly positive.[12]

Nonetheless, there are also plenty of data to support a negative assessment. Most importantly, there's the link between aid and growth: some of the countries that have seen the least amount of aid per capita—such as China and India—have seen the most impressive growth rates, while many of the countries that receive the highest relative amounts of aid, such as the Central African Republic, the Democratic Republic of Congo, Haiti, Papua New Guinea, and Somalia, have performed poorly. Dambisa Moyo, author of *Dead Aid*, writes that "as aid has increased over time, Africa's growth has decreased with an accompanying higher incidence of poverty."[13] Of course, this might be explained at least in part by poverty triggering aid, rather than aid causing poverty.

The link between aid and corruption has also been studied. A World Bank report uncovered a strong relationship between aid and deposits in secretive financial havens such as Switzerland and the Cayman Islands.[14] "Peter Singer keeps leaping into shallow ponds to 'help,' "[15] writes Angus Deaton, but rescuing people from shallow ponds encourages elites to generate more shallow ponds, into which they throw yet more people. Indeed, not just elites: "Not so long ago, you could find beggars in India who had actively crippled children as begging tools."[16]

The AIDS/HIV project in Kenya, mentioned above, failed on its own terms. However, there are many projects that seem to succeed. Charity workers can point to them. That new hospital, or that new road, that new school, or those new textbooks, that new truck or those new pipes, the new dam or the new water-well, the pills, and the vaccinations—they owe their existence to aid (though arguably they would have been built anyway). In theory, couldn't all aid projects produce similar results—positive and tangible?

The success of many micro-/individual projects, coupled with the insistence by some development economists that, at the macro-/general level, aid fails, would seem to present us with a paradox. Economists such as Angus Deaton have a theory about how this apparent paradox dissolves.

Born in Scotland, the grandson of a coal miner, as a boy Angus Deaton won a place at Fettes, a posh private boarding school in Edinburgh, on an open scholarship, then went to Cambridge to study mathematics, which he hated "because I was bad at it,"[17] switching to economics. He arrived at Princeton University, from Bristol University, in 1983. Huge and cheerful, the giant panda of economists, Deaton received a Nobel Prize in 2015, not for a single breakthrough in his discipline, but for contributions in several areas.

He is the bow-tied bête noire of effective altruism. For several years he skirmished with his Princeton colleague, Peter Singer. "There is no one who's more agreeable to disagree with," he's said.[18] Two years before winning his Nobel Prize he published *The Great Escape*, in which he argued that aid had all sorts of bad unintended consequences. Principal among them was the undermining of the relationship between citizen and state. If the government alone were responsible for meeting the needs and demands of the people, then, even in non-democracies, it would feel pressure to do so. Without inflows of foreign money, governments have to raise taxation, and to be alert to the priorities of their citizens. When foreign governments, or foreign institutions, deliver essential services, the government is off the hook. Aid is a dunghill fertilizer for corruption and incompetence.

Meanwhile, the aid industry, which in theory seeks to create the conditions to make itself redundant, has self-interested reasons not to highlight abuses, but rather to excuse, to turn a blind eye, to misreport. No doubt many aid workers could be more highly remunerated in other forms of employment, but still, aid is a career, and for aid workers from abroad, the expat life with its Land Rovers and subsidized accommodation has much to commend it. Some charities have themselves been implicated in serious wrongdoing: Oxfam workers, most notoriously, have been involved in the sexual abuse of minors.[19] The relationship between aid donors and aid recipients has been labeled "mutually parasitic."[20] Interestingly, the geographic locations in which many international NGOs operate are not as strongly correlated with poverty as one might expect: history, religious affiliation, and many other factors play a part—leading to some countries becoming "donor darlings."[21]

A distinction is often drawn between emergency aid and aid to deal with stubborn long-term needs. But aid can be unhelpful in either case. When there's a humanitarian disaster caused by a war, say, aid can be siphoned off, fall into the wrong hands, and further fuel conflict. Ethiopians did actually know it was Christmas;[22] but did the Band Aid concert boppers in 1984 foresee that the Ethiopian president Colonel Mengistu would deliberately restrict aid from reaching areas not controlled by the government? Did they know that the main reason for mass starvation was not drought, but Mengistu's counterinsurgency campaign?[23]

One egregious illustration of aid exacerbating war followed the genocide of Tutsis in Rwanda in 1994, when members of the government who had perpetrated the genocide, along with the remnants of the extremist Hutu militia group the Interahamwe, fled into Zaire. The population of Goma, just across the Rwandan border, swelled by a million.

Shocking details of the relief effort for these "refugees" are presented by Alex de Waal in *Famine Crimes*.[24] NGOs poured into the area to deliver aid worth tens of millions of dollars, much of which was stolen by the Interahamwe. This allowed them to consolidate, rearm, and continue their murderous campaign. But for charities, this global news event was a fundraising opportunity. De Waal quotes a representative from a leading charity: "For Save the Children Fund, it is a difficult question of either competing or staying away—in which case we lose out on both media coverage and money."[25]

Even when aid reaches its intended target, a positive outcome is not guaranteed. A magnificent, if depressing, book, *The Idealist*, by Nina Munk, recounts the story of the Millennium Villages Project, evangelized by Jeffrey Sachs. Villages in parts of Africa selected as laboratories for development, and showered initially with money, didn't see anything like the transformation that was predicted, the project being derailed by multiple and unforeseen complications, such as rats gnawing through bags of maize and sacks of mosquito nets.

Budgets are fungible. You might think you're building a power station, noted the economist Paul Rosenstein-Rodan, when actually you're building a brothel.[26] If NGOs are dealing with the aftermath of a crisis, local and national governments that might otherwise have had to bear this responsibility are freed to spend money on soldiers, guns, and bullets. In *Gambling on Development*, Stefan Dercon, the former chief economist at the UK's

Department for International Development (DfID), describes arriving in South Sudan. "The local commander who had welcomed us, wearing his tight-fitting size XXXL army fatigues, told us later that morning that he was pleased the NGOs looked after the people so he could focus on important matters."[27]

This is a variation of what is known as the "distortion of resources effect."[28] An NGO sets up, say, a medical facility to treat trachoma. Outcome assessors measure the impact. "During the past year, X number of operations have been successfully performed at a cost of Y." It seems hugely successful. But what the assessors don't measure are the spillover effects upon the rest of the healthcare system. To entice local doctors and nurses to work with them, the foreign body funding the trachoma program will have had to offer relatively attractive terms—a higher-than-market salary, for example. This switch of labor may boost trachoma stats, to the detriment of other health measures. In Botswana, many doctors were lured into a generously funded Gates Foundation AIDS program. It was probably no coincidence that, simultaneously, there was a spike in child mortality.[29]

Should we conclude that all aid is bad? That would be going too far. Even the most ardent critics of effective altruism recognize the possibility of effective aid. Moyo's criticism is primarily aimed at bilateral aid: government to government. This is Easterly's main target too. Moyo seems to endorse specific interventions, as too does Easterly: "Put the focus back where it belongs: get the poorest people in the world such obvious goods as the vaccines, the antibiotics, the food supplements, the improved seeds, the fertilizer, the roads, the boreholes, the water pipes, the textbooks, and the nurses."[30] Deaton has never argued against emergency humanitarian aid—and there's even a passage in his book *The Great Escape* that acknowledges the success of campaigns to eliminate smallpox, river blindness, and polio.[31]

This seems to give the effective altruists all the intellectual wiggle room they need. After all, effective altruists can grant the contentious premise that aid is on balance bad. They might even argue that that's precisely why the rigorous analysis of philanthropic programs is so vital. All the effective altruist has to claim is that there are some programs that are indisputably beneficial.

Where does that leave the extreme aid skeptic? Angus Deaton denounces "the EA folks" for "extracting their own self-satisfaction at the expense of the people in poor countries." He compares them (as have others) to colonialists. There is "a grave moral wrong in both cases. I am old enough to have been brought up on 'our Empire story' and the immense amount of good we were doing in the world. It sounded then just the same as the EA people now."[32]

A harsh judgment. The colonialists may have believed they were doing good—bringing civilization to the natives, and so on—yet they were also extracting resources. Effective altruists, by contrast, are giving, not stealing. Propelling Deaton's scorn, however, is the conviction that effective altruists do not treat the potential downsides of charity, especially the undermining of government, with sufficient gravity. There are no serious trade-offs at the Shallow Pond: the rescuer makes a negligible sacrifice (ruined shoes, muddy clothes), but for the child there is only an upside. Ordinary life, by contrast, is full of more complex trade-offs, some of which we're prepared to live with. Medicines are approved if they stop or reduce sickness, though they might carry the risk of acute side effects: chemotherapy is used to treat cancer though it leaves a patient exhausted. In the aid sector, decisions about what trade-offs to accept can be finely balanced. And often, since many programs are funded from abroad, the local population has limited power to determine for itself what is and what isn't acceptable.

A utilitarian can easily conclude that if a program saves five lives over here, then it's justifiable even at the cost of a different life over there. But if effective altruists insist—as many do—that they are not utilitarians, then they can't always treat lives in such an aggregative way, weighing the harm to and suffering of some against the benefits and happiness of others. It's not permissible to save five people drowning in ponds if a sixth person, as a result, is thrown into the water and dies.

The argument, then, will pivot around basic empirical claims. In these empirical debates, "the philosopher is a tourist."[33] The raison d'être of GiveWell is to investigate interventions: they're definitely not tourists. Still, the view from over a spreadsheet in San Francisco is not the same as that from a village in Senegal. Effective altruists maintain (and Angus Deaton vehemently denies) that positive programs can be identified, and that programs in which, say, teachers hand out deworming tablets to their class, or NGOs provide insecticide treated bed-nets, do little to interfere with the government's relationship with its citizens and cause no serious spillover harm. Your attitude to effective altruists should depend on whether, on this crucial point, you believe them.

As I write this, I'm listening to the radio. Médecins sans frontières (MSF: Doctors without Borders) is appealing for money. "This is the hospital you could help build. This is the doctor you could help train in the hospital you could help build. These are the drugs you could help buy, used by the doctor you could help train, in the hospital you could help build." MSF helps people in dozens of countries, from South Sudan to Syria, Haiti to Yemen,

Ukraine to Gaza. They have international brand recognition, like Oxfam and Save the Children. When pressed, the extreme skeptic is reluctant to concede—what seems to follow logically from their position—that these adverts should be ignored. And more: that if these aid organizations are causing harm, perhaps they should even be banned, like adverts for tobacco?

If we get rid of internationally administered aid, if we close down NGOs operating in the developing world, what then? Do the development economists who are skeptical about aid have a better way to help?

Again, there is no consensus. Some say what's needed is investment in health, education, and transport infrastructure, but different economists offer different prescriptions. Stefan Dercon believes the key component is the will of the elite. Enough members of the elite, who currently gain from plundering the existing system, have to gamble on growth, for which they'll potentially be rewarded with a slice of the expanded economic pie.

In their widely cited book *Why Nations Fail,* economists Daron Acemoglu and James Robinson have an alternative explanation for why some countries are economic basket cases, while others have powered ahead.[34] None of it has to do with aid. The most crucial ingredients are certain cultural norms about honesty and tax compliance, combined with property rights (so that property/income cannot be arbitrarily seized) and rules to enforce contracts. These, in turn, require a strong independent judiciary and a free press. If there's a simple way to sum the recipe for success up, it's that there's a need for what the authors call "inclusive institutions": institutions that do not lubricate embezzlement by an elite, but function fairly and equally for everyone. They agree with Dercon, at least, on the significance of the privileged class.

Similarly, LSE economist Tim Besley makes the claim that it's not lack of resources specifically that holds development back. What matters is the ability of a state to raise finances through a tax system and to fairly regulate markets through a legal system.[35] "There are no examples in human history of meaningful sustained economic development that were not accompanied by building a strong and capable state from within. (I would certainly be curious to know if anyone thinks that they can come up with a counter-example!)"[36]

Typical effective altruism projects—funding of mosquito nets, and suchlike—on a small scale might not interfere with the building of state capacity. However, on a large scale they might, not just in the passive sense of being a distraction from what is important in the long term, but in a more active sense that they may undermine aspects of state development. Crucial to state development is for citizens to evolve their own metrics in terms of what is important to them, rather than have these imposed from outside. Inevitably, when large-scale external funds flow into a country, these metrics become distorted. This is probably even more of a problem when these funds arrive not from NGOs, but from governments and financial institutions. One former World Bank economist, Ravi Kanbur, recalls that during his stint in Ghana, local policymakers felt more accountable to callow twenty-five-year-olds newly emerged from Ivy League universities than they did to their own citizens: part of what he calls the "de-responsibility of the local elite."[37] Some compensation for the local elite comes from business-class trips to air-conditioned meetings and canapé receptions in Washington, DC.

What, then, should somebody concerned about global poverty do? According to Stefan Dercon, aid might play a role in identifying and supporting the growth gamblers. If an earnest student approaches Angus Deaton for advice, he suggests involvement in lobbying to alter the terms of trade so that, for example, poor farmers are not forced to compete with subsidized farming in the West: the EU supports farmers to the tune of tens of billions of euros every year.[38] There are other options. Poor countries could benefit from the transfer of knowledge, scientific, medical, technical, and legal. Deaton says that trade treaties can be "unbelievably exploitative."[39] Mining companies often manage to extract substantial and long-lasting tax concessions in the developing world. In part that's because they can afford the sharpest lawyers, accountants, and negotiators. With help, negotiations could be conducted on a more level playing field.

Deaton believes that charities are "doing net harm, in effect encouraging bad governments to exist, and encouraging bad governments to put children in ponds to attract aid."[40] The more positive gloss, from other development economists, is that effective altruism is not, in principle, wrong. There are effective forms of assistance; however, some of these effective forms of assistance are not ones promoted by effective altruists.

18

Rattling the Can

THE PSYCHOLOGICAL CRITIQUE

> If I look at the mass, I will never act. If I look at the one, I will.
>
> —MOTHER TERESA

IN JULY 2017, a video emerged showing a group of teenagers watching a man struggle in a pond. They didn't wade in. They didn't call the emergency services. The video shows them laughing. The man, thirty-one-year-old Jamel Dunn, later drowned. According to the *New York Times*, which reported the story, one of the teenagers could be heard telling Dunn, "Ain't nobody going to help you, you dumb bitch. You shouldn't have got in there."[1]

It is the task of the moral philosopher to address how people *should* behave. The moral philosopher might be persuaded that we should give more of our wealth away—and that we should try to save not just the child in the Shallow Pond, but the child on the far side of the world. If possible, we should save more lives rather than fewer. But even if the philosopher is right about this, people don't always behave as they should.

The psychological critique is that human nature is incompatible with the kind of demands pressed upon it by Singer and the effective altruists. We all react to the Shallow Pond in much the same way. However, there are specific elements to the Shallow Pond that explain our reaction, but that don't generalize to the real world.

A Case of Identity

"Small Earthquake in Chile, Not Many Dead." These are the words that Claud Cockburn, a journalist for the British daily newspaper the *Times*, claimed won him an award among fellow *Times* journalists in the 1930s for dullest headline.[2] For who in the UK could possibly care about the death of a few people in a far-flung strip of South America? His thought experiment was tested when an earthquake struck off the coast of Chile, in the early hours of Saturday, February 27, 2010—except that, with a magnitude of 8.8 it was not so small; it resulted in around five hundred deaths, and in the immediate aftermath there were fears that a tsunami would surge across the Pacific.

As the desperate search began for bodies among the rubble, the tabloid *News of the World* responded to this catastrophe with the front-page headline "Lover Exclusive: My Secret Fling with Peter Andre."[3] The Chile story, "Quake Leaves World in Peril," does make an appearance, though, tucked away on page 16. It was a bigger, though still not front-page story in the broadsheet *Sunday Times*.

Chile has not always been a news turn-off. That same year, but six months later, the whole world was glued to a drama in the northern part of the country. It all began at around 2 p.m.

on August 5, when part of the main access tunnel in a copper and gold mine collapsed, trapping thirty-three men hundreds of meters underground. Rescuers began digging holes, but it was over two weeks before there was any communication with the miners, and we learned that they were all still alive. Their rations were running out, however, and the hope of a happy ending receded with every passing day. Plans were put in place to memorialize the dead miners with a gigantic cross.

Over a thousand journalists pitched up—newspaper, radio, and TV reporters; global interest in the story was insatiable. Through friends and relatives of the miners we heard details about their lives and characters. Fifty-year-old Yonni Barrios, for instance, had a wife and a mistress—the wife only found out about the mistress when both of them appeared at the vigil. Eventually, boring equipment completed a new tunnel, and on October 13 the miners, bearded, sweaty, and weak, were brought to safety one by one through a specially built capsule. Yonni Barrios was the twenty-first man to emerge. The two-month crisis was over—though it would take another few days for the media circus to disperse.

"Mining Accident in Chile, Nobody Dead" turned out to be one of the biggest stories of the year, eliciting far more interest than the earlier earthquake, the force of which had led to half a million houses being declared uninhabitable. On the day the miners emerged, the *Times* ran a ten-page rescue special. Why the fascination? Well, there was the obvious jeopardy—with the clock ticking, would they/wouldn't they be reached in time? But there was also something else—tied to an extensively studied psychological phenomenon: the Identifiable Victim Effect.

"Anyone here been raped and speaks English?" The inquiry, which makes the grimly sardonic title of a foreign correspondent's memoir,[4] is attributed to a BBC journalist who allegedly yelled it out to some Belgian nuns in 1964, during the civil war in the Republic of the Congo. Even if few journalists have heard of it, every journalist has worked out the Identifiable Victim Effect for themselves and internalized its message; they know that the way to engage the reader, listener, or viewer in an extensive tragedy is to humanize it by highlighting its impact on one individual or more—such as Yonni Barrios.

If there is a significant Identifiable Victim Effect there will be implications for philanthropy. In a famous 2007 study, paid participants were offered the chance to donate some of the money to Save the Children.[5] They were presented with one or the other of two appeals:

a) Any money that you donate will go to Rokia, a seven-year-old girl who lives in Zambia in Africa. Rokia is desperately poor and faces a threat of severe hunger, even starvation. Her life will be changed for the better as a result of your financial gift. With your support, and the support of other caring sponsors, Save the Children will work with Rokia's family and other members of the community to help feed and educate her, and provide her with basic medical care.
b) Food shortages in Africa are affecting millions of children. In Zambia, severe rainfall deficits have resulted in a 42% drop in maize production from 2000. As a result, an estimated three million Zambians face hunger. Four million Angolans—one-third of the population—have been forced to flee their homes. More than 11 million people in Ethiopia need immediate food assistance. They

> need your help now and by donating to Save the Children you can help.

You can guess the result: the first appeal was far more successful.

We can see an Identifiable Victim as containing three separate elements. There's a victim, there's only one victim, and there's identifiable information about this victim. It's not always easy to pull the "identity" and the "number" factors apart.[6] In one study, people were shown a picture of a child: would they help this child with some money? (Yes, of course.) Then they were shown a picture of another child: would they help this child? (Yes, of course.) Finally, they were shown two children and told that if they donate money it will go to one of these children, to be determined by the toss of a coin. Under these conditions, people didn't give to nearly the same extent. But was that because in this case there were twice as many people in need, or because the potential donors couldn't be sure (couldn't identify) who would benefit from their support?

There's also the issue of what counts as identifiable information. A face? A name? One laboratory study suggests that only a trifling amount of identification is required for the Identifiable Victim Effect to kick in. In this study, participants were given a sum of money and the option of passing a portion of it on to a receiver. Just being told the number of the receiver—"The money will go to Receiver 3," say—had the effect of increasing the amount participants handed over.[7]

A caveat: psychologists disagree about how powerful the Identifiable Victim Effect is, and caution with regard to psychological experiments is always advisable, in light of the so-called replication crisis, whereby studies when repeated have failed to produce the same result.[8] In any case, the Identifiable Victim

Effect is only one of many phenomena studied by psychologists researching altruism and charity. They've also looked into victim numbers.

Numbers

The number of victims matters. Small numerical differences have a big impact. Two victims are more off-putting than one. It's partly that we care about ratios. By rescuing the child in the Shallow Pond, we save 100 percent of those at risk; by rescuing one of two children we save 50 percent; and if there's a huge tragedy, we, as individuals, can come to the assistance of only a tiny fraction.

A related point concerns "Scope Insensitivity." If there are two children struggling in the Shallow Pond rather than one, the problem we face is twice as big, and that's easy to comprehend. But the difference between an earthquake that kills 46,146 and one that kills 49,635 goes unnoticed. Equally, although it's very satisfying to help one person, it's not ten times as satisfying to help ten people.

Here's another illustration of Scope Insensitivity. Suppose you are told that migrating birds are dying in waste oil ponds. The birds can be saved by covering these ponds with wire-nets, a job that comes at a financial cost. What cost would you be willing to pay? Presumably that will depend on how many birds are affected. But when different groups were asked about this, and given different numbers—two thousand, twenty thousand, two hundred thousand (numbers reflecting actual bird deaths in real-life oil spills), they gave more or less the same answer ($80, $78, and $88).[9] Of course, if we're comparing options ("Would you rather save twenty thousand or two hundred thousand?") we have no difficulty in selecting the one that helps the most people. But ordinarily that is not how evaluation works. If we're asked to donate to a cancer charity, any evidence of its effectiveness is not normally presented alongside evidence of the effectiveness of other charities.

Distinct from Scope Insensitivity is "Psychic Numbing":[10] when we are dealing with big numbers, we zone out. The Shallow Pond threatens one person, while absolute poverty affects hundreds of millions. Stalin probably never uttered this notorious "quote," but it captures a truth nonetheless: "The death of one man is a tragedy. The death of millions is a statistic."

Bystanders

When I still had a day job, I would cycle to and from work every day along busy London roads and then through Regents Park, past a lake on which there was a scattering of boats and pedalos (pedal boats), and then back into the congested city. I was a more or less law-abiding commuter, but the roads are treacherous for a two-wheeler and sometimes, at traffic-light junctions, it felt safer to be clear of the cars before the lights turned green. So I would jump a red light. This always induced a slight (I mustn't exaggerate) feeling of guilt. After a time, I began to reflect on my own behavior. This is what psychologists call meta-cognition. The frequency with which I broke the law was affected by many factors beyond concerns about safety: how cold it was, whether I was late for work, whether I had just spotted a police car and feared a reprimand. But I was most influenced by another element—were there other cyclists at the same light, and did they stick to the rules? If they did, I would too. If they didn't, I would follow their lead.

Psychologists have long known that our values, judgments, and decisions are powerfully shaped by those around us. Back in the 1950s, the psychologist Solomon Asch conducted his famous experiments about peer pressure. Subjects were told that they were taking part in a vision test. Along with others in a room, they were shown a card on which there were several lines. The task was simple: they had to say out loud which line of several on the right was equal to the line on the left—except there was a twist. The others in the room were secretly "actors" or "confederates." The confederates gave the right answer a couple of times, but then all of them gave what was clearly the wrong answer. Astonishingly, this influenced the majority of subjects—who repeated the wrong answer.[11]

Peer pressure is as present in philanthropy as in any other domain. It is not easy to persuade people to donate more of their income than other people: and most people give only a tiny percentage. If you do give more than others, you might feel like a mug—like the person who pays their due taxes when everyone else is cheating on theirs.

This is one way we're influenced by peers. There's also the related "Bystander Effect." You may have been in a road where someone is lying on the ground, or apparently injured or in distress. It turns out that the more people there are at such a scene, the less likely we are to assist. Partly this is because if we're not alone in being able to come to this individual's assistance, we feel less responsible. If I'm one of many adults walking past the Shallow Pond, I'm obviously not the only one who can save the child.[12]

But the Bystander Effect is not just produced by a feeling of reduced responsibility. As Asch discovered, we take our cues from others—if others are not helping, we assume that help is not required, or that we aren't obliged to help. This is perfectly rational. It makes sense to give credence to a conclusion that everyone else has reached. Why is nobody helping the child? Perhaps if, alone, I rush to the child's assistance, it will turn out that she was only playacting; I might embarrass myself by being seen to have overreacted.

Perhaps the least surprising finding in the psychological literature on philanthropy is this: the belief that a person in difficulty is responsible for their predicament will color our willingness to come to their aid. We don't hold children responsible for their actions, let alone for circumstances that endanger them and that they have had nothing to do with—war, disease, poverty.

The philosopher Daniel Dennett coined the phrase "intuition pump" for a thought experiment that leads those exposed to it to a particular conclusion. We can now see why the Shallow Pond is the perfect intuition pump. There is a particular, identifiable person who can be rescued. There are no other bystanders—it's your responsibility alone to save the child. Only one child is in peril; or, to put it another way, you have the opportunity to save the entire set of imperiled persons. And the child, being a child, is innocent. Each and every ingredient pumps the intuition that we must save the child.

Ineffective Semi-Altruism

The phenomena just described explain the psychological power of the Shallow Pond—and how it differs from the case of the distant stranger. The ideal effective altruist would be able to overcome these psychological barriers. But the ideal effective altruist would have to leap some other psychological hurdles as well.

For a start, people are poor at judging effectiveness. They're oblivious to the gulf in effectiveness between charities. And they place far too much weight on how much of a charity's money goes on overheads.[13] As Toby Ord spotted early on, a charity might devote only a tiny percentage of its money to staff costs, the electricity bill, and so on, and yet be hopeless at accomplishing anything worthwhile.

Even if people are aware of effectiveness differentials, the more fundamental problem is this: they don't believe that this really matters. They don't believe that philanthropic decisions should be taken on the basis of either effectiveness or impartial altruism.

It's striking how this attitude differs from our approach to other financial matters. When individuals reflect on which pension fund to invest in, they try to do so on the basis of hard data, objective numbers: which fund, for example, produces the best return. By contrast, support for charities is usually based on emotion and personal connections.[14] Since we have dogs and not pigs for pets, it's unsurprising that in a study in which participants had to choose how to allocate $100 between a dog and a pig charity, the canines received the bulk of the funds.[15] Researchers have discovered that people who choose charities on the basis of feeling rather than calculation are assessed as being more trustworthy.[16] One study asked whether an imaginary Mary should give money to the charity to which she's most emotionally attached, or the charity that's most effective. The majority thought Mary should give to the former.[17] Further evidence that effectiveness has a low priority comes from a study in which people rated charity volunteers more highly on their sacrifice than on their contribution.[18]

A small minority of people are happy to endorse the "impartial altruism" component of effective altruism: that we should be indifferent between the stranger far away and the person in front of us—or even that this impartial concern should extend to animals and future people (people not yet born). A small minority of people also believe that effectiveness is very important. But in the Venn diagram of charitable donors, the overlap between those who care about altruism and those who care about effectiveness is a tiny sliver.[19]

19

The Art of the Feel

THE MOTIVATIONAL CRITIQUE

Statistics are human beings with the tears wiped off.

—PAUL BRODEUR (SCIENCE WRITER)

AID AND PHILANTHROPY FUNCTION within a market economy. Just as commercial companies seek ways to attract customers, so charities aim to appeal to donors. Business schools have generated an enormous and ever increasing literature on how to peddle more life insurance policies, cars, package holidays, fizzy drinks, and soap powder. Although competition between charities can be cutthroat, the science of philanthropy is nowhere near as advanced (the discipline of making money appeals to more academics and students than that of giving it away). Still, as some of the philanthropic findings attest, it is a science that is growing and becoming ever more sophisticated. Charities are aware of the need to push the right psychological buttons—what one might call "the Art of the Feel."

The response to the psychological critique—the view that humans are simply not hardwired to respond to a faraway stranger in the way they would to the drowning child in front of them—is this: it is possible to tailor a message to potential donors that mimics elements of the Shallow Pond. It is possible to work with the grain of our cognitive biases. It is possible to persuade people that they should give a not insignificant percentage of their earnings away.

Notably, and distastefully, the emphasis of almost all the psychological literature is on the givers, rather than receivers. The receivers, especially those in the developing world, are viewed as passive receptacles for altruism. What do they feel about charity and aid? What do they think of the benefactors? In what form would they like to receive charity and aid, if at all? We know little.

By contrast, we know a great deal about the benefactors. There is plenty of evidence that giving money makes people happy. Participants in one study reported higher happiness levels in the periods in which they donated more to charity, and spent more money on gifts.[1] Spending money on others tends to induce a positive mood. At the same time, the moment at which one parts with money can be painful. A solution, adopted by effective altruists, is a form of precommitment. By taking a pledge, and signing away a percentage of future earnings, a psychological distance is created between the decision and the act of donation. Since the decision has already been made, the donor is only left with the much more gratifying role of determining where the money is to go.[2]

Other lessons to boost donations emerge from the previous chapter. People are scope insensitive, but they also like to be consistent. Charities can take advantage of this. Imagine a worthy charity has been established to help a group of twenty deprived children. Suppose one set of donors receives a request for financial support for the group as a whole, while a second set receives the same request, but only after being primed with an earlier question: "How much would you give to help just one of these needy children?" The latter group, it transpires, will donate considerably more. If we think we should give X to one child, then obviously if there are twenty children in a similar situation we ought to donate a sum greater than X. The psychologists who discovered this phenomenon labeled it "Unit Asking."[3]

This is not the same as the Identifiable Victim Effect, but philanthropic organizations can take advantage of this effect too. Most charities have not had to await the academic research to recognize the effectiveness on their marketing leaflets of the image of an individual child. The image matters. Images can have extraordinary power, as has been evident since the dawn of photography. Stark photographs of starving Indians—tough to look at, but hard to turn away from—spurred a relief effort for the Great Famine of 1876–78, though it was only after World War I that newspapers routinely began to feature photos.

When Peter Singer arrived in Oxford another famine was in the papers. The Biafran War had begun in May 1967 after Igbos in Nigeria's southeast declared the independence of the Republic of Biafra. But the conflict received minimal media coverage until the summer of 1968, when journalists and photographers showed up to report on the dire food shortages. The footage and photos of emaciated bodies prompted the tabloid *Sun* newspaper to describe the breakaway region as a "land of no hope," in a headline next to a photograph of a nurse cradling a tiny dying child in her arms.[4]

The dominance of image over word has been corroborated repeatedly. The Syrian civil war that broke out in 2011 created a refugee crisis. Some among the millions of displaced people attempted to reach Europe across the Mediterranean Sea, often risking their lives on overcrowded, rickety boats and inflatable dinghies. The mass exodus moved few people, until they saw a photograph, taken on September 2, 2015, of a dead three-year-old boy, Aylan Kurdi, wearing a red T-shirt, blue shorts, and sneakers, face down in the beach sand, as the surf gently washed over him. Researchers looked into the finances of one charity for Syrian refugees and calculated that the number of donations had rocketed a hundredfold.[5] Compassion fades though, like colors on washed clothes. Within a couple of months, donations had slumped back to pre-photo levels.

Evidently images have power. But what sort of image? The image of Aylan Kurdi was so overwhelmingly distressing that, at least in the short term, it jolted people into action. Sometimes charities use more optimistic images—smiling rather than sad faces. There's an ideological reason for that: a reaction against the presentation of Africans and others as mere passive victims. But the efficacy of facial expressions has also been examined by academics. Happy-faced ads work best with those already involved in the charity, according to one study, while sad-faced ads are more effective with those who have weak ties to it—with the implication that charities should alter their message depending on whom they're appealing to.[6]

Even effective altruists are susceptible to image. In the past, Will MacAskill has used images like a drug: as a stimulant to overcome psychological barriers, and to align his feelings and impulses with his rationally reached conclusions. As a young graduate, when he was dithering about how much he would commit to giving away, it wasn't solely philosophy articles that spurred him on. Instead, "I loaded up images on Google of children suffering from horrific neglected diseases, and in the course of making the decision I was looking at these photos." One photo was of a child with elephantiasis and a hideously swollen face. "I just thought, man, if my giving can just stop [the suffering of] . . . that child (putting aside the fact that probably it's hundreds of thousands of times that), it just seems worth it to me."[7]

Some of the psychological research is on the way intermediaries raise funds. Suppose you appeal to friends, family, neighbors, and colleagues for money to be paid to a charity of your choice. The norm is that they support you in return for a task or challenge, like running a marathon. This is doubly odd. First, why is such a challenge—often both time-consuming and costly—considered necessary? Second, it seems that to be successful you would do well to suffer for your cause. But why is it preferable to be sponsored for doing something tedious and/or painful, rather than interesting and enjoyable?

Part of the cynicism around events like Live Aid has to do with the juxtaposition of millionaire rock stars and adoring fans alongside appeals to help the starving—the incongruity of singing and dancing as a means to ease distress. The so-called "martyrdom effect" is the flip side of this: good luck asking friends to fund you to sunbathe on a beach; but put yourself through some horrendous feat of endurance that in and of itself will do nothing for the cause you're promoting (nobody benefits from you damaging your ligaments by running a marathon), and wallets will open.

Information on charities was once hard to gather and analyze. Now, vast sums of money are raised through online platforms such as Just Giving, and they offer a cheap, reliable, and rich seam of data for researchers to mine. The figures provide evidence for various theories: that the anchoring effect works (kick off with a large donation, and subsequent donors are swayed into stumping up more than they otherwise would);

that fundraising targets are useful (particular satisfaction seems to be derived from being the donor that hits the target); and that males compete to out-donate each other when the appeal is made by an attractive female: "If a male gives a large donation and it's a page with an attractive female, then another male landing on that same page is much more likely to respond with another large donation."[8] (Interestingly, the same effect is not observed among either sex when the fund requester is an attractive man.) There's evidence, too, that people love a "buy one, get one free" deal: they are more likely to give if there's the promise of matching funds from another source. Oddly, however, it is merely the fact, and not the scale, of this funding boost that matters: it makes little difference whether the donation is doubled, tripled, or quadrupled.

All of the tactics described above are ways to increase donations generally. But what about effective donations in particular? Are there psychological predispositions that the effective altruist could exploit to increase donations to demonstrably effective charities especially?

Could information help? The evidence is mixed. While a headline like "Earthquake in Chile: 500 Dead" doesn't tug at our heartstrings, it would be natural to assume that the perfect compassion-generating cocktail would combine an individual narrative with a dash of additional statistical information: "Isabella Martinez was one of the 500,000 people who lost their homes." But some researchers have found that context only succeeds in putting potential donors off.[9] The single story motivates some people to action, and they're then demotivated by the broader picture.

However, although "effectiveness" is easily eclipsed in the charity decision-making process by "personal connections," it turns out that informing people that one charity is more effective than another does have an impact.[10] People will reorient their giving, somewhat, toward effective organizations if they're informed about them.

A mass online study largely corroborates this finding.[11] Over a quarter of a million participants, from over two hundred countries, took 2.7 million decisions on an online test. They were given choices about where to donate $100. For example, would they prefer to donate to Charity A, saving the life of one girl in Western Europe by providing her with clean water, or Charity B, saving the lives of nineteen adult women in North Africa by providing them with clean water. Factors that might affect the choice included "who" (e.g., male or female, old or young, stranger or relative, one or more), "where" (near or far), "what" (the charitable cause: e.g., clean water), and the charity's branding (e.g., whether it was a well-known and respected organization, such as Save the Children). It took a benefit to six strangers to overcome a benefit to one relative. But in a choice between charities supporting strangers, it was the number of strangers that was the most decisive factor (followed by their age, with the young attracting the most support).

An ingenious scheme devised by two psychologists provides further evidence that people in the real world (not just in a laboratory setting) can be nudged toward effective charities. Starting in the laboratory, Lucius Caviola and Joshua Greene discovered that donors welcomed the chance to split donations between their favorite charity and an effective charity—the option to split increased the effective charity donations by 75 percent. Another set of subjects was then asked to assess donor decisions. Donors who gave exclusively to effective charities were deemed colder than those who gave exclusively to their favorite charities. But donors who split their donations were judged best of all—presumably because they had demonstrated measures of both competence and kindheartedness.

Caviola and Greene then built on research (see above) that donors, like shoppers, are pulled in by a "buy one, get one free" offer. Thus, they offered donations matching any money that donors allocated to effective charities of their choice.[12] This didn't require the backing of a zillionaire: these matching donations were provided by individual effective altruists, motivated purely by a desire to maximize funds for the best performing charities, and who could use their donations to leverage the donations of others.

The result is a website called GivingMultiplier.org: an online donation platform that encourages donors to split their contributions between a personal favorite charity and an effective charity of their choice, with the added benefit of having their donations matched. It's so far a small-scale project: as of 2024/2025 it had raised $3.3 million.

So much for nudges and psychological techniques. We haven't yet looked at the role of plain philosophical argument. The Shallow Pond has changed minds and behavior. The impact has been very concrete; Giving What We Can would not have existed without it. But do arguments of this kind tend to work for many people?

The evidence is inconclusive, but various experiments suggest it might. In one, run by the psychologist Fiery Cushman and philosopher Eric Schwitzgebel, an appeal was made for a rational, unemotional, and succinct argument to convince people to donate. Eventually the many entries were whittled down to the most promising five. Thousands of participants were then each shown one of these five arguments (selected at random). Participants were told that a few of them would receive an extra $10 for taking part in the study and asked whether, if they were one of the lucky few to receive this bonus, they would like to donate a portion of it to one of several named charities.

It turned out that each argument to some degree worked. Those who were exposed to any one of the five arguments gave notably more than participants in the control group, who were not. The most successful argument, in terms of generating the most money, was proposed by a young American philosopher, Matthew Lindauer, and a certain Peter Singer.[13]

> Many people in poor countries suffer from a condition called trachoma. Trachoma is the major cause of preventable blindness in the world. Trachoma starts with bacteria that get in the eyes of children, especially children living in hot and dusty conditions where hygiene is poor. If not treated, a child with trachoma bacteria will begin to suffer from blurred vision and will gradually go blind, though this process may take many years. A very cheap treatment is available that cures the condition before blindness develops. As little as $25, donated to an effective agency, can prevent someone going blind later in life.
>
> How much would you pay to prevent your own child becoming blind? Most of us would pay $25,000, $250,000, or even more, if we could afford it. The suffering of children in poor countries must matter more than one-thousandth as much as the suffering of our own child. That's why it is good to support one of the effective agencies that are preventing

blindness from trachoma, and need more donations to reach more people.

The distinction between "rational" and "emotional" is a slippery one, tough if not impossible to draw. Nonetheless, there is growing evidence that ethical arguments, stripped of highly emotive language, can be persuasive.[14] The model for such an approach is the Shallow Pond.

Why the Hate? Alien Minds

This chapter is the place to explain—or attempt to explain—something that has long intrigued me. Why do effective altruists arouse such ire and scorn? The puzzle is this. Here are a bunch of mostly well-intentioned people, donating a not insubstantial amount of their income with the objective of improving the lives of strangers. Yet any trawl through social media will net a slew of ad hominem vitriol directed at the movement itself, and prominent figures within it. Articles about effective altruism are routinely accompanied by abusive language, such as "the dumbest idea of the century."[15] This is not normal in philosophical debate. The fact that there are perfectly legitimate criticisms of effective altruism hardly seems sufficient to justify the contempt.

When FTX went bankrupt, Will MacAskill, who'd been so influential in persuading Sam Bankman-Fried to work in finance, came in for particular contumely. He was accused of being a bad person, and (worse!) a bad philosopher. But hostility toward EA existed long before anybody had even heard of FTX. So the latter's bankruptcy cannot be the whole story.

One theory is that the movement makes us feel challenged. It holds a mirror up to our levels of self-sacrifice, and compared to those involved in effective altruism what is reflected back looks mean and selfish. Effective altruists are reluctant to condemn those who give away less than they do (in part because this would not itself be effective: it would not be good for "business"). Nonetheless, their behavior is an implicit rebuke to our own. Naturally, that makes people defensive.

There's the politics too. Politically, effective altruism falls between stools. To the conservative, effective altruists are interventionist do-gooders; to the socialist, individualist, atomistic neoliberals. Then there's the—often unfair—perception of arrogance. To outsiders, effective altruists can come across as smug and self-righteous, like the religious believer who out of politeness resists the urge to proselytize, but deep down knows that you'll fry in hell for eternity. It doesn't help that, as we have seen, EA members are predominantly Western, White, male, and highly educated: their earnestness can be interpreted as condescension, and the titles of their affiliated organizations—the (now defunct) Future of Humanity Institute, the Global Priorities Institute, and so on—as puffed-up and pompous.

Fourth, although most money from effective altruism continues to go toward international development, the growing emphasis on Longtermism, existential risks, and, especially, AI, further alienates some people, for whom EA has come to be seen as a plaything of the rich and a front for their interests.

Fifth is the allegation of many detractors of effective altruism, that it's a cult.[16] How seriously should we take this? A cult is what Wittgenstein would call a "family resemblance" term. That is to say, among all the organizations or movements that one might reasonably call cults, there is no single characteristic that they all share—there are merely sets of overlapping similarities. Cults may involve charismatic leaders, accusations from nonmembers of "brainwashing," atypical sexual practices, the requirement that members sustain the organization with substantial donations, apocalyptic fears or prophecies, threats toward or harsh punishment of potential or actual defectors. They are often life-dominating (in that they're central, rather than peripheral, to the lives of their members); they might have a strict moral code, or idiosyncratic rituals, chants, or terminology; they might have a revered text; they're often secretive and closed to outsiders.

No doubt some of this applies to EA. The recent emphasis on existential risk, for example, ticks the apocalyptic box. It may be a stretch to call them all charismatic, but everyone can identify the high-status individuals within effective altruism. Jargon is ubiquitous: blog posts and conversations are dotted with talk of "cause-prioritization," "expected value," "infra-Bayesianism," and "fuzzies" (a fuzzy is a unit of measurement for the warm fuzzy feeling arising out of the belief that something morally worthwhile has been done).

EA is also close knit: some members live together, or date one another. There have been a few allegations of sexual misconduct within the community, though not disproportionately so in relation to the wider world. There is a culture among a minority of effective altruists of polyamory, with individuals having multiple sexual partners with the full consent of all parties involved. Polyamory comes naturally to the effective altruist, who believes that our greater concern for the child in the pond than the stranger far away is part of our irrational evolutionary inheritance; so too is our jealousy when it comes to sexual partners being with others. The effective altruist likes to interrogate and reexamine traditional ways of thinking and acting.

All this is cult-like, or cult-lite. But calling the movement a cult is a cheap and lazy insult. There are clear disanalogies between effective altruism and the archetypal cult. Most obviously, compared to most organizations, effective altruism is remarkably transparent. Internal arguments are held online and in public, for everyone to see. Indeed, the culture of open and robust debate often lands the movement in trouble. At the same time, there is a willingness to abandon old positions; errors are usually owned up to, lessons learned.

My own theory as to why effective altruists provoke disdain—and the reason why this digression fits into this chapter—is this: the animosity is psychological. Approaching the intractable problem of extreme poverty with spreadsheets makes effective altruists seem like extraterrestrials. Their dispassionate hyper-rationalism feels alien. In fact, around the effective altruist/rationalist movement there is an unusual degree of neural diversity: so it may actually be true that many effective altruists have atypical responses to the world.

While many effective altruists give a portion of their income to charity, aid workers—those who work for Oxfam, say—are spending all their working hours in the same cause. If, as Angus Deaton and some other development economists contend, aid is often actually harmful, then one might expect the same opprobrium, or even more, to be directed toward aid workers as toward the effective altruists. But, of course, this doesn't happen. Aid workers get a pass. At worst they're accused of being naive or misguided. Why the difference? Aid workers seem recognizably human, gaining sympathy and acknowledgment of their good intentions, while effective altruists just seem odd.

Kant's "Can"

As the famous formula (attributed to Immanuel Kant) has it, "ought implies can." That is, a person can't be required to do something if they're in fact unable to do it. It would be unreasonable to condemn a person for failing to come to the aid of another if they're locked in a room and powerless to help. As a result, in appraising the ambitions of effective altruism, much will hinge on our view of human nature. How malleable is it? Is effective altruist morality too exacting?

It is worth drawing attention again to the distinction between effective altruism and utilitarianism. Utilitarianism is very demanding; effective altruism much less so. The pledge of 10 percent of income is in line with religious norms and, as we have seen, there are ways of encouraging a shift toward more donations that are judged "effective."

Besides, it is surely possible to modify behavioral norms. In a world in which people give little it seems wild to suggest they give far more. But in other cultures, at other times, this would not have appeared so alien. Singer quotes Aquinas quoting the fourth-century theologian Saint Ambrose: "the bread which you withhold belongs to the hungry; the clothing you shut away, to the naked, and the money you bury in earth is the redemption and freedom of the penniless."[17]

POSTSCRIPT

Singer's Swan Song

READERS OF PROFILES of Peter Singer, of which there have been dozens over the years, might be forgiven for supposing that his actual given name was "Controversial Philosopher."

After Oxford, and his two years at NYU, Singer returned to Australia in 1975 to take up a position first at La Trobe University and then at Monash, where he was appointed to the chair of philosophy aged only thirty. He would stay and teach in Melbourne for a quarter of a century. By the time he left, in 1999, the adjective "controversial" and its conceptual siblings—"provocative," "notorious," "scandalous"—were indelibly glued to his reputation. Sometimes he was the "controversial utilitarian philosopher," "utilitarian" having evolved (like "Zionist") to become a term of abuse.

The primary justification for the adjective "controversial" was Singer's unflinching application of philosophical arguments to whichever issue he was writing about. In a series of books and articles, he reiterated the point made in his 1975 book *Animal Liberation* that what made humans morally distinct from animals was not their being "human" per se. Most of the traits that make us "persons"—beings worthy of special moral status—develop slowly after human conception and are absent at the embryo stage.

The implications for the abortion debate are self-evident. But Singer went further. Some nonhuman animals, he wrote, have more "rationality, self-consciousness, awareness, capacity to feel etc." than any human baby—leading the controversial philosopher to conclude that "the life of a newborn is of less value than the life of a pig, a dog, or a chimpanzee."[1] Birth itself, Singer argued, was an irrelevant stage in development. The moral status of the fetus an hour before birth was no different from the moral status of the baby an hour after birth. And, in extreme cases where the baby was severely disabled (perhaps, for example, born with anencephaly), in great suffering, and destined to live for only a few years, and where the parents and doctors were in agreement, infanticide was permissible.[2] Sometimes, in such extreme cases, life-sustaining medical support is withdrawn; but since Singer rejected the moral distinction between an act and an omission, between killing and failing to save a life, this policy made no sense to him. If anything, allowing a baby to die more slowly, rather than actively terminating its life, was worse, since it simply prolonged the agony.

Singer's arguments around disability and infanticide were not totally outlandish within philosophical circles, but wildly transgressed traditional moral norms, and made his public-facing writings about charity and animal liberation seem anodyne by comparison. No doubt he was naive not to expect a backlash, but there had been barely a ripple when he first set out his views in a book chapter, nor when they reappeared in his popular introductory text *Practical Ethics*, published in 1979, and again in the coauthored *Should the Baby Live*, published in 1985.[3]

Trouble only really kicked off a few years later, in 1989, when he was invited to talk in Germany. A philosophy professor there, Dr. H. Kliemt, was forced to abandon a course that used a translation of *Practical Ethics* as a central text, after a sustained campaign of harassment. Further protests followed in Germany, with whistles and rattles used to drown out Singer's voice in lectures. The fear of violent disruption in other European countries led to the cancellation of other lectures and conferences. Although Singer's proposals bore no relationship to the eugenics project in Nazi Germany (for a start, he had always argued that euthanasia should never be a state decision), the German periodical *Der Spiegel* published a hostile article about him which was accompanied by a photograph of victims being sent to be "euthanized" during the Third Reich.

The irony of calling the son of Jewish refugees a Nazi eugenicist, as many did, was lost. In 1991, at the University of Zurich, in German-speaking Switzerland, when Singer was due to lecture on animal rights, a crowd began to chant "Singer raus, Singer raus" (Get out Singer, get out). Singer later wrote, "I had an overwhelming feeling that this was what it must have been like to attempt to reason against the rising tide of Nazism in the declining days of the Weimar Republic. The difference was that the chant would have been, not 'Singer raus,' but 'Juden raus.'"[4] Although he could not be heard over the din, Singer drew the parallel using the overhead projector—at which point a protestor jumped onto the podium on which Singer was standing, then tore off and stamped on his glasses. Singer remained unbowed and characteristically phlegmatic. "It was disturbing and upsetting. But even the guy who grabbed my glasses didn't touch me."[5]

Meanwhile, in Australia, the archbishop of Melbourne, Cardinal Pell, was so outraged by Singer's depravity that he labeled him "Herod's propaganda machine."[6] (Cardinal Pell himself later had a prison sentence for child abuse quashed on appeal, but, according to an inquiry, he'd known about and failed to take action on child abuse within the Church in the 1970s.)

Singer continued to campaign to improve animal lives, with *Animal Liberation* inspiring a broad movement. On one occasion, the Animal Liberation Front broke into Howard University's medical science building and freed more than two dozen cats—leaving behind a gift-wrapped copy of Singer's book.[7]

In 1992, Singer became one of the original members of the Greens in Victoria, and stood for election twice, the second time, in 1996, for the Australian senate. He was heavily defeated. In any case, a reluctance to compromise intellectually made him unsuited to politics. In the words of the *New Yorker*'s profiler, he was "hobbled by a compulsive honesty."[8] The following year, he was back on more familiar territory, as one of the founders of the Great Ape Project, which sought a declaration of basic rights for nonhuman great apes.

In 1999 Singer was offered a position at Princeton University's Center for Human Values. This prompted Bernard Williams to crack a typically acerbic joke: "I should have thought it would have sounded to him rather like a Center for Aryan Values." (Williams had a blind spot about animal welfare.) An outraged letter in the *Princeton Alumni Weekly* queried why, if Singer was so sure of the equality between chimpanzees and humans, he didn't go and teach in a zoo. "Until I moved to Princeton," Singer says, "nobody personally threatened to kill or maim me."[9]

Indeed, not since 1940 had a job offer in philosophy caused such a kerfuffle. Then, the proposed appointment of the outspoken atheist Bertrand Russell had had to be abandoned, after a suit brought to court by a religious parent of a student, whose lawyer accused the sixty-eight-year-old Englishman (due to teach courses in logic and the foundations of mathematics) of being "lecherous, libidinous, lustful, venomous, erotomaniac, aphrodisiac, irreverent, narrow-minded, untruthful and bereft of moral fibre."[10]

Singer's job offer was not withdrawn, but a major Princeton donor, the presidential candidate Steve Forbes, announced that as a result of his arrival he would cease to donate, and there were protests from a disability rights group, Not Dead Yet, whose leader described Singer as an advocate of genocide and the most dangerous man on earth. "Professor Pleasure—or Professor Death" was the headline of a *Wall Street Journal* article, which reluctantly conceded that there was "an impressive, if lunatic, consistency to his arguments."[11] The death threats against Singer were considered sufficiently credible for the university to provide him with a scanner that could detect bombs in his mail.

Assessing it in purely utilitarian terms, Singer regarded the furor over his disability writings as, on balance, positive. It certainly brought about a hike in his book sales (including in Germany) and thus aided the spread of his ideas. He insists that although he has always been attracted by topics that spark debate, he is never intentionally provocative. Still, again judged on a utilitarian calculus, the next controversy was a net negative, generating trouble for negligible reward. In 2001, he was approached by a little-known website to review a little-known book, *Dearest Pet: On Bestiality*.[12] The author, a Dutch biologist, had researched and compiled a history of human love for animals—"love" not in its usual meaning, as when someone reports that they love Rover, their pet labrador, but rather in the romantic sense.

Agreeing to comment on the book was, Singer says, possibly his biggest mistake:[13] after all, it was hardly an issue of widespread interest. Few people are romantically entangled with canine or feline domestic animals. In his review, Singer argued that sex with animals was just a taboo (as masturbation, sex outside marriage, and homosexuality had once been, and in some places still are), and that it was hard to see it as an offence so long as it was "consensual" and "mutually satisfying." The review contained graphic sexual details; even Singer's condemnation of some forms of bestiality was expressed in terms that must have discomfited readers.

> Some men use hens as a sexual object, inserting their penis into the cloaca, an all-purpose channel for wastes and for the passage of the egg. This is usually fatal to the hen, and in some cases she will be deliberately decapitated just before ejaculation in order to intensify the convulsions of the sphincter. This is cruelty, clear and simple. (But is it really worse for the hen than living for a year or more crowded with four or five other hens in a wire cage so small that they can never stretch their wings, and then being stuffed into crates to be taken to the slaughterhouse, strung upside down and killed? If not, then it is no worse than what egg producers do to their hens all the time.)[14]

The response was predictable, although not to Singer. "I was certainly aware that there could be some reaction but was surprised how strong it was. And people keep bringing it up. That was not something I anticipated."[15] One academic claimed that "[t]he philosophy that leads Singer to these and other antihuman conclusions—a form of utilitarianism—is rooted in an autistic faith in rationality at the expense of feelings of empathy and compassion."[16] Echoing the earlier hounding of Bertrand Russell, another article was subtitled "This Could Be Your Kid's Teacher." "Once an Ivy League professor is known to be a proponent of infanticide," the article began, "perhaps nothing he says or writes should thereafter raise eyebrows."[17]

In March 2017, a talk Singer was giving on effective altruism at Canada's University of Victoria was disrupted by protestors claiming he supported eugenics and chanting "Disabled lives matter." In 2022, an Auckland venue initially agreed to host Singer, when he was on a speaking tour of New Zealand, but then, following an outcry, canceled, claiming that although in general they believed in the right to free speech, this right could not be upheld in this instance since Singer's views did not reflect their values of diversity and inclusivity.

This uproar too eventually subsided. For much of his career, protests against Singer have followed this pattern, rising and then ebbing away. The death threats still arrive, often clustered like London buses, so that months can pass without one, and then half a dozen appear at the same time. "You should be murdered. People like you should be tortured to death. . . . Die, die, die you scum."[18] They come by voicemail, by email, and by post, with the letter writers revealing a propensity for the use of capital letters and multicolored pens. Christian correspondents promise to pray for him, while reminding him, with regret, that he will burn in hell for eternity. Some academics have careers killed off by a single scandal. But Singer seems uncancelable.

Singer insists that he has no problem with protestors waving placards, handing out leaflets, and so on. "That's fine. I have a problem only when they try to prevent me speaking. I think we should respect each other's right to express our views."[19] In 2021 Singer and two fellow-ethicists, Jeff McMahan and Francesca Minerva, launched an unusual peer-reviewed publication, the *Journal of Controversial Ideas*. It was established amid concern that free speech was under increasing threat, and the worry that many academics and journals were petrified of tackling contentious topics that might incite a popular backlash, especially via social media. Minerva had herself suffered a torrent of abuse after coauthoring an article (drawing on Singer) arguing that neither the fetus nor the newborn had the relevant capacities associated with moral status—and hence both abortion and infanticide were permissible.[20] That brought the wrath of various newspapers down upon her, including the *Daily Mail*; multiple death threats via mail and email followed. Singer supported her and, when she was wavering, advised her against retracting the article.

The *Journal of Controversial Ideas* aims to publish rigorous peer-reviewed articles that can't find a home elsewhere because the arguments are considered too explosive. Authors worried about their safety, or the subsequent outrage, are permitted to publish pseudonymously. A few readers seem to have missed the point, and have expressed shock that some of the ideas expressed in the *Journal of Controversial Ideas* are controversial. Singer himself was back in the headlines when he recommended that people "read and ponder" an article that defended zoophilia,[21] the *New York Post* describing him as "the absurd academic."[22]

Amidst all the abuse there has been a gentle trickle of accolades. In 2005, *Time* magazine named Singer as one of the world's one hundred most influential people. In 2012, he became a Companion of the Order of Australia (AC), roughly comparable to a knighthood in Britain. The citation mentioned his "eminent service to philosophy and bioethics," and the honor was supported by a reference from his old university friend, the politician Gareth Evans: "What has been most extraordinary, in many ways, is that his success . . . has been achieved not by flamboyant campaigning but by relentlessly careful, methodical argument. . . . He has sometimes been a controversial figure, but that has not been because he has courted controversy in any voracious way: it's simply a function of the many very sensitive and difficult social policy issues with which he has intellectually wrestled."[23]

In 2021, the launch year of the *Journal of Controversial Ideas*, Singer was the recipient of a lucrative and relatively new philosophy honor, the Berggruen Prize, worth around $1 million. He immediately announced that he would give away the entire amount. There have been other baubles too, though it's notable that while some philosophers with much less fame and influence have been garlanded with honorary degrees,[24] Singer has received only two, quite probably because universities are nervous about the resulting flak.

He retired from Princeton in 2024, but there was no slowing down. Shortly after his "retirement" he undertook a four-week lecture tour of China, speaking at twenty-five events across nine different cities. China has more animals crowded into factory farms than any other country,[25] so Singer thought that an opportunity to talk about this was not one he could turn down. His list of written, cowritten, or edited books by then stretched to over fifty titles. And he embarked on a new project: a podcast series of interviews copresented with Polish philosopher Katarzyna de Lazari-Radek, it aimed to probe what it is to live a good life.

A remarkable fact about Singer's own life is that the intellectual terrain of his twin intellectual preoccupations was mapped out by his late twenties. He was twenty-nine when *Animal Liberation* was published. Since then, interest in animal welfare and animal rights has grown steadily. Prior to 1970, when Singer inquired about his friend's rejection of the meat option at an Oxford lunch, he'd never met a vegetarian. Now restaurants in the UK routinely offer at least one vegetarian dish and often there's a vegan option too. An updated edition of *Animal Liberation* appeared in 2023.

This acknowledged that there had been progress in farm practices (for which Singer justifiably claims some credit) while regretting that it had been slow and patchy. Singer expressed bafflement that most humans still don't care, or else turn a blind eye, to the terrible animal conditions that persist. "The core argument I was putting forward," Singer wrote, "seemed so irrefutable, so undeniably right, that I thought everyone who read it would surely be convinced by it."[26] Yet today a higher percentage of our food comes from factory farming than in 1975.

Among the minority of humans for whom the conditions of life for nonhumans really do matter, Singer is not uniformly hailed as an ally. Within this minority there has emerged another minority, who have come to regard Singer's pragmatic, incremental approach to bettering the lives of animals as compromising and itself immoral—akin to responding to the slave trade not by demanding a total ban on slavery and refusing to have anything to do with slave owners, but instead by pushing for an improvement in the conditions of the slaves.[27]

As for Singer's second major interest, and the subject of this book, his efforts to boost charitable giving have continued unabated. He continues to seek converts to his ideas, in lectures and talks. He rarely declines an interview, though since the emergence and explosion of podcasts he can no longer satisfy every request. During interviews, he never raises his voice, however provocative the question. For interviewers more used to talking to politicians skilled in the art of dissembling, it must be unnerving to interrogate a man who tackles each question head on. In interviews, Singer is often asked about the Shallow Pond; he likens it to fans demanding of the Rolling Stones that they play "Satisfaction" at every concert.

In 2009, the publication of *The Life You Can Save* was accompanied by the establishment of a new organization, of the same name, encouraging people to donate, and with a website that made it easy to support a set of recommended high-impact charities. This foundation was the main beneficiary of Singer's Berggruen prize money (with other charities, including animal charities, also benefiting).

As further proof of the enduring appeal of "Famine, Affluence, and Morality," it was published in book form in 2016, this time with a foreword by Bill and Melinda Gates. The evidence that we have the power to prevent bad things (like the death of children) from happening, claimed the Gateses, "is much stronger now than it was in 1972."[28] A notable development since 1972 has been the decline in the percentage of those living in extreme poverty. When "Famine, Affluence, and Morality" was written, it is estimated that there were 1.87 billion people in this category, or about half of the global population. The total population size has since more than doubled, but now only around 9 percent, or approximately 690 million, live in extreme poverty.[29] This is 690 million too many, though a startling improvement. The decline in child mortality—those dying under the age of five—has been equally astounding.[30] Still, the article remains relevant, and a staple of ethics courses. The Shallow Pond has even, and rather beautifully, been set to choral music.[31] With the exception, perhaps, of John Rawls's *A Theory of Justice*, it's hard to think of another modern philosophical paper or book that has had such an impact on the non-philosophical world.

The effective altruism movement is one legacy. The movement as a whole took time to recover from the Sam Bankman Fried fiasco. The collapse of FTX led to a sharp collapse in EA morale. Until then, there had been an exponential growth in the numbers taking the pledge. That growth slowed markedly. For a time, it looked like effective altruism might implode altogether.

Will MacAskill wrote for himself (as a sort of therapy) a short story, in which a character helps to construct an entire system to rescue drowning people in shallow ponds, including cranes that scoop them out. These saved individuals are eventually numerous enough to constitute an entire town. Then, one day, a bomb goes off, and the town, with all its inhabitants, is destroyed. The character walks away devastated from the apocalyptic scene—before passing a shallow pond, in which a child is drowning. What to do . . . ?

The answer, of course, is that you save the child. And while MacAskill considered the post-FTX period as the "low point in my mood and mental health,"[32] he didn't abandon effective altruism. He did, however, decide to step back from some of his official responsibilities and public-facing roles. The scandal continued to reverberate. There was a court order for the Effective Ventures Foundation (EVF), the umbrella organization of various effective altruist offshoots, to return money donated by FTX and, in acknowledgment that the purchase of the grand Oxfordshire manor house, Wytham Abbey, had been a terrible look, it was put up for sale. EVF was then shut down, and its individual components, such as Giving What We Can, became discrete legal entities. Again, reputation was a major consideration. Separating the organizations was equivalent to the installation of fire doors, so that if in future the flames of controversy were fanned in one place, they would not automatically spread to others.

The expansion of effective altruism into causes beyond philanthropy—in particular human extinction and animal rights, but also research to reduce cognitive biases—has proved vastly contentious. Alongside concerns about artificial intelligence, however, tackling global poverty is still ranked as the most important priority among EA supporters.[33]

By no means have all the donations inspired by effective altruist ideas been channeled through EA affiliated organizations; but as of 2024, in addition to the £400 million from Giving What We Can, the $2 billion from GiveWell, the $1 billion from the private charity of Dustin Moskovitz, plus the more tenuous connection with the Giving Pledge of billionaires, which could unleash billions more, around $ 141 million has been raised by Singer's organization The Life You Can Save.

As for Singer's personal giving: well, from one perspective he is impressively munificent, far more generous than the average person. He donates between a third and a half of his income. Of course, judged by the ideal standards of his own utilitarian philosophy, he is a morally flawed figure. He still indulges in "unnecessary" luxuries—meals out and so on. He still retains resources that he could give away without sacrificing anything of importance. "Perhaps I've become too complacent," he says. "Certainly I'm no saint."[34]

What should we conclude about the Shallow Pond? The moral case for helping distant strangers, and to do so as effectively as we can, is difficult to deny. Nor is this a trivial point, as some allege.

But the practical implications are more contentious. Good intentions are not good enough. There are some bafflingly weak criticisms of the effective altruism project, but the objections of serious development economists, such as Angus Deaton and William Easterly, are not so easily dismissed. On balance, aid (especially government aid) may have been bad for those it is supposed to help. It may well be that the effective altruists, at least when it comes to international development, should pursue their objectives through other means—and that their reliance on measures such as randomized control trials biases them in favor of micro-interventions and against those that address the bigger picture. Still, I find it hard to believe that there are not some narrowly focused and limited measures, particularly in the realm of health—vaccinating children, for example—that are, firstly, identifiable, and secondly, do vastly more good than harm. Almost all actions have downsides, and for some actions it is reasonable to conclude that the downsides are insufficiently grave to rule the actions out.

The Shallow Pond was devised in the wake of the crisis in 1971 as Bangladesh (then East Pakistan) fought for independence. It was about the rich world's obligation to the poor world. But even if we were convinced by critics of aid that aid did more harm than good, that wouldn't give us an entirely free pass. "If it is in our power to prevent something bad from happening, without thereby sacrificing anything of comparable moral importance, we ought, morally, to do it." That was Singer's compelling premise. And if sending money to the other side of the world would not prevent anything bad from happening, well, we could still choose to spurn the expensive meal, eschew designer clothes, forsake a luxury holiday. For there are plenty of worthwhile causes close to home that would make worthwhile use of additional resources.

The fundamental ethical point is that the Shallow Pond asks for more than almost all of us are prepared to deliver. It therefore poses a challenge. Are we—we humans—psychologically equipped to embrace an obligation that few of us currently acknowledge?

NOTES

Preface and Acknowledgments

1. Jacobson (2024).

Introduction: Death and the Shallow Pond

1. Singer (2009), 3.
2. Singer (2016 [1972]), 5–6.
3. Wenar (2024).
4. Robinson (2022).

1. Vienna, Melbourne

1. Singer (1980), 1.
2. Singer (2003).
3. Singer (2003), 173.
4. Gutman (1990), 455.
5. See Rutland (2005), 59.
6. Singer (1984 [1968]), 271. This particular translation runs, "for the animals it is an eternal Treblinka."
7. I discuss similar cases in chapter 11 of Edmonds (2013).
8. See Kahneman (2012).
9. Peter Singer, interview with author.
10. Woods (2006), 606.
11. Haigh (2007).
12. Gareth Evans, email to author.

2. Oxford: Philosophy Awakes

1. Peter Singer, interview with author.

2. For easily the best and most comprehensive account of Austin's wartime service, see Rowe (2023).

3. Rowe (2023), 382.

4. Austin (1979 [1956]), 181–82.

5. Austin (1979 [1956]), 185.

6. Austin (1979 [1956]), 185.

7. This Austin example is cited in Rowe (2023), 418.

8. For a description of the Kindergarten, see Mac Cumhaill and Wiseman (2022), 166.

9. John Passmore in Edwards (1967), 52–57.

10. Subsided, rather than having been extinguished. As a postgraduate in Oxford, I recall a portion of one tutorial dedicated to distinguishing a cup from a mug, and "almost" from "nearly."

11. I would not wish to give the impression that this snobbish attitude has wholly dissipated, even now, however.

12. For more on the tribunal, see Monk (2000), 469–71.

13. *Time Magazine*, quoted in Katz (1982), 174.

14. Quoted in Katz (1982), 175.

15. Travis (2000).

16. The Beatles' track "Revolution," released a year earlier, had been more lyrically ambiguous.

17. I won't dwell at length here on the Trolley Problem; for interested readers, one author (but who would do this?) has devoted an entire book to it: see Edmonds (2013).

18. Singer (2017).

19. I describe this case too in Edmonds (2023), where you can read more about this seminar series, and in particular Parfit's writings on future people.

20. Here we need a short note on terminology. There are some countries where average wealth is high, and other countries where it is low: there is a huge disparity in average income between, say, Spain and Sierra Leone; and the average person in the United Kingdom is around forty times as rich as the average person in Niger. In the literature, there is no standard way of expressing this gap. "Rich and poor"; "developed and developing countries"; "the Global North and the Global South": there are obvious drawbacks to each of these dichotomies (rich Australia is in the South, for instance). And sometimes terms that start off neutral became value-laden over time. But I've not stuck rigidly to any one set of labels, since nothing of much importance hinges on this. What matters is that there are some people with desperate material needs, and other people in a position, in theory, to meet some of these needs.

21. Thomson (1971), 48–49.

22. Nagel (1979 [1972]), 74.

3. Vietnam, East Pakistan

1. Singer (1973).
2. Singer (1980) and Singer (2001b).
3. Rée et al. (2022), 4.
4. Rée (1972b), 31.
5. Rée et al. (2022), 4.
6. Rée (1972a), 2.
7. Peter Singer, interview with author.
8. Godlovitch, Godlovitch, and Harris (1971).
9. Singer (1975), ix.
10. Singer (1975), 97.
11. Bentham (1970 [1789]), 283n.
12. Singer (2016 [1972]), 31–32.
13. Peter Singer, interview with author.
14. Mascarenhas (1971), 5. There is some disagreement about the exact timing of the order. Bennett Jones (2002), 167 has it being given as soon as General Yahya Khan reached West Pakistan airspace.
15. The Hamoodur Rehman Commission, quoted in Bennett Jones (2002), 167.
16. Quoted in Bennett Jones (2002), 147.
17. Bass (2014), 77.
18. Mascarenhas (1971), 119.
19. August 5, 1971, quoted in Bass (2014), 212.
20. Singer (2016 [1972]), 6–7.

4. Bob's Bugatti

1. Smith (2012 [1776]), 445 (Book 4, ch. 2). The invisible hand metaphor receives an equally brief mention in Smith's earlier work *The Theory of Moral Sentiments*.
2. See Singer (1979a), ch. 8.
3. Singer (1979a), 168.
4. Singer (2009), 5.
5. Singer (2016 [1972]), 7.
6. Singer (1979a), 165.
7. Singer (1979a), 171.
8. Singer (2016 [1972]), 10. We will return to this argument below, in chapter 12.
9. Unger (1996), 8.
10. Unger (1996), 24–25.
11. Unger (1996), 25.
12. Unger (1996), 114.

13. See Unger (1996), 135–36.

14. A check (British "cheque") was a paper bill, ordering a bank to pay money to the person named from the account of the signee—a form of payment commonly used by *Homo sapiens* in the twentieth century.

15. Nussbaum (1997).

5. From the Pond to the World

1. Toby Ord, blog (no longer available), March 11, 2006.
2. Toby Ord, blog (no longer available), March 11, 2006.
3. Singer (1979a), 181.
4. See Parfit (1987), 32–39.
5. Parfit (1987), 32.
6. Toby Ord, blog (no longer available), February 26, 2006.
7. Toby Ord, blog (no longer available), March 11, 2006.
8. Toby Ord, interview with author.
9. See Caviola et al. (2014).
10. Toby Ord, interview with author.
11. Toby Ord, email to author.
12. Harris (2020).
13. Singer (2006). For more on this topic, see chapter 14 below.
14. Elie Hassenfeld, interview with author.
15. GiveWell (2024a).
16. Pliskin (1974), 109.
17. Zeckhauser and Shepard (1976).
18. Datum valid for 2024.

6. Turning Point in the Grave

1. William MacAskill, recorded on Giving What We Can (website), https://www.givingwhatwecan.org/about-us/history.
2. William MacAskill, recorded on Giving What We Can (website), https://www.givingwhatwecan.org/about-us/history.
3. William MacAskill, interview with author.
4. William MacAskill, interview with author.
5. William MacAskill, interview with author.
6. Lewis-Kraus (2022).
7. William MacAskill, interview with author.
8. William MacAskill, interview with author.

9. William MacAskill, interview with author.

10. William MacAskill, interview with author.

11. William MacAskill (@willmacaskill) on Twitter, September 4, 2023.

12. William MacAskill, quoted in Lewis-Kraus (2022).

13. Not to mention sheep-, pig-, crocodile-, and bull-penis pizza: https://www.thesun.co.uk/tv/24799180/im-a-celebrity-nigel-farage-four-penis-pizza/ (accessed Jan. 9, 2025).

14. John Lennon had a very brief spell at the Liverpool College of Arts.

15. It is now Unlimit Health, an independent charity.

16. Alan Fenwick, interview with author.

7. Growing Pains

1. William MacAskill, quoted in Edmonds (2016), 84.

2. Unger (1996), 151.

3. Singer (2013).

4. Michelle Hutchinson, interview with author.

5. Michelle Hutchinson, interview with author.

6. Michelle Hutchinson, interview with author.

7. William MacAskill, speaking on the Tim Ferriss Show: see Ferriss (2018), 13.

8. Toby Ord, interview with author.

9. This honorific is awarded to non-Jews who risked their lives to save Jews during the Holocaust.

10. MacAskill (2016), 244.

11. MacAskill, interview with author.

12. Parfit (1987), 68.

13. MacAskill, interview with author.

14. For non-UK readers, "the man on the Clapham omnibus" is a supposedly ordinary person holding reasonable views.

8. Longtermism

1. The following section draws heavily on Edmonds (2023), where you can read much more about the strange life and times of Derek Parfit.

2. An example adapted from BBC Radio 4 (2022a).

3. I owe this example to Tyler Cowen, also on BBC Radio 4 (2022a).

4. Parfit (1987), 453–54.

5. See Schubert, Caviola, and Faber (2019). The authors put a modified version of Parfit's question to subjects. They were able to alter this result, by, for example, asking participants to reflect on the long term.

6. Parfit (2011), 616.

7. The pledge now reads, "I recognise that I can use part of my income to do a significant amount of good. Since I can live well enough on a smaller income, I pledge that for the rest of my life or until the day I retire, I shall give at least ten percent of what I earn to whichever organisations can most effectively use it to improve the lives of others, now and in the years to come. I make this pledge freely, openly, and sincerely."

8. Singer (1981).

9. For an argument along these lines, see Beckstead (2013).

10. See Syropoulos, Law, and Young (2024).

11. According to an EA survey in 2022, around one in five effective altruists believes in research as the way to make the most impact. See Moss and Sleegers (2023).

12. Bostrom (2002), 3.

13. Bostrom (2014), 123.

14. This foundation is called Good Ventures. It channels the philanthropic donations of Tuna and Moskovitz. These days, the causes it supports are those identified by GiveWell and Open Philanthropy.

15. Peter Singer, interviewed: Corbyn (2023).

9. Laboratory in the Mind: The Thought Experiment Critique

1. Quoted in *The Oxfordshire Weekly News*, November 13, 1889. Further details of this case as reported in *Jackson's Oxford Journal*, June 22, 1889, can be found at https://www.oxfordhistory.org.uk/streets/inscriptions/south_west/drowning.pdf (accessed Jan. 10, 2025).

2. To hear Frank Jackson speak about this experiment, go to the podcast Edmonds and Warburton (2011).

3. See chapter 10 below.

4. Unger (1996), 67.

5. See Warburton and Singer (2015). Nigel Warburton asked whether it would be right to let the drowning child die if instead you could sell the extremely expensive shoes you are wearing, which would otherwise be ruined in the pond, sending the money raised to charity, and thus saving two lives.

6. Temkin (2022), 67–68.

7. Temkin (2022), 67.

8. Temkin (2022), 68.

9. Williams (1981 [1976]), 18.

10. Quoted in Williams's obituary in *The Times*, June 14, 2003.

11. Fraser and MacAskill (2015).

12. World Health Organization (2024).

10. Shallow Ponds in Deep Waters: The Utilitarian Critique

1. See https://www.cryptobahamas.com/ (accessed Jan. 10 2025).

2. Bambysheva (2022) (which also features a photo of the trio).

3. Fried (2020), xv.

4. Cowen (2022).

5. On BBC Radio 4 (2022b).

6. Ehrlich and Peterson-Withorn (2021).

7. The paradox was analyzed in the eighteenth century by Daniel Bernoulli, who lived in St. Petersburg.

8. Wiblin and Harris (2022) (interview with Bankman-Fried).

9. Wiblin and Harris (2022).

10. I presented BBC Radio 4 (2022b).

11. Sam Bankman-Fried, quoted in Rushe (2022).

12. Rushe (2022).

13. Michael Lewis, quoted in Sandbu (2023).

14. Lewis-Kraus (2022).

15. Thompson (2015).

16. This is consistent with support for an inegalitarian distribution of goods. Although utilitarianism rejects the notion that one life is more intrinsically valuable than any other, it might, in theory, be the case that utility is maximized in a very unequal society.

17. Caroline Ellison at the trial, and quoted in Lewis (2024a).

18. Whether those who endorse "utilitarian" judgments in these sacrificial dilemmas (kill one to save five) are actually motivated by utilitarian thinking is a complex and contested matter: see Kahane et al. (2015).

19. Recall Clare in chapter 5 above.

20. See Schubert and Caviola (2023).

21. Lewis (2024b), 72.

22. Smart and Williams (1973), 97–98.

23. Smart and Williams (1973), 116.

24. Singer (2015), 49.

25. See chapter 18 below.

26. The phrase is from Robinson (2022).

27. Lichtenberg (2015).

28. Toby Ord, speaking at Ord and MacAskill (2016).

11. Moral Math, Play Pumps, and Microloans: The Numbers Critique

1. Chan (2007).

2. I came across the Helmsley example in Jeff McMahan's excellent essay, MacMahan (2018).

3. Data from Giving USA (2024).

4. IUPUI Lilly Family School of Philanthropy (2021).

5. List (2011).

6. Email to author from Open Philanthropy. See also GiveWell (2024b).

7. See Giving USA (2024).

8. See Giving USA (2024).

9. Bruce Leslie, interview with author, 2014.

10. See Giving USA (2024).

11. Alexander (2013).

12. See MacAskill (2016), 3–7.

13. A World Bank Development Marketplace Award, in the year 2000.

14. For some of the difficulties involved in measuring poverty and drawing country comparisons, see Deaton (2020).

15. World Bank Group (2024).

16. MacAskill (2016), 28.

17. I am indebted to Kieran Setiya for drawing my attention to this quote, which he discusses at BBC Radio 4 (2022b).

18. "Condition X" might be a "mental" illness, such as depression.

19. As with all EA-related issues, there are dissenting voices within the movement. There are effective altruists critical of the reliance on RCTs. See, for example, Hillebrandt (2020).

20. Yunus (1998), foreword (no page number).

21. See, for example, Banerjee, Karlan, and Zinman (2015).

22. Esther Duflo, interviewed by the author for *The Big Idea: Economics and Mosquito Nets* (BBC World Service, May 31, 2020).

23. Cited in Breeze (2021), 95.

24. Angus Deaton, email to author.

25. Kinstler (2024).

26. Berger and Penna (2013).

27. In fact, people generally do view charity and policy differently: see Berman et al. (2018).

28. See Lewis-Kraus (2022).

29. For a lively discussion of the Wytham Abbey purchase on the EA Forum, see Willems (2022).

12. Mrs. Jellyby and Groundhog Day: The Demandingness Critique

1. William MacAskill, quoted in Kinstler (2022). This mirrors a line in Sachs (2005), 1: "Every morning our newspapers could report, 'More than 20,000 people perished yesterday of extreme poverty.' "

2. Dickens (1985 [1852]), 36.

3. Dickens (1985 [1852]), 33.

4. How I wish this were a hypothetical example.

5. This position has been taken in Sterri and Moen (2021).

6. Murphy (2000), esp. chs. 5 and 6.

7. Pummer (2023), ch. 6, esp. pp. 133–34. See also Cullity (1995) for a related, and earlier, treatment of this same issue.

8. Wolf (2009 [1982]).

9. Wolf (2009 [1982]), 130.

13. The New White Man's Burden: The Institutional Critique

1. Marx and Engels (1998 [1848]), 52.

2. Srinivasan (2015).

3. Nussbaum (1997).

4. Sebastian (2023), 27.

5. Srinivasan (2015).

6. Sanbonmatsu (2023), 211.

7. As ranked at "QS World University Rankings 2025," https://www.topuniversities.com/world-university-rankings (accessed Jan. 14, 2025).

8. Figures from Moss and Sleegers (2023).

9. Criado Perez (2019), 186–91.

10. Adams (2023), 135.

11. Chambers (2022).

12. Singer (2016), 69.

13. MacAskill (2016), 158–63.

14. Quoted in Tett (2022).

15. See, for example, Chambers (2022).

16. See Sen (2001).

17. Srinivasan (2015).

18. See https://thehumaneleague.org.uk/ (accessed Jan. 14, 2025).

19. *National Pork Producers Council et al. v. Karen Ross, . . . Secretary of the California Department of Food and Agriculture, et al.*

14. The Mega-Rich and the Pearly Gates: The Billionaire Critique

1. Collins and Flannery (2022), 5.

2. The usual caveat should be made about measurement complexities; but this datum is from https://inequality.org/facts/global-inequality/ (accessed Jan. 14, 2025).

3. Quoted in Nevins (1953), 167.

4. Nevins (1953), 167.

5. Gates was soon also put in charge of Rockefeller's investments.

6. Gates (1977), 161.

7. Gates (1977), 163.

8. Gates to John D. Rockefeller, June 3, 1905, quoted in Schenkel (1995), 38.

9. Quoted in Gates (1977), 134.

10. Gates (1977), 161.

11. Bill Gates (@BillGates) on Twitter, June 25, 2015.

12. Frederick T. Gates to John D. Rockefeller, April 24, 1905, quoted in Chernow (1998), 314.

13. Teddy Roosevelt, quoted in Reich (2018), 4.

14. Quoted in Blake (2010).

15. I'm grateful to Alexander Berger for drawing my attention to this example. See too Eig (2015).

16. Cari Tuna, email to author.

17. Cari Tuna, email to author.

18. Melinda Gates on the Charlie Rose show, June 16, 2010.

19. Figures sent to the author by the Giving Pledge media team.

20. Singer (2006).

21. Wiblin, Koehler, and Harris (2019) (interview with Peter Singer).

22. As discussed in chapter 11 above.

23. Kaspersen and Wallach (2022).

24. Elon Musk (@elonmusk) on Twitter, August 22, 2022.

25. Wenar (2024).

26. Toby Ord, interview with author.

27. William MacAskill, quoted in Kulish (2022).

15. Righting Past Wrongs: The Historical Injustice Critique

1. For a vivid description of the rubber plunder, see Hochschild (2006), 158–66.

2. Foot (1993), 7 (original emphasis).

3. Peter Singer, interview with author.

16. Distance and Dignity: The Power Critique

1. The Victorians habitually drew a distinction between the deserving and the undeserving poor. See Himmelfarb (1991).

2. Smirl (2015), xii.

3. Smirl (2015), 90.

4. Moyo (2010), 26.

5. Michael Buerk, BBC News, October 23, 1984.

6. This point is covered in Deveaux (2015).

7. Quong (2020), 101.

8. Wiesel (1993), quoted in Saunders-Hastings (2022), 134.

9. See Banerjee et al. (2023). For a summary of research findings relating to UBIs (monthly universal basic incomes), see GiveDirectly (2023).

10. Angus Deaton, interview with author.

17. The Harm You Do: The Effectiveness Critique

1. Three donations is the maximum chain length in the UK.

2. See GiveWell (2024c).

3. Cari Tuna, note to author.

4. Human Rights Watch (2008).

5. Wrong (2009), 189.

6. Wrong (2009), 189.

7. Moyo (2010), 47.

8. Bauer (1972).

9. Easterly (2006) and Moyo (2010), respectively.

10. Sachs (2006) (review of Easterly [2006]).

11. Sachs (2005).

12. Mekasha and Tarp (2019).

13. Moyo (2010), 46.

14. Andersen, Johannesen, and Rijkers (2020).

15. Angus Deaton, email to author.

16. Angus Deaton, email to author.

17. Angus Deaton, email to author.

18. Angus Deaton, speaking at Peter Singer's farewell conference, Princeton University, May 14, 2024.

19. See, for example, BBC News (2019).

20. Wrong (2009), 183.

21. Koch (2009), esp. 163–64

22. See chapter 16 above.

23. For a full account of what really caused the drought, and how foreign governments and agencies were complicit, see de Waal (1997), ch. 6.

24. De Waal (1997).

25. John Seaman, quoted in de Waal (1997), 196.

26. Quoted in Deaton (2013), 275.

27. Dercon (2023), 191–92.

28. See Deaton (2013), 292.

29. See Piller and Smith (2007).

30. Easterly (2006), 322.

31. Deaton (2013), 104–5. There are other books that are hostile to aid and philanthropy as it currently functions, but with proposals for how it could work much better in future: for example, Riddell (2007).

32. Angus Deaton, email to author.

33. Leif Wenar, interview with author.

34. Acemoglu and Robinson (2013).

35. See, for example, Besley and Persson (2011).

36. Tim Besley, conversation with author.

37. Ravi Kanbur, conversation with author.

38. See European Parliament (2021).

39. Angus Deaton, email to author.

40. Angus Deaton, email to author.

18. Rattling the Can: The Psychological Critique

1. Chokshi (2017).

2. Cockburn (1956), 131. Cockburn claims that the headline had to be genuine, but in fact this one appears to have been fictitious.

3. *News of the World*, February 28, 2010. Andre had achieved fame in the UK as a singer and star of reality television.

4. Behr (1981).

5. Small, Loewenstein, and Slovic (2007); also quoted in Singer (2009), 45–46.

6. For a teasing apart of the effect of a single identifiable victim from that of several identifiable victims, see Kogut and Ritov (2005).

7. Small and Loewenstein (2003).

8. Some studies have raised doubts about the Identifiable Victim Effect: for example, Maier, Wong, and Feldman (2023).

9. This study is described in Desvousges et al. (2010).

10. A term invented by Paul Slovic: see Slovic (2007).

11. The interpretation of the data is disputed. Although peer pressure affected how subjects responded, they may not have actually believed the answer they gave.

12. It's even claimed that merely thinking about being in a group ("Imagine that you're out to dinner with ten friends") will influence our charitable impulse. See Garcia et al. (2002).

13. See Caviola et al. (2014).

14. Small and Simonsohn (2008).

15. Caviola, Everett, and Faber (2019).

16. Montealegre et al. (2020). See also two other papers: Everett et al. (2018), and Law, Campbell, and Gaesser (2022).

17. Berman et al. (2018).

18. Berman and Silver (2022).

19. For a fuller treatment of this point, see the excellent Schubert and Caviola (2024).

19. The Art of the Feel: The Motivational Critique

1. See Anik et al. (2011), 7.

2. For more on precommitment, see Meyvis, Bennett, and Oppenheimer (2011).

3. Hsee et al. (2013). In this study, the primed group's donation was almost double that of the unprimed. See also Maier et al. (2023).

4. *The Sun*, front page, June 12, 1968.

5. Slovic et al. (2017). The charity was the Swedish Red Cross.

6. Cao and Jia (2017).

7. William MacAskill interviewed by Ali Abdaal: Abdaal (2022).

8. Prof. Sarah Smith of Bristol University, on BBC Radio 4 (2016).

9. See Small, Loewenstein, and Slovic (2007).

10. See Schubert and Caviola (2024), 101–4.

11. Awad et al. (2024).

12. See Caviola and Greene (2023).

13. See Schwitzgebel (2020) for a description of the contest.

14. For further evidence of this, see Lindauer et al. (2020).

15. McGoey (2023).

16. See, as one of numerous examples, Orlowski (2023).

17. *Summa theologica* II-II.Q66.A7C (Aquinas [1948], 171), quoted in Singer (2016), 23.

Postscript: Singer's Swan Song

1. Singer (1979a), 122–23.

2. Later he modified this view slightly, suggesting that disability groups should also be consulted.

3. Singer (1979b), Singer (1979a), and Kuhse and Singer (1985), respectively.

4. Singer (1991).

5. Peter Singer, interview with author.

6. See the *New Yorker* profile of Singer, Specter (1999).

7. This took place during the Christmas period in 1982.

8. Specter (1999).

9. Peter Singer, interview with author.

10. Edmonds and Eidinow (2001), 31.

11. Schaefer (1998).

12. See Singer (2001a), a review of Dekkers (1994) originally written for the website www.nerve.com.

13. Peter Singer, interview with author.

14. Singer (2001a).

15. Peter Singer, interview with author.

16. Hamilton (2012).

17. Lopez (2001).

18. Email to Peter Singer, March 9, 2024.

19. Peter Singer, interview with author.

20. This article went further than Singer, who had argued that infanticide was permissible for babies in pain and destined not to live long.

21. Peter Singer (@PeterSinger) on Twitter, November 9, 2023.

22. Court (2023).

23. Details of this reference were sent to the author by Gareth Evans.

24. Martha Nussbaum has been awarded over sixty.

25. See Ormandy (2024).

26. Peter Singer, quoted in Barber (2023).

27. Gary Francione takes this position. You can hear an interview with him on the podcast Edmonds and Warburton (2012).

28. Singer (2016 [1972]), viii.

29. Figures from World Bank PIP (2024).

30. See UNICEF (2024).

31. "The Life You Can Save," composed by Gustav Alexandrie. A performance by the Södra Latin Chamber Choir, conducted by Jan Risberg, can be watched at https://www.youtube.com/watch?v=UKIzPawLiNM (accessed Jan. 15, 2025).

32. William MacAskill, interview with author.

33. See the survey E [*sic*] and Moss (2024).

34. Peter Singer, interview with author.

BIBLIOGRAPHY

Abdaal, Ali. 2022. "Ethics of Giving Back." *Deep Dive*, August 11. https://www.youtube.com/watch?v=YkdI8ztqWZc (accessed Jan. 15, 2025).

Acemoglu, Daron, and James A. Robinson. 2013. *Why Nations Fail: The Origins of Power, Prosperity, and Poverty*. Profile.

Adams, Carol J. 2023. "A Feminist-Ethics-of-Care Critique of Effective Altruism." In *The Good It Promises, the Harm It Does: Critical Essays on Effective Altruism*, edited by Carol J. Adams, Alice Crary, and Lori Gruen. Oxford University Press.

Alexander, Scott. 2013. "Efficient Charity: Do unto Others . . ." *Effective Altruism Forum*, September 3. https://forum.effectivealtruism.org/posts/2iAwiBQm535ZSYSmo/efficient-charity-do-unto-others (accessed Jan. 10, 2025).

Andersen, Jorgen Juel, Niels Johannesen, and Bob Rijkers. 2020. "Elite Capture of Foreign Aid: Evidence from Offshore Bank Accounts." World Bank Group Policy Research Working Paper 9150, February.

Anik, Lalin, Lara B. Aknin, Michael I. Norton, and Elizabeth W. Dunn. 2011. "Feeling Good about Giving: The Benefits (and Costs) of Self-Interested Charitable Behavior." In *The Science of Giving: Experimental Approaches to the Study of Charity*, edited by Daniel M. Oppenheimer and Christopher Y. Olivola. Taylor & Francis.

Aquinas, Thomas. 1948. *Selected Political Writings*. Edited by A. P. d'Entrèves and translated by J. G. Dawson. Blackwell.

Austin, J. L. 1979 [1956]. "A Plea for Excuses." In *Philosophical Papers*, 3rd ed., edited by J. O. Urmson and G. J. Warnock. Oxford University Press.

Awad, Edmund, Erez Yoeli, Iyad Rahwan, and Zoe Rahwan. 2024. "Heterogeneity in Charitable Giving Preferences from over 2 Million Decisions Worldwide." OSF Preprints. https://doi.org/10.31219/osf.io/28g3z.

Bambysheva, Nina. 2022. "Royal Flush: Inside Crypto's Most Exclusive Gathering." *Forbes*, May 3. https://www.forbes.com/sites/ninabambysheva/2022/05/03/royal-flush-inside-cryptos-most-exclusive-gathering/ (accessed Jan. 10, 2025).

Banerjee, Abhijit, Michael Faye, Alan Krueger, Paul Niehaus, and Tavneet Suri. 2023. *Universal Basic Income: Short-Term Results from a Long-Term Experiment in Kenya*. https://conference.nber.org/conf_papers/f192616.pdf (accessed Jan. 14, 2025).

Banerjee, Abhijit, Dean Karlan, and Jonathan Zinman. 2015. "Six Randomized Evaluations of Microcredit: Introduction and Further Steps." *American Economic Journal: Applied Economics* 7 (1): 1–21.

Barber, Elizabeth. 2023. "What Would It Mean to Treat Animals Fairly?" *New Yorker*, December 16.

Bass, Gary J. 2014. *The Blood Telegram: Nixon, Kissinger, and a Forgotten Genocide*. Hurst.

Bauer, Peter T. 1972. *Dissent on Development: Studies and Debates in Development Economics*. Harvard University Press.

BBC News. 2019. "Oxfam Criticised over Haiti Sex Claims." June 11. https://www.bbc.co.uk/news/uk-48593401 (accessed Jan. 14, 2025).

BBC Radio 4. 2016. "The Charitable Impulse." June 27. https://www.bbc.co.uk/programmes/b07h6zg7 (accessed Jan. 15, 2025).

BBC Radio 4. 2022a. "Why Worry about Future Generations?" February 13. https://www.bbc.co.uk/programmes/m00146pp (accessed Jan. 10, 2025).

BBC Radio 4. 2022b. "Can Effective Altruism Really Change the World?" October 24. https://www.bbc.co.uk/programmes/m001ddfv (accessed Jan. 10, 2025).

Beckstead, Nicholas. 2013. "On the Overwhelming Importance of Shaping the Far Future." PhD diss., Rutgers University. https://rucore.libraries.rutgers.edu/rutgers-lib/40469/PDF/1/play/ (accessed Jan. 10, 2025).

Behr, Edward. 1981. *Anyone Here Been Raped and Speaks English?: A Foreign Correspondent's Life behind the Lines*. Hamish Hamilton.

Bennett Jones, Owen. 2002. *Pakistan: Eye of the Storm*. Yale University Press.

Bentham, Jeremy. 1970 [1789]. *An Introduction to the Principles of Morals and Legislation*. Edited by J. H. Burns and H.L.A. Hart. Continuum.

Berger, Ken, and Robert M. Penna. 2013. "The Elitist Philanthropy of So-Called Effective Altruism." *Stanford Social Innovation Review*, November 25. https://doi.org/10.48558/fts4-6040.

Berman, Jonathan Z., Alixandra Barasch, Emma E. Levine, and Deborah A. Small. 2018. "Impediments to Effective Altruism: The Role of Subjective Preferences in Charitable Giving." *Psychological Science* 29 (5): 834–44.

Berman, Jonathan Z., and Ike Silver. 2022. "Prosocial Behavior and Reputation: When Does Doing Good Lead to Looking Good?" *Current Opinion in Psychology* 43: 102–7.

Besley, Timothy, and Torsten Persson. 2011. *Pillars of Prosperity: The Political Economics of Development Clusters*. Princeton University Press.

Blake, Heidi. 2010. "Carlos Slim: Profile of the World's Richest Man." *Daily Telegraph*, March 11. https://www.telegraph.co.uk/finance/7419211/Carlos-Slim-profile-of-the-worlds-richest-man.html (accessed Jan. 14, 2025).

Bostrom, Nick. 2002. "Existential Risks: Analyzing Human Extinction Scenarios and Related Hazards." *Journal of Evolution and Technology* 9 (1): 1–31.

Bostrom, Nick. 2014. *Superintelligence: Paths, Dangers, Strategies*. Oxford University Press.

Breeze, Beth. 2021. *In Defence of Philanthropy*. Agenda Publishing.

Cao, Xiaoxia, and Lei Jia. 2017. "The Effects of the Facial Expression of Beneficiaries in Charity Appeals and Psychological Involvement on Donation Intentions." *Nonprofit Management and Leadership* 27 (4): 457–73.

Caviola, Lucius, Jim A. C. Everett, and Nadira S. Faber. 2019. "The Moral Standing of Animals: Towards a Psychology of Speciesism." *Journal of Personality and Social Psychology* 116 (6): 1011–29.

Caviola, Lucius, Nadira Faulmüller, Jim A. C. Everett, Julian Savulescu, and Guy Kahane. 2014. "The Evaluability Bias in Charitable Giving: Saving Administration Costs or Saving Lives?" *Judgment and Decision Making* 9 (4): 303–16.

Caviola, Lucius, and Joshua D. Greene. 2023. "Boosting the Impact of Charitable Giving with Donation Bundling and Micromatching." *Science Advances* 9 (3). https://doi.org/10.1126/sciadv.ade7987.

Chambers, Luke. 2022. "Why EA's Talent Bottleneck Is a Barrier of Its Own Making." *Effective Altruism Forum*, May 27. https://forum.effectivealtruism.org/posts/qXLvnGFQ5FfGjDhgk/monthly-overload-of-ea-june-2022.

Chan, Sewell. 2007. "Leona Helmsley's Unusual Last Will." *New York Times*, August 29. https://archive.nytimes.com/cityroom.blogs.nytimes.com/2007/08/29/leona-helmsleys-unusual-last-will/ (accessed Jan. 10, 2025).

Chernow, Ron. 1998. *Titan: The Life of John D. Rockefeller, Sr.* Little, Brown.

Chokshi, Niraj. 2017. "Teenagers Recorded a Drowning Man and Laughed." *New York Times*, July 21. https://www.nytimes.com/2017/07/21/us/video-drowning-teens-florida.html (accessed Jan. 14, 2025).

Cockburn, Claud. 1956. *In Time of Trouble*. Rupert Hart-Davis.

Collins, Chuck, and Helen Flannery. 2022. *Gilded Giving 2022: How Wealth Inequality Distorts Philanthropy and Imperils Democracy*. Institute for Policy Studies. https://ips-dc.org/wp-content/uploads/2022/07/Report-Gilded-Giving-2022.pdf (accessed Jan. 14, 2025).

Corbyn, Zoë. 2023. "Philosopher Peter Singer: 'There's No Reason to Say Humans Have More Worth or Moral Status than Animals.'" *Guardian*, May 21. https://www.theguardian.com/world/2023/may/21/philosopher-peter-singer-theres

-no-reason-to-say-humans-have-more-worth-or-moral-status-than-animals (accessed Jan. 10, 2025).

Court, Andrew. 2023. "Princeton Professor Sparks Outrage by Calling Journal Article about Sex with Animals 'Thought Provoking': 'Someone Check His Hard Drive.'" *New York Post*, November 11. https://nypost.com/2023/11/11/ (accessed Jan. 15, 2025).

Cowen, Tyler. 2022. *Conversations with Tyler*, episode 145 (January 6): "Sam Bankman-Fried on Arbitrage and Altruism." https://conversationswithtyler.com/episodes/sam-bankman-fried/ (accessed Jan. 10, 2025).

Criado Perez, Caroline. 2019. *Invisible Women: Exposing Data Bias in a World Designed for Men*. Chatto and Windus.

Cullity, Garrett. 1995. "Moral Character and the Iteration Problem." *Utilitas* 7 (2): 289–99.

De Waal, Alex. 1997. *Famine Crimes: Politics and The Disaster Relief Industry in Africa*. James Currey.

Deaton, Angus. 2013. *The Great Escape: Health, Wealth, and the Origins of Inequality*. Princeton University Press.

Deaton, Angus. 2020. "Price Indexes, Inequality, and the Measurement of World Poverty." *American Economic Review* 100 (1): 5–34.

Dekkers, Midas. 1994. *Dearest Pet: On Bestiality*. Verso.

Dercon, Stefan. 2023. *Gambling on Development: Why Some Counties Win and Others Lose*. Hurst.

Desvousges, William H., F. Reed Johnson, Richard W. Dunford, Kevin J. Boyle, Sara P. Hudson, and K. Nicole Wilson. 2010. *Measuring Nonuse Damages Using Contingent Valuation: An Experimental Evaluation of Accuracy*, 2nd ed. RTI International Press.

Deveaux, Monique. 2015. "The Global Poor as Agents of Justice." *Journal of Moral Philosophy* 12 (2): 125–50.

Dickens, Charles. 1985 [1852]. *Bleak House*. The Folio Society.

E, Jamie, and David Moss. 2024. "EA Survey: Cause Prioritization." *Effective Altruism Forum*, May 15. https://forum.effectivealtruism.org/posts/sK5TDD8sCBsga5XYg/e (accessed Jan. 15, 2025).

Easterly, William. 2006. *The White Man's Burden: Why the West's Efforts to Aid the Rest Have Done So Much Ill and So Little Good*. Oxford University Press.

Edmonds, David. 2013. *Would You Kill the Fat Man?* Princeton University Press.

Edmonds, David, ed. 2016. *Philosophers Take On the World*. Oxford University Press.

Edmonds, David. 2023. *Parfit: A Philosopher and His Mission to Save Morality*. Princeton University Press.

Edmonds, David, and John Eidinow. 2001. *Wittgenstein's Poker*. Faber.

Edmonds, David, and Nigel Warburton (hosts). 2011. "Frank Jackson on What Mary Knew." *Philosophy Bites* podcast, August 26. https://philosophybites.com/2011/08/frank-jackson-on-what-mary-knew.html (accessed Jan. 10, 2025)

Edmonds, David, and Nigel Warburton (hosts). 2012. "Gary Francione on Animal Abolitionism." *Philosophy Bites* podcast, October 13. https://philosophybites.libsyn.com/gary-francione-on-animal-abolitionism (accessed Jan. 15, 2025).

Edwards, Paul, ed. 1967. *The Encyclopedia of Philosophy*. Vol. 5. Macmillan.

Ehrlich, Steven, and Chase Peterson-Withorn. 2021. "Meet the World's Richest 29-Year-Old: How Sam Bankman-Fried Made a Record Fortune in the Crypto Frenzy." *Forbes*, October 6.

Eig, Jonathan. 2015. *The Birth of the Pill: How Four Pioneers Reinvented Sex and Launched a Revolution*. Macmillan.

European Parliament. 2021. "Common Agricultural Policy: How Does the EU Support Farmers?" September 22, updated November 30. https://www.europarl.europa.eu/topics/en/article/20210916STO12704/common-agricultural-policy-how-does-the-eu-support-farmers (accessed Jan. 14, 2025).

Everett, Jim A. C., Nadira S. Faber, Julian Savulescu, and Molly J. Crockett. 2018. "The Costs of Being Consequentialist: Social Inference from Instrumental Harm and Impartial Beneficence." *Journal of Experimental Social Psychology* 79: 200–216.

Ferriss, Tim. 2018. *The Tim Ferriss Show*, episode 120. Transcript available at https://tim.blog/wp-content/uploads/2018/08/120-william-macaskill.pdf (accessed Jan. 9, 2025).

Foot, Philippa. 1993. *Justice and Charity*. Oxfam.

Fraser, Giles, and Will MacAskill. 2015. *Intelligence Squared* debate, November 30, hosted by Kamal Ahmed. Viewable at https://www.youtube.com/watch?v=Qslo4-DpzPs (accessed Dec. 22, 2024).

Fried, Barbara H. 2020. *Facing Up to Scarcity: The Logic and Limits of Neoconsequentialist Thought*. Oxford University Press.

Garcia, Steven M., Kim Weaver, Gordon B. Moskowitz, and John M. Darley. 2002. "Crowded Minds: The Implicit Bystander Effect." *Journal of Personality and Social Psychology* 83 (4): 843–53.

Gates, Frederick Taylor. 1977. *Chapters in My Life*. The Free Press.

GiveDirectly. 2023. "Early Findings from the World's Largest UBI Study." https://www.givedirectly.org/2023-ubi-results/ (accessed Jan. 14, 2025)

GiveWell. 2024a. "How Much Does It Cost to Save a Life?" (February version, published April). https://www.givewell.org/how-much-does-it-cost-to-save-a-life (accessed Jan. 9, 2025).

GiveWell. 2024b. "How We Produce Impact Estimates" (updated February). https://www.givewell.org/impact-estimates#Impact_metrics_for_grants_to_GiveWells_top_charities (accessed Jan. 10, 2025).

GiveWell. 2024c. "Our Impact" (updated December). https://www.givewell.org/about (accessed Jan. 14, 2025).

Giving USA. 2024. *Giving USA Annual Report on Philanthropy*. https://givingusa.org/ (accessed Jan. 10, 2025).

Godlovitch, Stanley, Roslind Godlovitch, and John Harris, eds. 1971. *Animals, Men and Morals: An Inquiry into the Maltreatment of Non-Humans*. Gollancz.

Gutman, Israel, ed. 1990. *Encyclopedia of the Holocaust*. Macmillan.

Haigh, Gideon. 2007. "The Principle of Necessity." *The Monthly*, November. https://www.themonthly.com.au/node/711/wrap-function (accessed Jan. 8, 2025).

Hamilton, Clive. 2012. "Cory Bernardi Is Right, in Peter Singer's Anti-Human World." *The Conversation*, September 24. https://theconversation.com/cory-bernardi-is-right-in-peter-singers-anti-human-world-9774 (accessed Jan. 15, 2025).

Harris, Sam, host. 2020. *Making Sense*, episode 208 (podcast, June 23): "Existential Risk: A Conversation with Toby Ord." https://www.samharris.org/podcasts/making-sense-episodes/208-existential-risk (accessed Jan. 9, 2025).

Hillebrandt, Hauke. 2020. "Growth and the Case Against Randomista Development." *Effective Altruism Forum*, January 16. https://forum.effectivealtruism.org/posts/bsE5t6qhGC65fEpzN/growth-and-the-case-against-randomista-development (accessed Jan. 10, 2025).

Himmelfarb, Gertrude. 1991. *Poverty and Compassion: The Moral Imagination of the Late Victorians*. Alfred Knopf.

Hochschild, Adam. 2006. *King Leopold's Ghost: A Story of Greed, Terror and Heroism in Colonial Africa*. Pan Books.

Hsee, Christopher K., Jiao Zhang, Zoe Y. Lu, and Fei Xu. 2013. "Unit Asking: A Method to Boost Donations and Beyond." *Psychological Science* 24 (9): 1801–8.

Human Rights Watch. 2008. "A Question of Life or Death: Treatment Access for Children Living with HIV in Kenya." December 16. https://www.hrw.org/report/2008/12/16/question-life-or-death/treatment-access-children-living-hiv-kenya (accessed Jan. 14, 2025).

IUPUI Lilly Family School of Philanthropy. 2021. *Overview of Overall Giving, Based on Data Collected in 2019 about Charitable Giving in 2018*. https://generosityforlife.org/wp-content/uploads/2021/07/Overall-Giving-2019-PPS.pdf (accessed Jan. 10, 2025).

Jacobson, Gavin. 2024. "Thomas Piketty: 'The Labour Party Is Too Conservative.'" *New Statesman*, March 15–21.

Kahane, Guy, Jim A. C. Everett, Brian D. Earp, Miguel Farias, and Julian Savulescu. 2015. "'Utilitarian' Judgments in Sacrificial Moral Dilemmas Do Not Reflect Impartial Concern for the Greater Good." *Cognition* 134 (January): 193–209.

Kahneman, Daniel. 2012. *Thinking, Fast and Slow*. Penguin.

Kaspersen, Anja, and Wendell Wallach. 2022. "Long-termism: An Ethical Trojan Horse." *Carnegie Council for Ethics in International Affairs*, September 29. https://www.carnegiecouncil.org/media/article/long-termism-ethical-trojan-horse (accessed Jan. 14, 2025).

Katz, Barry. 1982. *Herbert Marcuse: The Art of Liberation*. Verso.

Kinstler, Linda. 2022. "The Good Delusion: Has Effective Altruism Broken Bad?" *Economist*, November 15. https://www.economist.com/1843/2022/11/15/the-good-delusion-has-effective-altruism-broken-bad (accessed Jan. 14, 2025).

Kinstler, Linda. 2024. "How Poor Kenyans Became Economists' Guinea Pigs." *Economist*, March 1. https://www.economist.com/1843/2024/03/01/how-poor-kenyans-became-economists-guinea-pigs (accessed Jan. 14, 2025).

Koch, Dirk-Jan. 2009. *Aid from International NGOs: Blind Spots on the Aid Allocation Map*. Routledge.

Kogut, Tehila, and Ilana Ritov. 2005. "The Singularity Effect of Identified Victims in Separate and Joint Evaluations." *Organizational Behavior and Human Decision Processes* 97 (2): 106–16.

Kuhse, Helga, and Peter Singer. 1985. *Should the Baby Live: The Problem of Handicapped Infants*. Oxford University Press.

Kulish, Nicholas. 2022. "How a Scottish Moral Philosopher Got Elon Musk's Number." *New York Times*, October 12.

Law, Kyle Fiore, Dylan Campbell, and Brendan Gaesser. 2022. "Biased Benevolence: The Perceived Morality of Effective Altruism across Social Distance." *Personality and Social Psychology Bulletin* 48 (3): 426–44.

Lewis, Michael. 2024a. "Sam Bankman-Fried: A Personal Verdict." *Washington Post*, August 20.

Lewis, Michael. 2024b. *Going Infinite: The Rise and Fall of a New Tycoon*. Penguin.

Lewis-Kraus, Gideon. 2015. "Peter Singer's Extremely Altruistic Heirs." *New Republic*, November 30. https://newrepublic.com/article/124690/peter-singers-extremely-altruistic-heirs (accessed Jan. 10, 2025).

Lewis-Kraus, Gideon. 2022. "The Reluctant Prophet of Effective Altruism." *New Yorker*, August 8.

Lichtenberg, Judith. 2015. "Peter Singer's Extremely Altruistic Heirs." *New Republic*, November 30. https://newrepublic.com/article/124690/peter-singers-extremely-altruistic-heirs.

Lindauer, Matthew, Marcus Mayorga, Joshua Greene, Paul Slovic, Daniel Västfjäll, and Peter Singer. 2020. "Comparing the Effect of Rational and Emotional Appeals on Donation Behavior." *Judgment and Decision Making* 15 (3): 413–20.

List, John A. 2011. "The Market for Charitable Giving." *Journal of Economic Perspectives* 25 (2): 157–80.

Lopez, Kathryn Jean. 2001. "Peter Singer Strikes Again." *National Review*, March 5. https://www.nationalreview.com/2001/03/peter-singer-strikes-again-kathryn-jean-lopez/ (accessed Jan. 15, 2025).

Mac Cumhaill, Clare, and Rachael Wiseman. 2022. *Metaphysical Animals: How Four Women Brought Philosophy Back to Life*. Chatto and Windus.

MacAskill, William. 2016. *Doing Good Better*. Faber & Faber.

MacAskill, William. 2022. *What We Owe the Future*. Oneworld.

MacMahan, Jeff. 2018. "Doing Good and Doing the Best." In *The Ethics of Giving: Philosophers' Perspectives on Philanthropy*, edited by Paul Woodruff. Oxford University Press.

Maier, Maximilian, Lucius Caviola, Stefan Schubert, and Adam J. L. Harris. 2023. "Investigating (Sequential) Unit Asking: An Unsuccessful Quest for Scope Sensitivity in Willingness to Donate Judgements." *Journal of Behavioral Decision Making* 36 (4). https://doi.org/10.1002/bdm.2335.

Maier, Maximilian, Yik Chun Wong, and Gilad Feldman. 2023. "Revisiting and Rethinking the Identifiable Victim Effect: Replication and Extension of Small, Loewenstein, and Slovic (2007)." *Collabra: Psychology* 9 (1). https://doi.org/10.1525/collabra.90203.

Marx, Karl, and Friedrich Engels. 1998 [1848]. *The Communist Manifesto*. Monthly Review Press.

Mascarenhas, Anthony. 1971. *The Rape of Bangla Desh*. Vikas Publications.

McGoey, Linsey. 2023. "Elite Universities Gave Us Effective Altruism, the Dumbest Idea of the Century." *Jacobin*, January 19. https://jacobin.com/2023/01/effective-altruism-longtermism-nick-bostrom-racism (accessed Jan. 15, 2025).

Mekasha, Tseday Jemaneh, and Finn Tarp. 2019. "Meta-Analysis of Aid Effectiveness: Revisiting the Evidence." *Politics and Governance* 7 (2): 5–28.

Meyvis, Tom, Aronté Bennett, and Daniel M. Oppenheimer. 2011. "Precommitment to Charity." In *The Science of Giving: Experimental Approaches to the Study of Charity*, edited by Daniel M. Oppenheimer and Christopher Y. Olivola. Taylor & Francis.

Monk, Ray. 2000. *Bertrand Russell: 1921–1970; The Ghost of Madness*. Jonathan Cape.

Montealegre, Andres, Lance S. Bush, David Moss, David Pizarro, and William Jimenez-Leal. 2020. "Does Maximizing Good Make People Look Bad?" PsyArXiv Preprints. https://doi.org/10.31234/osf.io/2zbax.

Moss, David, and Willem Sleegers. 2023. "EA Survey 2022: Demographics." *Effective Altruism Forum*, May 25. https://forum.effectivealtruism.org/posts/AJDgn PXqZ48eSCjEQ/ea-survey-2022-demographics (accessed Jan. 10, 2025).

Moyo, Dambisa. 2010. *Dead Aid: Why Aid Is Not Working and How There Is Another Way for Africa*. Penguin.

Munk, Nina. 2013. *The Idealist*. Anchor Books.

Murphy, Liam B. 2000. *Moral Demands in Nonideal Theory*. Oxford University Press.

Nagel, Thomas. 1979 [1972]. "War and Massacre." In *Mortal Questions*. Cambridge University Press.

Nevins, Allan. 1953. *Study in Power: John D. Rockefeller, Industrialist and Philanthropist*. Vol. 2. Charles Scribner's Sons.

Nussbaum, Martha. 1997. "If Oxfam Ran the World." *London Review of Books*, September 4.

OECD. 2021. *How Was Life?* Volume 2: *New Perspectives on Well-Being and Global Inequality since 1820*. OECD Publishing.

Ord, Toby, and Will MacAskill. 2016. "Opening Keynote: EA Global, San Francisco 2016." YouTube video, August 5. https://www.youtube.com/watch?v=VH2Lh-Sod1M4 (accessed Jan. 10, 2025).

Orlowski, Andrew. 2023. "Sam Altman and the Cult of Effective Altruism." *Spiked*, November 26. https://www.spiked-online.com/2023/11/26/sam-altman-and-the-cult-of-effective-altruism/ (accessed Jan. 15, 2025).

Ormandy, Elisabeth. 2024. "Announcing Our 2024 Charity Recommendations." *Animal Charity Evaluators*, November 12. https://animalcharityevaluators.org/blog/announcing-our-2024-charity-recommendations/ (accessed Jan. 15, 2025).

Parfit, Derek. 1987. *Reasons and Persons*. Oxford University Press.

Parfit, Derek. 2011. *On What Matters*. Vol. 2. Oxford University Press.

Piller, Charles, and Doug Smith. 2007. "Unintended Victims of Gates Foundation Generosity." *Los Angeles Times*, December 16. https://www.latimes.com/nation/la-na-gates16dec16-story.html (accessed Jan. 14, 2025).

Pliskin, Joseph S. 1974. "The Management of Patients with End-Stage Renal Failure: A Decision Theoretic Approach." PhD diss., Harvard University.

Pummer, Theron. 2023. *The Rules of Rescue: Cost, Distance, and Effective Altruism*. Oxford University Press.

Quong, Jonathan. 2020. *Liberalism Without Perfection*. Oxford University Press.

Rée, Jonathan. 1972a. "Professional Philosophers." *Radical Philosophy*, no. 1. https://www.radicalphilosophy.com/issues/001 (accessed Jan. 9, 2025).

Rée, Jonathan ["JVR"]. 1972b. "Reports from Kent, London, Oxford: Oxford." *Radical Philosophy*, no. 1. https://www.radicalphilosophy.com/issues/001 (accessed Jan. 9, 2025).

Rée, Jonathan, Sean Sayers, Christopher J. Arthur, Kate Soper, Diana Coole, and Stella Sandford. 2022. "*Radical Philosophy* Turns 50." *Radical Philosophy*, series 2, no. 13. https://www.radicalphilosophy.com/article/radical-philosophy-turns-50 (accessed Jan. 9, 2025).

Reich, Rob. 2018. *Just Giving: Why Philanthropy Is Failing Democracy and How It Can Do Better*. Princeton University Press.

Riddell, Roger C. 2007. *Does Foreign Aid Really Work*? Oxford University Press.

Robinson, Nathan J. 2022. "Defective Altruism." *Current Affairs*, September 19. https://www.currentaffairs.org/news/2022/09/defective-altruism (accessed Jan. 8, 2025).

Rowe, M. W. 2023. *J. L. Austin: Philosopher and D-Day Intelligence Officer*. Oxford University Press.

Rushe, Dominic. 2022. "FTX Billionaire Sam Bankman-Fried Funneled Dark Money to Republicans." *Guardian*, November 30. https://www.theguardian.com/technology/2022/nov/30/ftx-billionaire-sam-bankman-fried-dark-money-republicans (accessed Jan. 10, 2025).

Rutland, Suzanne D. 2005. *The Jews in Australia*. Cambridge University Press.

Sachs, Jeffrey. 2005. *The End of Poverty: Economic Possibilities of Our Time*. Penguin.

Sachs, Jeffrey. 2006. "How to Help the Poor: Piecemeal Progress of Strategic Plans?" *Lancet* 367 (9519).

Sanbonmatsu, John. 2023. "Effective Altruism and the Reified Mind." In *The Good It Promises, the Harm It Does: Critical Essays on Effective Altruism*, edited by Carol J. Adams, Alice Crary, and Lori Gruen. Oxford University Press.

Sandbu, Martin. 2023. "Effective Altruism Was the Favoured Creed of Sam Bankman-Fried: Can It Survive His Fall?" *Financial Times*, December 29. https://www.ft.com/content/128f3a15-b048-4741-b3e0-61c9346c390b (accessed Jan. 10, 2025).

Saunders-Hastings, Emma. 2022. *Private Virtues, Public Vices: Philanthropy and Democratic Equality*. University of Chicago Press.

Schaefer, Naomi. 1998. "Professor Pleasure—or Professor Death?" *Wall Street Journal*, September 25.

Schenkel, Albert F. 1995. *The Rich Man and the Kingdom: John D. Rockefeller, Jr., and the Protestant Establishment*. Fortress Press.

Schubert, Stefan, and Lucius Caviola. 2023. "Virtues for Real-World Utilitarians." In *An Introduction to Utilitarianism*, edited by R. Y. Chappell, D. Meissner, and

W. MacAskill. https://www.utilitarianism.net/guest-essays/virtues-for-real-world-utilitarians (accessed Jan. 10, 2025).

Schubert, Stefan, and Lucius Caviola. 2024. *Effective Altruism and the Human Mind*. Oxford University Press.

Schubert, Stefan, Lucius Caviola, and Nadira S. Faber. 2019. "The Psychology of Existential Risk: Moral Judgments about Human Extinction." *Scientific Reports* 9, art. 15100. https://doi.org/10.1038/s41598-019-50145-9.

Schwitzgebel, Eric. 2020. "Contest Winner! A Philosophical Argument That Effectively Convinces Research Participants to Donate to Charity." *The Splintered Mind* (blog), June 23. https://schwitzsplinters.blogspot.com/2020/06/contest-winner-philosophical-argument.html (accessed Jan. 15, 2025).

Sebastian, Christopher. 2023. "Anti-Blackness and the Effective Altruist." In *The Good It Promises, the Harm It Does: Critical Essays on Effective Altruism*, edited by Carol J. Adams, Alice Crary, and Lori Gruen. Oxford University Press.

Sen, Amartya. 2001. *Development as Freedom*. Oxford University Press.

Singer, Isaac Bashevis. 1984 [1968]. "The Letter Writer." In *The Penguin Collected Stories of Isaac Bashevis Singer*. Penguin.

Singer, Peter. 1973. *Democracy and Disobedience*. Oxford University Press.

Singer, Peter. 1975. *Animal Liberation*. Avon Books.

Singer, Peter. 1979a. *Practical Ethics*. Cambridge University Press.

Singer, Peter. 1979b. "Unsanctifying Human Life." In *Ethical Issues Relating to Life and Death*, edited by John Ladd. Oxford University Press.

Singer, Peter. 1980. *Marx: A Very Short Introduction*. Oxford University Press.

Singer, Peter. 1981. *The Expanding Circle*. Farrar, Straus & Giroux.

Singer, Peter. 1991. "On Being Silenced in Germany." *New York Review of Books*, August 15.

Singer, Peter. 2001a. "Heavy Petting." *Prospect*, April 19. https://www.prospectmagazine.co.uk/opinions/56258/heavy-petting (accessed Jan. 15, 2025).

Singer, Peter. 2001b. *Hegel: A Very Short Introduction*. Oxford University Press.

Singer, Peter. 2003. *Pushing Time Away: My Grandfather and the Tragedy of Jewish Vienna*. Ecco.

Singer, Peter. 2006. "What Should a Billionaire Give—and What Should You?" *New York Times Magazine*, December 17.

Singer, Peter. 2009. *The Life You Can Save*. Picador.

Singer, Peter. 2013. "The How and Why of Effective Altruism." TED talk, posted online May 20. https://www.ted.com/talks/peter_singer_the_why_and_how_of_effective_altruism?subtitle=en (accessed Jan. 9, 2025).

Singer, Peter. 2015. *The Most Good You Can Do: How Effective Altruism Is Changing Ideas about Living Ethically*. Yale University Press.

Singer, Peter. 2016. *One World Now: The Ethics of Globalization*. Yale University Press.

Singer, Peter. 2016 [1972]. *Famine, Affluence, and Morality*. Oxford University Press [originally published in *Philosophy & Public Affairs* 1 (3): 229–43].

Singer, Peter. 2017. "A Life That Mattered." *Project Syndicate*, March 15. https://www.project-syndicate.org/commentary/life-that-mattered-derek-parfit-by-peter-singer-2017-03 (accessed Jan. 8, 2025).

Singer, Peter. 2023. *Animal Liberation Now: The Definitive Classic Renewed*. Harper.

Slovic, Paul. 2007: "'If I Look at the Mass I Will Never Act': Psychic Numbing and Genocide." *Judgment and Decision Making* 2 (2): 79–95.

Slovic, Paul, Daniel Västfjäll, Arvid Erlandsson, and Robin Gregory. 2017. "Iconic Photographs and the Ebb and Flow of Empathic Response to Humanitarian Disasters." *Proceedings of the National Academy of Sciences of the United States of America (PNAS)* 114 (4): 640–44.

Small, Deborah A., and George Loewenstein. 2003. "Helping a Victim or Helping the Victim." *Journal of Risk and Uncertainty* 26 (1): 5–16.

Small, Deborah A., George Loewenstein, and Paul Slovic. 2007. "Sympathy and Callousness: The Impact of Deliberative Thought on Donations to Identifiable and Statistical Victims." *Organizational Behavior and Human Decision Processes* 102 (2): 143–53.

Small, Deborah A., and Uri Simonsohn. 2008. "Friends of Victims: Personal Experience and Prosocial Behavior." *Journal of Consumer Research* 35 (3): 532–42.

Smart, J.J.C., and Bernard Williams. 1973. *Utilitarianism, For and Against*. Cambridge University Press.

Smirl, Lisa. 2015. *Spaces of Aid: How Cars, Compounds and Hotels Shape Humanitarianism*. Zed Books.

Smith, Adam. 2012 [1776]. [*An Inquiry into the . . .*] *Wealth of Nations*. Wordsworth Editions.

Specter, Michael. 1999. "The Dangerous Philosopher." *New Yorker*, September 6.

Srinivasan, Amia. 2015. "Stop the Robot Apocalypse." *London Review of Books*, September 24. https://www.lrb.co.uk/the-paper/v37/n18/amia-srinivasan/stop-the-robot-apocalypse (accessed Feb. 2, 2025).

Sterri, Aksel Braanen, and Ole Martin Moen. 2021. "The Ethics of Emergencies." *Philosophical Studies* 178 (8): 2621–34.

Syropoulos, Stylianos, Kyle Fiore Law, and Liane Young. 2024. "Caring for Present and Future Generations Alike: Longtermism and Moral Regard across Temporal and Social Distance." *Group Processes & Intergroup Relations* 27 (8). https://doi.org/10.1177/13684302241242115.

Temkin, Larry S. 2022. *Being Good in a World of Need*. Oxford University Press.

Tett, Gillian. 2022. "Philosopher William MacAskill: 'The World Is a Darker Place than It Was Just Five Years Ago.'" *Financial Times*, September 9. https://www.ft.com/content/091862f9-985f-4769-aa37-1aed32636329 (accessed Jan. 15, 2025).

Thompson, Derek. 2015. "The Greatest Good." *Atlantic,* June 15. https://www.theatlantic.com/business/archive/2015/06/what-is-the-greatest-good/395768/ (accessed Jan. 10, 2025).

Thomson, Judith Jarvis. 1971. "A Defense of Abortion." *Philosophy & Public Affairs* 1 (1): 47–66.

Travis, Alan. 2000. "Student Rebels Were 'Frighteningly Radical.'" *Guardian,* May 31. https://www.theguardian.com/uk/2000/may/31/freedomofinformation.politics (accessed Jan. 9, 2025).

Unger, Peter. 1996. *Living High and Letting Die: Our Illusion of Innocence.* Oxford University Press.

UNICEF. 2024. "Under-Five Mortality." March update. https://data.unicef.org/topic/child-survival/under-five-mortality/ (accessed Jan. 15, 2025).

Warburton, Nigel, and Peter Singer. 2015. "What's the Most Good You Can Do?" *London Thinks,* June 8. Available (YouTube video and transcript) at http://opentranscripts.org/transcript/whats-the-most-good-you-can-do/ (accessed Feb. 2, 2025).

Wenar, Leif. 2024. "The Deaths of Effective Altruism." *Wired,* March 27. https://www.wired.com/story/deaths-of-effective-altruism/ (accessed Jan. 8, 2025).

Wiblin, Robert, and Keiran Harris. 2022. "Sam Bankman-Fried on Taking a High Risk Approach to Crypto and Doing Good." *80,000 Hours,* episode 127 (podcast, April 14). https://80000hours.org/podcast/episodes/sam-bankman-fried-high-risk-approach-to-crypto-and-doing-good (accessed Jan. 10, 2025).

Wiblin, Robert, Arden Koehler, and Keiran Harris. 2019. "Peter Singer on Being Provocative, EA, How His Moral Views Have Changed, and Rescuing Children Drowning in Ponds." *80,000 Hours,* episode 66 (podcast, December 5). https://80000hours.org/podcast/episodes/peter-singer-advocacy-and-the-life-you-can-save/ (accessed Jan. 14, 2025).

Wiesel, Elie. 1993. *A Passover Haggadah.* Pocket Books.

Willems, Jeroen. 2022. "Why Did CEA Buy Wytham Abbey?" *Effective Altruism Forum,* December 6. https://forum.effectivealtruism.org/posts/xof7iFB3uh8Kc53bG/why-did-cea-buy-wytham-abbey (accessed Jan. 14, 2025).

Williams, Bernard. 1981 [1976]. "Persons, Character, Morality." In *Moral Luck: Philosophical Papers 1973–1980.* Cambridge University Press.

Wolf, Susan. 2009 [1982]. "Moral Saints." In *Exploring Ethics,* edited by Steven M. Cahn. Oxford University Press [originally published in *The Journal of Philosophy* 79 (8): 419–39].

Woods, Randall B. 2006. *LBJ: Architect of Ambition.* Free Press.

World Bank Group. 2024. "Poverty: Overview." Updated October 15. https://www.worldbank.org/en/topic/poverty/overview (accessed Jan. 10, 2025).

World Bank PIP. 2024. *The World Bank Poverty and Inequality Platform*. https://pip.worldbank.org/home (accessed Feb. 2, 2025).

World Health Organization. 2024. "Drowning." December. https://www.who.int/news-room/fact-sheets/detail/drowning (accessed Jan. 10, 2025).

Wrong, Michela. 2009. *It's Our Turn to Eat: The Story of a Kenyan Whistleblower*. Fourth Estate.

Yunus, Muhammad (with Alan Jolis). 1998. *Banker to the Poor: The Story of the Grameen Bank*. The University Press.

Zeckhauser, Richard, and Donald Shepard. 1976. "Where Now for Saving Lives?" *Law and Contemporary Problems* 40 (4): 5–45.

INDEX

A NOTE ON THE TYPE

This book has been composed in Arno, an Old-style serif typeface in the classic Venetian tradition, designed by Robert Slimbach at Adobe.